SHAME

The
Power
of
Caring

SHAME
The
Power
of
Caring

Third Edition,
Revised and Expanded

Gershen Kaufman

Schenkman Books, Inc.
Rochester, Vermont

Copyright © 1980, 1985, 1992

Schenkman Books, Inc.
118 Main Street
Rochester, Vermont 05767

Library of Congress Cataloging in Publication Data

Kaufman, Gershen.
    Shame: the power of caring/ Gershen Kaufman.—
    Third edition (revised and expanded)

    Includes bibliographical references and index.
    1. Shame. 2. Self. 3. Affect (Psychology) 4. Psychology,
        Pathological.
    I. Title.

    BF575.S45K38 1991
    152.4—dc20
    91–13825

    ISBN 0-87047-052-3
    ISBN 0-87047-053-1

Printed in the United States of America.

To Bill Kell
Who showed me the path
I needed to walk, not his path, but my own.

To Dinny Kell
Who showed me how
a more competent self was possible.

Preface to the 1992 Edition

In the decade since the original publication of *Shame: The Power of Caring* there has been an explosion of interest in the topic of shame, a topic previously neglected for almost a century.

There has also been an increase in concern with the varied phenomena of addiction: drugs, alcohol, and other forms of addiction—even sex and relationship addiction. The aftermath of addiction, particularly sexual and physical abuse, has recently become a focus for concern as well.

A populist mental health phenomenon, the recovery movement has also been sweeping through the country in the last ten years. Like some new age Joshua at the walls of Jericho, this movement is shaking the foundations of traditional mental health treatment. These developments are by no means unrelated phenomena. But understanding their interrelation requires an examination of shame, though shame itself is larger in significance than either addiction or the recovery movement, as we will see.

We will concern ourselves first with the nature of shame, that misunderstood and neglected emotion. We must begin by illuminating and then suspending the categories we have inherited for describing inner experience, the names for inner states we inherited from our culture and from our science.

General psychological theories include more specific theories of personality, psychopathology, and psychotherapy. But theories also contain general assumptions about the determinants of personality: primary motives, organizing principles, and critical developmental events. Equally imbedded in all psychological theories, though hidden and too often denied, is an *ideology* about the nature of human beings and the cosmos. That ideology consists of a vision of optimal development; a vision of the interface between human beings and the universe; a vision of the interaction between psyche and soma, mind and body, consciousness and brain; a vision of what is good and what is bad. Each theory is a specific language of inner experience; each has its own starting point.

When examining the domain of inner experience, the self, from the perspective of any given theory, we must carefully consider the nature of the self's development by identifying crucial developmental events. We must furthermore attend to the nature of motivation itself by illuminating the goals of human activity. And we must articulate the nature of the self's organization or structure by studying what shapes and patterns the self. Finally, we must carefully explore the nature of the process by which the self changes, evolves or becomes transformed, as in psychotherapy.

When our focus shifts instead to examining not the self, but various psychological theories of the self, we must be able to identify each theory's central constructs, its definitions, and its phenomenological/observable referents, as well as the interrelationships among constructs. Without such precision and specificity, theories lack utility. And when we address the implications derived from different theories, we must work toward constructing a dictionary of translation for moving between competing theories. Without such a dictionary, there is no way to be certain of the specific phenomenological referents connected to various theoretical constructs. But with it, we will be able to more accurately make observations and test predictions derived from different theories, thereby accumulating support for one or another competing view of the nature of the self.

All theories function essentially as languages for describing nature, and our psychological theories are more accurately understood as languages for describing the domain of the self, the inner life: from Freud's *libidinal drives,* Harry Sullivan's patterns of *interpersonal relations,* Erik Erikson's *identity crises,* and W. R. D. Fairbairn's *internal objects,* to Eric Berne's *ego states,* Albert Ellis' *irrational thoughts,* and Viktor Frankl's *will to meaning.* Each of these theories constitutes a rearrangement of experience, to use Jacob Bronowski's phrase, a new imaginative grouping. But these categories also determine perception. The language we use for describing inner experience inevitably shapes the actual perception of that experience.

Consider the problem of accurately perceiving affect as one observable among many others within the domain of inner experience. Without an accurate language for affect or emotion, there is no way to partition affect from drive, nor affect from either cognition, interpersonal relations, or the existential search for meaning. The particular categories of thought that we use inevitably shape the perception of all other related phenomena. When the construct of drive is conceived to be primary, all other observables are necessarily viewed from that perspective; then affect becomes simply a derivative of the drives. But affect becomes a derivative of cognition when *that* is the foremost organizing principle of the self. In neither case is affect conceived to be independent in its functioning.

The categories we employ for describing inner experience act as a filtering mechanism: the names we use for inner states actually filter our experience of them. The language we are taught for naming inner events either sharpens perception of those events or else masks them. This is true in the family when a girl is told by her mother, "You're not angry, you're just tired," or when a boy is told by his father, "Real boys don't cry, be strong, take it like a man." In each case the child's experience is being shamed and thereby disavowed, misidentified and eventually misfiled in memory. It is lost to conscious awareness, no longer as freely available for expression.

This use and misuse of language likewise occurs in all forms of relationship and in all modes of psychotherapeutic intervention. Counselors, psychologists, social workers, and psychiatrists inevitably work *through* language to enable psychological healing and regrowth. Without accurate names for inner events—affects and needs, for example—perception remains clouded. Indeed the failure to attend to shame within scientific psychology and the mental health field until now is the result, partially, of the failure of language, that is, the failure of our scientific psychological language to accurately partition the domain of inner experience.

The language we use must be precise in meaning, specific in definition, clear in its description of inner events, and teachable to anyone, including children. If we are truly to prevent addiction, for example, then we must begin by teaching our children about affect and shame, and how best to both tolerate and effectively overcome this most deeply disturbing experience of the self by the self. My own partitioning of inner experience, and resulting language of shame, begins with the *affect system* originated by Silvan Tomkins. This is my starting point for examining shame, illuminating its centrality in human development and interpersonal relations; understanding its significance for self-esteem, identity, and intimacy; and exploring the varied phenomena of addiction, abuse, and so-called dysfunctional family systems. It is affect that is primary over all other motivating subsystems within the human being, according to Tomkins. It is affect, therefore, to which we must turn in order to understand shame.

Shame is one of nine innate affects comprising the affect system, and all human beings inherit subcortical programs for these innate affects. Affects furthermore comprise correlated sets of responses; affect captures first the face, next the viscera and skeletal apparatus. We experience affect primarily and initially on the face and it is the feedback from our own face which produces the distinctive feel of affect.

Affect is primary over the drives and also over cognition or language. Tomkins' theory of affect is a direct challenge to both classical psychoanalysis and cognitive-behaviorism. Each has posited a different starting point, a different organizing principle. Our understanding of shame changes fundamentally depending on the particular filtering mechanism utilized by a given theory. Cognitive-behaviorism makes affect in general, and therefore shame in particular, an inevitable derivative of cognition. Classical psychoanalysis views affect in general, and shame in particular, necessarily as a derivative of the drives, either singly or in combination with the ego, whose function it is to accommodate between libidinal aims and reality constraints. Other variants of psychoanalysis such as interpersonal theory, object-relations theory, and self psychological theory likewise view affect largely as derivative of something else. Shame is therefore frequently tied to failings of the ideal self. Recent formulations of narcissism[1] represent attempts to account for shame-related phenomena by theories lacking a place for the affect system. Only a theory of affect yields a precise language for partitioning shame.

Tomkins' pioneering study of the emotions provides us with the missing key: a new theory, a new imaginative grouping, a radical rearrangement of experience. All of our psychological theories are like planets revolving about a common center, in this case, not the sun but the self. Viewing the self from the unique perspective offered by any given theory provides us with a particular, and different, view of the self. As we shift from one theory to another, in effect we change our vantage point, our essential position of observation, as though we had actually shifted our position from Mercury to Mars or from the Earth to Saturn when viewing the sun. Each psychological theory, including this one, offers only a *relative* view of the self, neither fixed, final, nor absolute. Fundamentally, then, our theories are never immutable, but instead must remain open and changing languages for describing the self.

Viewing shame from the perspective of affect theory means that, first of all, shame is an affect—an emotion or feeling—not a thought, drive, or interpersonal phenomenon per se. While shame may of course include self-evaluative thoughts or become expressed inter-personally, it begins as and remains an affect. As such, shame functions to amplify our awareness, connecting whatever event activated shame with any responses that follow it, including con-structed thoughts, motor actions, and retrieved memories. The se-quence of experience as it is lived therefore involves, in Tomkins' view, the creation of a *coassembly* of activator—affect—response. The event which generates shame, whether innate or learned, be-comes inexorably linked with any or all responses that follow shame.

---

[1]Morrison, A.P., *Shame: The Underside of Narcissism.* Hillsdale, N.J.: Analytic Press, 1989.

Broucek, F.J., *Shame and the Self.* New York: The Guilford Press, 1991.

The affect imprints the responses to it with the same amplification exerted on its own activator.

What are the implications of an affect theory perspective on shame?

1. Shame is an innate universal affect which has inherently adaptive, and therefore distinctly positive features. Shame is crucial to the development of identity, conscience, and to a sense of dignity. Shame is equally central to the development of self-esteem and intimacy.

2. Shame invariably begins as a partial, temporary experience, neither inherently global nor automatically crippling.

3. Shame can be experienced in the absence of a watching or shaming other. It does not require the presence of others.

4. Shame is observable from birth throughout the life cycle to death. It is not confined to the mother-child relationship, nor even to the family exclusively.

5. The critical distinction is between shame as an innate affect that functions simply to amplify awareness and shame that has become internalized and magnified to the point that it now progressively captures and dominates the self.

6. The continuing debate concerning shame vs. guilt is rendered obsolete and irrelevant.

7. The distinction between shame and guilt is equivalent to the distinction between shame and shyness: these are different manifestations of shame, variants of one and the same affect.

8. Shame is not the same as, nor is it simply the product of, negative cognitive self-appraisals. Affect is innate. It exists prior to, and is primary over, cognition or language.

9. Shame is not the result of dysfunctional families alone. It is not just the consequence of disturbed interpersonal relations.

10. The centrality of shame in human affairs extends well beyond our contemporary concern with the problems of addiction and abuse, the emergent reality of dysfunctional family systems, or even the current ascendance of the recovery movement. The significance of shame lies in its profound impact on personality, psychopathology, and interpersonal relations, as well as in its role in minority group relations, minority identity development, national identity development, and international relations.

These implications of affect theory make evident that three erroneous assumptions concerning shame continue to cloud our knowledge. The first of these concerns shame as it relates to guilt. Other perspectives continue to view shame and guilt as two distinctly different affective states. Implicit in these mistaken notions is the assumption that shame is always about the self, whereas guilt is always about *actions* of the self. It is consequently believed, both in our culture and in our science, that in shame the focus is on the self whereas in guilt the focus is only on the actions involved. Shame is thereby conceived as global, with guilt inevitably rendered partial and specific. Likewise, shame is considered to be both visual and public whereas guilt is seen as auditory and private. From such a view, shame inherently becomes a much more crippling experience while guilt remains necessarily a healthier one.

The error in such a view is not immediately apparent, however. We are so heavily influenced by the linguistic categories of thought we have inherited that we rarely suspend these names for labeling inner states and observe the phenomenon anew. If we study the literature of both this country and Great Britain over the past several centuries, for example, we will discover infinitely more references to shame than to guilt, and references as well to shame specifically in response to moral transgression.

After all, in Nathaniel Hawthorne's *The Scarlet Letter,* Hester Prynne was made to wear the scarlet letter "A," which stood for adulteress, and she wore it directly on her bosom. She was shamed publicly for her transgression. Not only was she required by Puritan justice to wear the scarlet letter, but she was also forced to stand upon the platform of the pillory before the assembled crowd with her head confined and thereby held up to public gaze. In Chapter Two of Hawthorne's novel, the narrator says: "There can be no outrage, methinks, against our common nature—whatever be the delinquencies of the individual—no outrage more flagrant than to forbid the culprit to hide his face for shame; as it was the essence of this punishment to do."

Frequent references to shame in literature continue into the early decades of this century. For example, in Raphael's illuminating study of Edith Wharton, shame emerges as an important though completely neglected theme in her fiction.[2] Owing partly to the influence of Sigmund Freud, the awareness of shame was buried, and guilt was reified as *the* salient phenomenon worthy of interest and intellectual scrutiny. Freud's attention to the drives oriented him toward examining the inevitable clashes that occurred between the primordial drives—eros and thanatos, the life and death instincts—and both the external and internal representations of culture, reality and the ego. Starting with the drives as an organizing principle thus orients us more toward examining guilt than shame. Furthermore, guilt is largely a Western concept. In the East, the experience is nonetheless viewed as shame, and it is shame that will be experienced, expressed, and so labeled in the East, even in response to transgression. Here we see once again the relativity of language in describing the domain of inner experience, along with the impact of culture on shaping perception through its particular linguistic categories. Language filters experience through the lens of culture, just as a prism filters light.

The second, newly ascendant though equally erroneous assumption is that shame is the necessary cause of addiction. While shame is certainly central to much that ails human beings, it is not the only

---

[2]Raphael, L., *Edith Wharton's Prisoners of Shame: A New Perspective on Her Neglected Fiction.* New York: St. Martin's Press, 1991.

source of disturbance and dysfunction. The principal cause of addiction from an affect theory perspective is the experience of overwhelming negative affect, shame included. The developing addict first of all becomes dependent on a sedative for intense negative affect. While any combination of negative affects may be involved here, shame is likely to play a prominent role as well. In addition to primary shame, the shame that precedes the development of addictive dependency, there is also secondary shame, the inevitable shame about being addicted to anything. Addicts are controlled by their addiction which, in turn, thereby reproduces shame and also further fuels the addictive process.

Addiction is rooted first in sedation of intense negative affect, next in an ever-increasing reliance upon the sedative, and finally in reliance upon the sedative to sedate panic, the overwhelming negative affect generated by the sudden absence of the previously reliable sedative. In addition to this form of addiction, there is another type of addictive process in which the addiction is not to sedation of negative affect, but instead to the pursuit of ever-increasing affect pay-offs. Here, affect pay-off governs the choice of objects for affect investment. One example of this form of addictive cycle is the individual who indiscriminately pursues excitement affect. Such a person is driven to seek ever-higher levels of excitement, independent of its source. Any of the affects, positive or negative, can function in this manner, resulting in an addictive-like process.

The third erroneous assumption regards the necessary relationship between dysfunctional family systems and shame. It is certainly the case that dysfunctional families are a breeding ground for shame. Dysfunctional families *are* shame-based families. But shame does not require dysfunctional families to grow in intensity, duration, or frequency. Dysfunctional families are not necessary to the magnification of shame or to the development of a shame-based syndrome. Neither are dysfunctional families necessary to the development of addiction. Dysfunctional families certainly do generate shame, and shame certainly does generate addiction. However, shame can magnify in the absence of dysfunctional families or even disturbed interpersonal relations. And the same holds true for addiction. The sources of shame are much broader in scope than dysfunctional family relations. One can become overwhelmed by shame even when interpersonal relations are intact or thriving, just as one can develop an addiction even when family relationships remain sound and effective. Even when the recovery movement has begun to fade—and concepts like "dysfunctional families," "adult children," and "codependency" begin to fade along with it—shame will remain a phenomenon of profound importance because of the multiplicity of its impact. Shame strikes deepest into the human psyche; it is a sickness within the self, a disease of the spirit, however brief or lasting.

Inherent in the recovery movement is a fundamental dilemma. The recovery movement has significantly facilitated the dissolution of the secondary shame surrounding such syndromes as alcoholism, addiction, bulimia, physical abuse, and sexual abuse. In accomplishing this, the recovery movement has begun to lift this culture's taboo on shame which still exists in contemporary society. But while identifying oneself as a recovering alcoholic, recovering drug addict, recovering bulimic, recovering sex addict, etc., certainly releases shame, it yields only a partial identity. And continuing to identify oneself as a *recovering something* necessarily remains an incomplete identity. Unless one moves on to an as yet unspecified "thirteenth step," involvement in twelve-step groups can become simply another addiction. Overcoming shame requires its complete assimilation. While this means transforming those early governing scenes of shame, it also means moving beyond recovery as an identity. Only by embracing a new vision of self are we able to create a coherent and integrated identity, one that is fundamentally *self-affirming*.

There is one final implication of an affect theory perspective that requires some discussion. For those clinicians and researchers pursuing biochemical answers to addiction, and to other psychological phenomena as well, we must turn the question around. We must also consider the likely biochemical consequences of the chronic magnification of any affect, shame included. Affect and its suppression result in distinct endocrine changes. The question we must ask, and which has not been asked, is this: Could affect produce permanent changes in brain chemistry?

Research evidence demonstrating distinctive patterns of autonomic correlates accompanying the activation of different affects is now accumulating, as Tomkins had originally hypothesized.[3] Affect magnification can feed equally well on the expression or suppression of affect. One important consequence of rapidly magnified affect and its suppression is *backed-up affect*. Endocrine changes are a further consequence of backed-up affect. In response to chronic affect suppression, the resulting endocrine changes may become permanent. This cycle is an important one. When affect is systematically suppressed, the inevitable result is backed-up affect, and endocrine changes are a further consequence of backed-up affect. It is the experience of backed-up affect along with its resulting endocrine changes, like the elevation of blood pressure in suppressed rage, that actually produces the effects typically and ambiguously referred to as "stress." Therefore, psychosomatic illness is a direct consequence of backed-up affect and stress itself is mediated by affect.

In a similar vein, we must pursue the long-term biochemical consequences of the chronic magnification or suppression of each of the affects. Certain biochemical changes are likely to be the consequence, not the cause, of affect. The affect mechanism is also likely to directly impact the immune system, with positive affect enhancing immune functioning and negative affect suppressing it. Consciousness and brain chemistry are *correlated* domains. LeShan and Margenau argue that reducing the phenomena of consciousness to the phenomena of brain chemistry is an error: "The brain no more secretes consciousness than consciousness secretes the brain. Different domains have different observables."[4]

---

[3]Ekman, P., Levenson, R.W., and Friesen, W.V., "Autonomic Nervous System Activity Distinguishes Among Emotions." *Science*, 1983, 221, pp.. 1208-1210.

[4]LeShan, L., and Margenau, H., *Einstein's Space and van Gogh's Sky: Physical Reality and Beyond*. New York: Macmillan, 1982.

If we are to solve the problem of addiction and if we are to repair dysfunctional family systems, then we must begin with an understanding of how the self develops, actually functions, and also changes, evolves, or becomes transformed. We will never solve the problem of addiction by concentrating on addiction alone. The key is affect or emotion, and the affect that is central both to addiction and to dysfunction in general is shame.

The disturbance within the self produced by shame impacts not only self-esteem, but also the development of identity and the pursuit of intimacy. Self-esteem, identity, and intimacy are three important dimensions of personality that are profoundly influenced by the experience of shame. Self-esteem, identity, and intimacy are each vulnerable to the disruptive effects of shame when shame becomes internalized and subsequently magnified, progressively capturing and dominating the developing personality. Then shame grows like an emotional cancer within the self.

Gershen Kaufman
East Lansing, Michigan
March 1991

Preface to the 1985 Edition

When I first wrote *Shame*, I had no idea whether others would find it of value; I had no conception of the impact it would have. To further the knowledge of the psychology of shame and its healing, this revised edition contains new sections which extend shame theory. The eventual goal is to create a language of the self by integrating *interpersonal theory* (Sullivan and Kell), *object-relations theory* (Fairbairn) and *affect theory* (Tomkins).

The struggle for identity is one of the recurring problems of our age. Each individual inevitably searches for answers to the questions: *"Who am I?" "Where do I belong?"* Inner security depends on feeling whole, worthwhile, and valued from within. Identity is rooted both in wholeness of self and essential belonging or identification with others.

The need to identify is the need for rootedness, connectedness, belonging. It is a need to feel identified with, to belong to particular individuals or groups. From identification spring loyalties, and loyalties create allegiances—to family, friends, religions, nations. The need to belong to something larger than ourselves—to a group, a cause, or an idea—is one principal source of identity.

Shame is another principal source of identity. We will examine the interplay of shame and identification in the unfolding of identity, and their profound impact upon the self.

If we are to understand the self, the sources of splitting and self-hatred, and the evolving process of identity, then we must begin with shame. Shame, however, remains under taboo in contemporary society, where achievement and success are dominant values.

Shame itself is an *entrance* to the self. It is the affect of indignity, of defeat, of transgression, of inferiority, and of alienation. No other affect is closer to the experienced self. None is more central for the sense of identity. Shame is felt as an inner torment, a sickness of the soul, in the words of Silvan Tomkins. It is the most poignant experience of the self by the self, whether felt in the humiliation of cowardice, or in the sense of failure to cope successfully with a challenge. Shame is a wound made from the inside, dividing us both from ourselves and from one another. Shame is the *affect* which is the source of many complex and disturbing inner states: depression, alienation, self-doubt, isolating loneliness, paranoid and schizoid phenomena, compulsive disorders, splitting of the self, perfectionism, a deep sense of inferiority, inadequacy or failure, the so-called borderline conditions and disorders of narcissism. These are phenomena which are rooted in shame. But how?

Shame so disturbs the functioning of the self that eventually distinct syndromes of shame can develop. Each is rooted in significant interpersonal failure. Each variant of a shame-based personality has a characteristic pattern for reproducing shame. Each evolving syndrome further distorts the self, creating such varied disorders of self-esteem. Each developmental variant of shame undergoes further transformation.

Experiences of shame become internalized through imagery. Internal images or *scenes*, as Silvan Tomkins describes them, of shame-inducing events may come to govern further development. Scenes of shame become linked to each other partially via language, but they also can fuse together directly, thereby magnifying one another. Language further transforms scenes of shame, creating both particular meanings about the self and distinct language patterns for reproducing shame, for continually re-making images of shame. Affect, imagery, and language are the central processes shaping the self and identity.

Gershen Kaufman
East Lansing, Michigan
August 1984

Preface to the 1980 Edition

All of us embrace a common humanity in which we search for meaning in living, for essential belonging with others, and for valuing of who we are as unique individuals. We need to feel that we are worthwhile in some special way, as well as whole inside. We yearn to feel that our lives are useful, that what we do and who we are do matter. Yet times come upon us when doubt creeps inside, as if an inner voice whispers despair. Suddenly, we find ourselves questioning our very worth or adequacy. It may come in any number of ways: *"I can't relate to people." "I'm a failure." "Nobody could possibly love me." "I'm inadequate as a man/woman."* When we have begun to doubt ourselves, and in this way to question the very fabric of our lives, secretly we feel to blame; the deficiency lies within ourselves alone. Where once we stood secure in our personhood, now we feel a mounting inner anguish, a sickness of the soul, as Silvan Tomkins puts it. This is shame.

Above all else, shame reveals the self inside the person, thereby exposing it to view. To feel shame is to feel *seen* in a painfully diminished sense. This feeling of exposure constitutes an essential aspect of shame. Whether all eyes are upon me or only my own, I feel deficient in some vital way as a human being. And in the midst of shame, an urgent need to escape or hide may come upon us.

This is a book which probes the inner experience of shame, its interpersonal origins as well as later internalization, and the violation shame does to our essential dignity as human beings. Furthermore, through identification, interpersonal learning in the family becomes the model for the gradually unfolding relationship which the self comes to have with the self; this we call our identity. Shame, which is first experienced at the hands of others, now can be wholly generated internally. Herein lies the significance of shame for identity. It is the unfolding conception of shame as a central motive in human development and interpersonal relations which provides the foundation for an emerging theory of identity development.

While this is a book about the inner deficiency that is shame, it is also a book about caring and the search for wholeness. However inadvertently, our most vital human relationships may unfortunately become ruptured emotionally. Herein lies the genesis of shame interpersonally. But shame is not so much to be avoided as to be understood and coped with. Relationships are restorable and mistakes in a relationship can be overcome, if we but face them honestly. While in caring certainly lies the seeds of shame, in caring also lies its healing.

Societally, we have for the most part never evolved accurate symbolizations for the felt inner experience of shame. In part this has been due to the wordless nature of the affect concerned, and to the speech-binding effects of exposure itself. It has also been due to the fact that human beings typically hide their own shame and avoid approaching anyone else's. To accomplish the task at hand, the approach I have taken essentially is a phenomenological one. In this endeavor I have drawn on three distinct sources: clinical observation, personal experience, and the writing and observations of other investigators and theorists. These sources are interwoven in an attempt to convey the inner experience of shame and gradually to evolve a language of the experienced self that, while precise, nevertheless keeps close to actual inner experience. The reader is invited to join directly in the exploration in order to verify through his or her own experience the essential accuracy or value of these ideas and of the particular language evolving here.

Intentionally, I have written the book in a conversational style. This is an effort to engage the reader more directly and to facilitate the understanding of the ideas presented. Writing in such a conversational vein additionally bridges the void between an author and reader who must remain unseen to one another. While the interrelation among shame, identification, and the self is likely to be of particular interest to other professionals in the mental health field, the relevance of shame for both the personality and interpersonal living may hold appeal for anyone concerned with human welfare.

It is my hope that the book articulates the central dimensions of shame in a way that communicates their essential relevance to the functioning of the self, internally as well as interpersonally. By evolving a language which more accurately reflects shame, further observation, investigation, and research can proceed. It is my hope to stimulate fruitful lines of inquiry into the processes of shame and identification, their interplay in the unfolding of identity, and their profound impact upon the self.

Gershen Kaufman
East Lansing, Michigan
August 1979

Acknowledgments

My understanding of shame began through Dr. Bill Kell, who for four years until his untimely death was my deeply valued friend, colleague, and consultant. To him I shall be forever indebted. He opened the door that enabled me to begin to grasp the significance of shame as a dynamic in human development. That unleashed for me a process of furthering my own understanding of shame.

To Dinny Kell with whom I picked up in so many ways where Bill and I left off. Our relationship deepened and broadened my understanding of internal as well as interpersonal functioning. Many ideas I have since come to hold I first learned from her. She will remain one of my most cherished teachers in living.

To Dr. Silvan Tomkins whose own writing and correspondence with me contributed significantly to the growth of my thinking. Silvan Tomkins died in June 1991, and he will be greatly missed. Hopefully, his great work will live on in this book.

To Lev Raphael, my dearest friend and writing partner, for countless helpful suggestions and for his critical reading of the two revised editions. His love, support, guidance, and generosity in time and labors spent over both of the revised editions have given me the courage to continue the work begun in the first edition. Our partnership in writing continues to nourish me and fire my imagination.

To Drs. Cecil Williams, Douglas Miller, Charles Bassos, and Sue Jennings, colleagues with whom discussions provided stimulating thought as well as clarified a number of my ideas.

To Rick Shipman, Mary Tonsager, Jayne Hoey, and Suzanne Clay who patiently assisted in typing the many drafts of the original manuscript.

To Ellie Flood who assisted in typing the new sections for the second revised edition.

And last, to all those clients who have shared deeply with me and in so doing have been a vital part of the process.

Introduction

The full range of what I have called the primary affects has not yet become common knowledge. The importance of aggression and anxiety was ineradicably established by the enormous authority of Freud. All the remaining affects were either unrecognized or misidentified by him. Distress, and especially the birth cry, was mistakenly identified as the prototype of anxiety despite the obvious fact that children cry without being anxious, and become anxious without crying. The superego was regarded as a turning of aggression inward against the ego, failing to recognize the critical roles of shame, contempt, and disgust, and misidentifying them as aggression. The positive affects of excitement and enjoyment were misidentified as sexuality, despite the fact that the excitement affect in sexual excitement is no different than excitement affect about anything under the sun. He had failed to recognize the fusion of affect and drive in sexuality and so failed to understand that sexuality required amplification by excitement for potency, but that excitement did not require amplification by sexuality to seize the human being.

Freud's failure to appreciate the primacy of the affects over drives made it more difficult to discover the missing affects, and a great deal of psychotherapy today is handicapped by insufficient sensitivity to the full spectrum of the primary affects.

In the case of shame there are some special problems which have prevented an appreciation of its centrality. Just as sexuality was tabooed in Freud's time, shame is still under taboo today. The paradox about shame is that there is shame about shame. It is much easier to admit one is happy or sad than one feels ashamed. In part this is because of the close association between shame and inferiority. One is ashamed to announce shame as one is ashamed to announce the fact of one's inferiority. It is a self-validating affect (or so believed) insofar as one believes one should try to conceal feelings of shame. This is particularly amplified in a culture which values achievement and success.

In order to understand shame one must have experienced deep shame and confronted it sufficiently to have assimilated it personally, and pursued it cognitively wherever it led, and finally, to have had the courage to risk further shame by exposing oneself in writing. This latter is unusual. Freud did it in *The Interpretation of Dreams,* but Galton, for example, would not: "It would be very instructive to print the actual records at length, made by many experimenters . . . but it would be too absurd to print one's own singly. They lay bare the foundations of a man's thoughts with more vividness and truth than he would probably care to publish to the world."

We are dependent for the understanding of each of the primary affects on the special sensitivities of each psychologist. For one, anxiety may have been dominant, for another aggression, for another (as in the case of Freud) anxiety and aggression. Whatever affect has been magnified in the life history of a psychologist will necessarily assume major significance in his understanding of human beings. We are indebted to Gershen Kaufman for his special sensitivity to the role of shame and its contribution to affect theory, requiring as it did conjointly, affect sensitivity, personal integrity, cognitive depth, and not least, personal courage in exposing his own self to the professional community.

Silvan S. Tomkins
January 1980

Contents

PART III: EXTENDING SHAME THEORY
IN NEW DIRECTIONS

PART I
A Developmental
Theory of Shame and Identity

The Interpersonal Origins of Shame

Those conceptualizations which have changing impact upon a person's life are rare. For me, shame counts among these. Though I have always lived with shame, I had not really known it as such. Only relatively recently have I become conscious of shame as a dynamic motive in the human endeavor. As shame has become understandable to me personally, I have begun to recognize the multiplicity of its impact upon the inner life and to grasp its relevance for interpersonal as well as internal living. Increasingly, I have come to appreciate the significance of shame as a central motive in human development, interpersonal relations, and the psychotherapeutic venture.

BEGINNING OF THE SEARCH: A PHENOMENOLOGICAL APPROACH

Shame had not been at all significant for me until one day, it was in late fall of 1972 I believe, a day when I had one of those usual talks with Bill Kell about a client with whom I was having some difficulties. For four years Bill had been my colleague and consultant, my friend, and my teacher.

The situation was this. The client, whom we'll call Tina, had been in therapy with me for a couple of years. While it had taken us a long time to get through all the impasses, at last, we secured our relationship but progress was still slow. Then Tina had to leave on a graduate internship. We reached a stopping point, she knowing that we might resume therapy when she returned a year later to finish her degree.

Some months later, she wrote me a long letter expressing loneliness, scared feelings, being unsure of how to relate to men (a recurring conflict), not knowing what to do in this new, unsettling situation she was in. She asked me to reply and to help her know what to do. For some unclear reasons, I did not answer her letter for a long time.

After several months, I received a second letter. Instead of the positive attachment to me expressed months earlier, there was now a profound distress. Some real fear that I had deserted her. What was wrong? Why hadn't I answered her plea for guidance, some response to an urgent need? Did I not care?

At that I felt confused as to what had happened and what to do. I went to see Bill Kell. I told him all that had happened and had him read the two letters. Bill first said that she probably had needed something from me and that it probably wasn't very much to begin with. I had felt an insatiable need coming from her against which I had been defending. What Bill was saying was this: in replying, all I need have said was that I still had a few feelings about her and thought of her now and then.

It was rather off-handed and as we were getting to be done that Bill asked if he had told me what he had figured out about the connection between shame and rage. I sort of settled back down for more talking. Bill then proceeded to recount what he had figured out. We had discussed shame some months ago, so his remark wasn't totally unexpected. The notion had been brought to us by a mutual colleague of ours, Dr. Sue Jennings, who first pointed us to the meaningfulness of shame. Bill began thinking about it when Sue asked him, "What's the connection between shame and rage?" When she kept after him, this set Bill to thinking.

"I think a sequence of events happens," Bill said, "when a child has a need which doesn't get responded to appropriately. It could be a need for anything. When, for example, a boy lets his dad know of some need and dad doesn't understand or reacts badly, then the need begins to convert into a bad feeling. Since the father, as all parents, is seen as infallible by a child, the child begins to feel that he's bad. There's something wrong with *him* or else dad would have met his need."

"Then what happens?" I broke in.

"Well, let's say later that dad recognizes his son needed something. If father then approaches his boy, the child reacts with rage because he feels exposed. The interpersonal bridge is broken."

"What do you do when that happens?"

"You say something like 'I guess I was late, but I'm here now.'"

Now I knew what I needed to do with my client: late as I was, I needed to respond to her need. At the same time that I realized this about my client, I became flooded with personal images—memories of my own growing up. Things I had never understood about myself suddenly came clear. Peculiar patterns of my own which always seemed to mysteriously "happen to me," became understandable and strangely somehow more manageable. The connection between shame and rage had opened an inner door which left me flooded.

Listening to the discovery Bill made had definitely unleashed a process of profound inner discovery of my own because its impact was still with me months later. I began to have a grasp on shame within myself. The experience which happened to me that day began for me a process of discovering the significance of shame, a process of which this book is an outgrowth.

As for my client? Well, I answered her letter and later received her reply. Such a burst of rage and hatred I had scarcely ever received. Again perplexed, I sought Bill out. I told him I got another letter from that client. He said, "I bet she blasted you," as he broke up laughing. I was surprised he had known. "How did you know she'd blast me?" Bill went on: "Remember? When you approach and attempt to restore things, you get the rage 'cause they feel so exposed." "Well, what do you do?" I asked. He said, "You just accept it and let them know you have no need to kick them back."

That meeting with Bill and living out the situation with my client had impact for me. At the time I had no idea where the door that had opened within me would lead.

Bill died in June 1973.

*　*　*　*　*　*　*

As a psychotherapist, I have found myself becoming an observer of, as well as participant in, the process of human growth. That process dissolves into several discernible dimensions. First, there is the process by which we come to be who we are; this I see as essentially developmental in focus. Then, there is the process of the self, i.e., the inner life or internal functioning of the self. Third, there is the interpersonal process, i.e., living outside ourselves. Together, these three dimensions can be construed as dynamic in focus. And lastly there is the process of change, call it psychotherapy or whatever, which is, in point of fact, regrowth. Discovering the sources of shame within myself led me to an investment of my energies in a continuing exploration of the development and dynamics of shame and of the process of change needed to reverse the developmental sequence. Those individuals who permitted me to enter their inner worlds by virtue of their being my clients have been the principal, though not exclusive, sources of my observations and formulations. Without them this book could not have been written.

In exploring shame and identity, I decided to rely upon myself as the instrument of observation, knowing full well the potential for error and bias involved, knowing also that no method is without its own special error. I know that one individual's observations constitute but a set of abstractions from the common ground of human experience. It is the continuing interplay of observation and theoretical formulation, along with repeated rechecking of those observations, from which understanding and knowledge gradually unfold. This book is an outgrowth of a number of years of study, observation, and thinking about shame and identity, two dynamic processes in human development and psychotherapy.

I offer this book not as a finished product but as a stopping point for reflection in an ongoing exploration, not as inviolate truth or knowledge but as one man's evolving view. Certainly, there can be a number of ways of viewing the same set of phenomena. The view presented here has been instrumental in my own development, personally and professionally, and has enabled me to become increasingly effective with others who have embarked upon their own inner search toward self-understanding, growth, and change. I offer it because it has shown itself useful, and what is useful ought to be communicated. It is from such shared communications that we move toward ever more accurate understandings of the complex and complicated processes that are involved in human development and human interaction.

My intent is to engage the unseen reader in conversation with me. By so joining with me in the ensuing exploration—and this is my hope—the reader may be stimulated to search through his or her own experience, whether it be as therapist, researcher, teacher, parent, or simply as a human being, in order to verify, refine, or even to discard the ideas presented here.

SHAME: THE ALIENATING AFFECT

Shame is as central to the human experience as anxiety or suffering, yet is far more elusive in nature. We have in the last half century begun to evolve a language for anxiety. We know, for example, how to describe our inner trembling in the face of life's uncertainties, whether it be childbirth, old age, or unprovoked attack in the night. We know in spite of ourselves that fear in some form is inevitable throughout life. We have been especially cautioned by psychologists and psychiatrists, our secular priests, to look for irrational or unconscious sources of what frightens us into backing away from living. In recent years, we have even begun to approach a psychology of human suffering, whether through facing death and dying more openly and honestly in our culture or through approaching the reality of human pain however it may manifest.

Not so with shame. Shame lies hidden behind inaccurate words, symbols that fail to grasp the inner experience of the self. Even the word, shame, is a rather poor one, though I know none better, for it fails to convey either the feeling of exposure inherent to the experience or the sense of despair and anguish that can accompany extreme moments of utter worthlessness. But we shall attempt in these pages to evolve just such a language, one that keeps close to actual inner experience, in the hope that shame can be rendered thereby both more understandable and, ultimately, more manageable.

Before launching into a discussion of the phenomenology of shame, something of a theoretical overview might enable the reader to better orient to what will follow. A basic thesis to be elaborated upon later is that shame originates interpersonally, primarily in significant relationships, but later can become internalized so that the self is able to activate shame without an inducing interpersonal event. Interpersonally induced shame develops into internally induced shame. Through this internalizing process, shame can spread throughout the self, ultimately shaping our emerging identity. Prior to internalization, shame remains a feeling which is generated and then passes on, whereas following internalization, shame can be prolonged indefinitely. Our identity is that vital sense of who we are as individuals, embracing our worth, our adequacy, and our very dignity as human beings. All these can be obliterated through protracted shame, leaving us feeling naked, defeated as a person and intolerably alone.

There are important developmental differences between early childhood shame experiences and later adolescent-adult ones. Language as a symbolic function unfolds rather slowly, making shame quite difficult to label with words until our ability to symbolize inner experience sufficiently matures. Thus, the signs of shame most notable with young children are the external, nonverbal ones which consist of lowering the eyes, hanging the head or blushing. With an adolescent or adult, whose capacity to symbolize inner experience has already greatly matured, we can more directly seek to approach shame as it occurs internally. When we have learned how to symbolize about symbols, in the Piagetian sense, conceptual and abstract thought become possible, enabling us to refine our symbols of inner experience. Thus, childhood shame experiences certainly feel bad and cause us to hide from others even if momentarily. Yet the capacity to translate those shame experiences into words and then link those words together, creating meanings about the self, has not matured, and until it does, shame and identity do not become linked.

Let us turn directly to the inner experience of shame. To feel shame is to feel *seen* in a painfully diminished sense. The self feels exposed both to itself and to anyone else present. It is this sudden, unexpected feeling of exposure and accompanying self-consciousness that characterize the essential nature of the affect of shame. Contained in the experience of shame is the piercing awareness of ourselves as fundamentally deficient in some vital way as a human being. To live with shame is to experience the very essence or heart of the self as wanting.

Shame is an impotence-making experience because *it feels as though* there is no way to relieve the matter, no way to restore the balance of things. One has simply failed as a human being. No single action is seen as wrong and, hence, reparable. So, *"there is nothing I can do to make up for it."* This is impotence.

The binding effect of shame involves the whole self. Sustained eye contact with others becomes intolerable. The head is hung. Spontaneous movement is interrupted. And speech is silenced. Exposure itself eradicates the words, thereby causing shame to be almost incommunicable to others. Feeling exposed opens the self to painful, inner scrutiny. It is as though the eyes inexplicably turn inward. We are suddenly watching ourselves, scrutinizing critically the minutest detail of our being. The excruciating observation of the self which results, this torment of *self*-consciousness, becomes so acute as to create a binding, almost paralyzing effect upon the self.

Imagine along with me a time of being bound by self-consciousness. We are watching ourselves in painful scrutiny. Yet it seems to us that it is, instead, the people around us who are watching and seeing into our very souls, finding us lacking, insufficient. This experience of apparent transparency, which is often referred to in regard to shame, and hence needs some explanation, is in my view created precisely by already feeling exposed. It is not so much that others are, in fact, watching us. Rather, it is *we* who are watching ourselves, and because we are, it *seems* most especially that the watching eyes belong to others. Exposure heightens our awareness of being looked at or seen.

Beyond exposure itself, how is one to openly express what must seem one's inescapable flaw as a human being? This alienating, isolating effect of shame also prevents us from conversing directly about the experience. However much we long to approach, to voice the inner pain and need, we feel immobilized, trapped, and alone in the ambivalence of shame.

Shame can occur in a wide range of intensity and depth, and in a variety of forms or manifestations. It is not so simply a singular experience. Rather, shame carries a multiplicity of *meanings* for the self depending upon a host of factors such as the actual importance to the person of the part of the self that has been exposed or shamed, the significance to the self of whatever other persons are involved in the shaming, whether one is shamed publicly or privately, the repetitiveness of shaming, capacity to cope effectively with the sources of shame, and capacity to literally tolerate the affect of shame itself.

Shame at the hands of a stranger may well carry less import than disparagement at the hands of one's father. Public humiliation creates a far deeper wound than does the very same action done entirely in private. Who has not at some time been laughed at by a group of one's peers? Remember how humiliating this felt? To have a mother shame us is one thing. But to do so directly in the presence of our friends is another. Not only have we lost dignity in our own eyes, but also in the eyes of those friends as well. The felt meaning of the shame experience differs in the two situations. And to be exposed and laughed at for something which I have already decided is trivial is yet again to be distinguished from exposure of a part of myself which I hold to be very dear, even essential, to my inner well-being.

To illustrate the power of the shame experience, I should like to recall here an instance drawn from my own life. This will further-more highlight the important role that can be played by the peer group and school setting in the development of shame, additionally to the family. The instance occurred when I was to participate in a ninth grade panel discussion before the assembled student body of my junior high school. Admittedly anxious as I was, I went ahead with this first attempt at public speaking. We were seated in the front row, my fellow panelists and I. The teacher heading us introduced the theme and members, who then walked to the stage to take their seats as he called each name. I was last to go up. The moment came and went. The moderator then proceeded to the program, forgetting me. I squirmed in my seat not knowing whether to go up anyway or to wait. Then he discovered his omission amid scattered peals of laughter as he called my name. This assemblage of my peers loudly broke out laughing as one, as I walked to the stage. Then, as I crossed to my seat, I tripped over the microphone wires which only sent them all howling the more. At last, I sank into my seat as though it were the very floor. I wished desperately I could just hide from all those staring eyes. Then our esteemed moderator turned to *me* to start things rolling for the panel. I was to be first to speak off-the-cuff on our topic of parent-teenager relations. Well, I sat there just paralyzed. I couldn't move, my mind was blank, I was speechless! I could think of nothing to say. And if that were not bad enough, the moderator, who now looked a bit bewildered himself, began to prompt me by asking questions, hoping to get me going. But not one word came to mind. I could not think of what to say, not one word. So I sat there, dumbly looking down at the table, wishing I could sink into the floor. I felt trapped, speechless, and intolerably alone. Before everyone I had to see daily I felt exposed as a simpleton, deficient for all to see. They would say, "There goes the laughing stock of the school!" I held my head and eyes down for the rest of the program. And later, when it was over, I could look no one in the face, least of all myself. That experience left its mark.

The foregoing incident highlights several key dimensions of shame. Most notable are the binding effects of exposure upon the self, culminating in such utter self-consciousness that speech can become silenced. It is rare to observe such a gross shame reaction so publicly. As a general rule we are able to either leave the situation or have attention focused elsewhere and so escape from the watching eyes of others.

The effects of shame upon the self, profound as these can be, may be concealed from the view of others. There may be only a trace of reaction to tell the onlooker of the pain or torment taking place within the individual experiencing shame. What may instead become manifested are the secondary reactions which can accompany or follow shame: fear, distress, or rage. Feeling exposed is often followed by fear of further exposure and further occurrences of shame. That feeling of distress more commonly referred to as hurt frequently accompanies shame. And the instant flash of rage, whether expressed or merely held inside, vitally protects the self against further exposure. When rage predominates in reaction to shame, all that one is shown when approaching the shame-experiencing individual is that very self-protective rage, as though the self were vehemently saying "Keep away!" In this manner the self protects itself yet paradoxically fights against either comforting of the inner wound or reunion, thereby preventing escape from the inner loneliness. In such a dilemma lies the so often felt hopelessness of the shame-experiencing self. Shame is a most ambivalent affect.

By way of summary, the root of shame lies in sudden unexpected exposure. We stand revealed as lesser, painfully diminished in our own eyes and the eyes of others as well. Such loss of face is inherent to shame. Binding self-consciousness along with deepening self-doubt follow quickly as products of shame, immersing the self further into despair. To live with shame is to feel alienated and defeated, never quite good enough to belong. And secretly we feel to blame. The deficiency lies within ourselves alone. Shame is without parallel a sickness of the soul, to echo Silvan Tomkins.

THE SHAME-INDUCING PROCESS: BREAKING THE INTERPERSONAL BRIDGE

The need for relationship with others is basic to us all from infancy on. To be in relationship with a consistent individual, usually mother, or some other person providing mothering, is the infant's primary need. As the growing new person's awareness differentiates self from mother, followed by mother from others, maternal caretaking likewise differentiates into providing for the young child's changing needs. Physical needs for food, warmth, sleep, protection, tactile and sensory stimulation, and bodily contact gradually come to share the focus with those emerging, less readily identifiable and more interpersonally based needs.

Needing a relationship with someone else translates into needing to *feel* that that other person who has now become significant also wants a relationship with us. *Mutuality of response* is indispensable to feeling that one is in a real relationship with another, in a word, to feeling wanted for oneself. The child needs to feel that the parent truly wants a relationship with him or her as a separate human being. Such an experience of being in relationship to a significant other of necessity conveys to children that they are loved as persons in their own right and in some fundamental way that they are special to that significant other.

Relationships begin when one person actively reaches out to another and establishes emotional ties, much as we might go about the process of taming a strange animal. Such a process entails the establishing of a bond. In this way relationships gradually evolve out of reciprocal interest in one another along with shared experiences of trust. Trusting essentially means that we have come both to expect and to rely upon a certain mutuality of response. An emotional bond begins to grow between individuals as they communicate understanding, respect, and valuing for one another's personhood, needs and feelings included. That bond deepens along with trust and makes possible experiences of openness and vulnerability. The bond which ties two individuals together forms an *interpersonal bridge* between them. The bridge in turn becomes a vehicle to facilitate mutual understanding, growth, and change. These vital processes are disrupted whenever that bridge becomes severed.

The interpersonal bridge which spans the gulf between strangers conveys to each person that the relationship is wanted by the other. Each feels wanted as a person in his or her own right. Over time, involving sufficient and reciprocal experiences of one person trusting and having the other person prove trustworthy, a sense of certainty about the relationship emerges. In such a manner, individuals relinquish their strangeness, establish emotional ties, and become significant to one another. This happens between adults who are strangers to one another, and a parallel though certainly not identical process can be observed between children and parents. The key point is that some attention must be paid to the establishing of emotional ties, grounded in trust and security, if a relationship is to mature.

Letting another person become significant to us means that person's caring, respect or valuing have begun to matter. We permit ourselves the vulnerability associated with needing something from that other person. We look to that person for something. And we expect some response to our needs, whether expressed clearly or not. Experiencing a need and expecting a response can be viewed as two sides of one and the same phenomenological event.

Because we are human, we behave in ways that have unintended impact even in our most important relationships. Whenever someone becomes significant to us, whenever another's caring, respect or valuing matters, the possibility for generating shame emerges. When we become significant to another individual, as happens when we are parent, friend, spouse, teacher, or therapist, then we can induce shame in that other person. It can happen intentionally or unintentionally, without even knowing it has happened. The critical step occurs when one significant person somehow breaks the interpersonal bridge with the other. This is the basic way in which shame is generated.

The interpersonal bridge is built upon certain expectations which we have come to accept and to depend upon. Learning to expect a certain mutuality of response is the basis for the trust we feel for someone significant to us. Shame is likely whenever our most basic expectations of a significant other are suddenly exposed as wrong. To have someone valued unexpectedly betray our trust opens the self inside of us and exposes it to view. "What a fool I was to trust him!" How familiar that reaction is. The anger evidenced is but a mask covering the ruptured self.

Imagine the following situation. A twelve-year-old boy has begun to value his relationship with a considerably older brother, even desiring to emulate him. The two make plans to purchase season football tickets, an activity highly prized by the older, for the coming year. This is in the fall and all throughout that next year the young boy expectantly looks ahead to the exciting adventure with his older brother. Little need be said of the forthcoming event, yet the boy has come to count on it. That spring, the older brother becomes engaged and marries later that summer. In the fall, with football season approaching, nothing more is said of their prior plan to go to the games. In fact, brother and his new wife purchase the coveted football tickets for themselves, with not a word being said to the young boy. The boy's expectations are smashed, suddenly exposed as wrong. The very thing he had come silently to depend upon is exposed as inconsequential to the deeply valued older brother. At once, the boy feels betrayed and his trust in brother shattered. Such betrayal of trust in a significant human relationship can be a potent generator of shame.

Repeatedly, we fail to take account of the impact that our actions have on those with whom we are in relationship. What may seem inconsequential or innocuous to us in what we do can have the most profound impact on another, be it friend, spouse, student, client, or child.

In order to elucidate the sequence of inner events which culminates in shame, let us consider a situation concerning a father and his son. Their relationship is a satisfying one, each often finding pleasure in the other. One day the father is rather preoccupied with his own pressing needs. He seems quite oblivious to what is happening around him. His son approaches and interrupts his internal preoccupation, asking father for some time together. Father is too preoccupied with himself to attend fully and responds to the boy with an abrupt, "Can't you see I'm busy? Don't bother me." Let us now enter this child's experience and see it from his perspective. The boy had been feeling quite upset and in need of special time with father, some attention immediately paid to him. And he had learned to expect some response to his need. Yet father neither responded to the boy's request directly nor responded in a way that acknowledged it while also communicating that father's needs had to come first. Responding appropriately does not necessarily mean either immediate or even delayed gratification of the need; however, it does mean openly acknowledging it in some way. Failure to fully hear and understand the other's need and to communicate its validity, whether or not we choose to gratify that need, breaks the interpersonal bridge and in so doing induces shame.

Let's reenter the boy's experience. (The following sequence of events was originally discerned by Dr. Bill Kell.) The boy's need went ignored and quickly began to convert into a bad feeling. Since his father, as all parents, is seen as infallible, the boy is left feeling that he is bad. "If I'm not bad, then my need would have been met," or "If there wasn't something wrong with my need, it would have been responded to." Later on, father is no longer preoccupied and comes looking for his son. Perhaps he even realizes that the boy may have needed something. The boy is off in his room alone behind a shut door. The father now tries to approach his son, but the boy reacts with rage. Because the interpersonal bridge is broken, his son now fears exposure not only of his badness but to another occurrence of shame as well. In this way, the boy feels trapped into remaining in his shame; he is unable to approach on his own. Though he must be approached first, he reacts with rage to any approach. This is an impossible situation for both father and son.

Rage serves a vital self-protective function by insulating the self against further exposure and by actively keeping others away to avoid further occurrences of shame. The boy's rage may even induce shame in his father through the very same process. In this event, a pattern of escalating rage can result, with each participant blaming the other as a way of protecting himself against exposure. What began as a friendly interaction turns into a raging battle that neither person wants yet feels helpless to stop.

The rupture is felt to lie either in the relationship, as happens when the interpersonal bridge becomes severed, in the very self of the individual, or in both. Interpersonal trust as well as internal security can be powerfully disrupted by the experience of shame.

There is a viable way out of the vicious spiral of shame and rage. In approaching the boy, all father need do is acknowledge being late in recognizing his son's need. Through openly acknowledging that he also had something to do with it, the father can relieve the boy's terrible burden of feeling that it was all his own fault. In such a way, the interpersonal bridge between them can be restored, thereby enabling the boy to move beyond his shame.

Even when that significant other fails to do what is needed, shame will likely pass, much as other feelings do. As with all feelings, shame will first pass on unless it becomes internalized, following which it is capable of being generated wholly from within.

PREVERBAL SHAME INDUCEMENT: THE ROLE OF EARLY PARENTAL ANGER

Shame can have origins at any point in the life cycle. The central idea to keep in mind is that the process by which shame originates in my view always involves some kind of severing of the interpersonal bridge. Language is certainly one of the most potent communicators of shame. Before looking at how this can occur, we shall first explore shame inducement in the preverbal child. An incident comes to mind. It occurred between my son and me when he was eleven months old. We were sitting in our home and he was playing on the floor. Then he did something that made me verbally angry at him. He sat up and instantly began crying with a most hurt look on his face. As he cried he raised up his arms, in this way reaching to be held. That was a moment of conflict for me. Everything I had ever learned taught me not to provide physical holding following anger, or else it would be too confusing for a child. In my anger was also a powerful, natural impulse to not hold him and even to walk away from him. But I acted contrary to my own feelings. I picked him up and simply held him close to me, while still verbalizing my anger at him. His crying gradually ceased and soon he wanted to be released. Something had clearly changed within him.

I puzzled over this incident for some time and finally came to a number of realizations. My anger at the boy severed the interpersonal bridge between us and my response to *his asking* to be held restored it. It seemed to make some sense that physical contact should not be denied a child out of anger. This does not mean one should offer it first. Anger directly followed by a parent's initiating close contact can indeed produce confusion for a child. But if the child spontaneously asks for holding in the midst of parental anger, he is needing to reestablish his sense of well-being. And at least prior to language development, this can only happen through physical holding, which communicates protection and security—the basis for trust.

To make this generally applicable, then, let us postulate a relationship involving some degree of adequate mothering. In such a case, the child's inner well-being is most notably a function of the maternal or parental climate. Though we can never know an infant's inner experience, imagine what it might be like for a young child to suddenly experience an outburst of anger from his principal caretaker. It seems at least plausible that the first occurrences of parental anger could powerfully disrupt a young child's sense of security and well-being. Certainly some anxiety or fear, perhaps even terror, might be generated. But even more than this, there is liable to be a critical tear in the fabric linking child with mother, that sense of bonding or attachment which the very young child depends upon for protection, for its very life. Such expressions of anger toward a preverbal child can, at times, though perhaps not always, sever the interpersonal bridge and thereby induce shame. Furthermore, it is parental failure to restore that bridge following expressions of anger toward the child which will critically intensify the rupture and leave the child feeling trapped in his or her shame. I am in no sense suggesting avoidance of expression of anger on the part of parents. Rather, we need to keep alert for the signs of shame, anxiety, and insecurity, particularly when these are of heightened proportions.

Without language, the only reparative means available to the young child is through physical contact. The rupture in the relationship will very likely be followed by the child's spontaneous, nonverbal request for holding. Reaching to be held at such a cataclysmic moment in the young child's life is his only way of reaffirming either himself or the relationship, thereby feeling restored. Asking to be held enables children to find out for certain through their own actions that they are still loved and wanted, to affirm their own value and well-being. That knowledge and security can come only through physical contact for the preverbal child.

In exploring the role anger plays in the shame-inducing process, two additional concepts have emerged: affirmation and physical holding. We shall return to these later when we consider a formulation of developmental needs in the context of shame internalization. For the time being, we have seen another way in which shame can subtly, even unknowingly be generated.

SHAME AND ABANDONMENT IN THE YOUNG CHILD

We have seen that shame is followed by a number of different feeling responses, the principal ones being fear of exposure, distress or hurt, and self-protective rage. We have also seen how the experience of shame violates trust and security, two phenomenological events which play a significant role in forming and maintaining relationships. There is another reaction which must be added to these.

Breaking the interpersonal bridge is the critical event which induces shame. The experience of shame itself further severs the bridge such that an ever-widening gulf emerges between the two individuals. Their relationship has indeed become ruptured. For the young child who is so acutely aware of depending upon his parents for his comfort, for his needs, for his very life, such a situation of intolerable yet unremediable isolation can generate the spectre of abandonment. What I am saying is that a young child, and a preverbal child, can directly experience shame as abandonment. This is not the case, of course, if the parent is reassuring, restores the bridge and in so doing reaffirms the relationship. On the other hand, the parent can react in one of the following three ways: by becoming emotionally unavailable as, for instance, through excessively long periods of silent withdrawal from the child, this being experienced by the child as a refusal to relate; or by becoming overtly contemptuous either facially or verbally, this being experienced as complete rejection of the offensive, disgusting child; or by in some manner overtly withdrawing love and prolonging this unreasonably. When the parental mood is molded by one of these reactions, whatever feelings of abandonment which may be lurking in the child can rapidly intensify to the point of sheer terror.

In all that has been covered so far, it must be emphasized that one or even several shame-inducing experiences do not launch a child on a path toward a shame-based identity. The experiencing of shame is even necessary if the growing individual is ever to develop the inner resources needed to effectively cope with shame in subsequent years. Avoiding necessary encounters with shame will only breed an individual lacking those essential resources, for shame is inevitable in life. It is the pattern of experiences within significant relationships over time that carries deepest and lasting impact. No one need be perfect, to respond appropriately always, and to live in fear of what might otherwise result. Relationships are restorable, however impaired they may have become. Mistakes in a relationship need not be feared and can even become growth experiences for the persons involved.

SHAME EXPERIENCES IN LATER CHILDHOOD

Not all shame is an unintended, unsought by-product of human interaction. Parents frequently seek to shame their children into desired behavior without understanding the disruptive impact shame is liable to have upon the self. Statements such as "Shame on you" or "You should be ashamed of yourself" are certainly obvious and blunt. Because of their obviousness, such statements are easier to defend against. Still, they can on occasion or with sufficient repetition wound the self.

Another most frequently occurring situation involves the discovery by the child that behavior which so far has been acceptable at home or in private suddenly and *unexpectedly* becomes bad when the family is in public. Unfortunately, there is no prior notice given that the rules must be different. I have often observed that much public parental shaming of children occurs as a result of parents themselves feeling exposed to their own peers through their children's behavior. Parents seemingly feel ashamed because their child is not adhering to some accepted adult norm, as though the child were merely an *extension* of the parent. At such a moment, the parent hurriedly looks around to see if anyone is watching and, anxiously expecting contemptuous glances from other parents, will suddenly shame the child.

Far more subtle is the use by the parents of their own shame or embarrassment as a shame-inducing mechanism. Let's imagine how this might occur. The child begins jumping up and down at the supermarket and mother shouts: "Stop that. You're embarrassing *me* in front of everyone." Immediately the child feels exposed, judged and shamed. Certainly the mother may be feeling some shame herself but whether or not she is, such communications at best induce shame in the child and at worst additionally burden the child with mother's shame as well.

Consider the following example. One young woman, Helen, recalled how her mother repeatedly would use such a mechanism to control the girl. She related the following incident, one of many, which had occurred when she was eleven years old. About fifty relatives had gathered for a celebration in their home. The paternal grandmother proceeded to give gifts to all the children. When grandmother did not hear Helen's all too quietly spoken "Thank you," grandmother unleashed a tirade of belittlement directed at Helen, before all the assembled relatives. The tirade culminated in grandmother saying to Helen that she "had not been brought up right," an insult aimed directly at Helen's mother. Helen could not bear the scene any longer and ran crying into the bathroom where she locked herself in. Mother came after her and demanded she unlock the door, insisting that Helen had made much more out of the situation than was warranted. Helen refused to come out until mother at last voiced to Helen: "You're embarrassing *me* in front of the family!" At this, Helen crumbled, opened the door and went over to apologize to grandmother.

Whenever mother would in similar ways openly voice being embarrassed by Helen's behavior, a pernicious tie became additionally fostered between the two of them which taught Helen to experience herself merely as an extension of her mother, never as a separate person in her own right responsible for her own behavior. Such a dynamic pattern in a family makes eventual separation all the more difficult. This was indeed the case for Helen, for while she had effected physical separation from home at the time I began working with her, she had not as yet been able to free herself emotionally from the entangled relationship with her mother, neither the continuing interpersonal one nor from the internalized mother within her.

Still another way to induce shame is to communicate to a child that he or she is a definite disappointment as a person to either one or both parents. Such communications convey a rather global accusation that one is fundamentally lacking. Saying something like, "How could you have done that! I can't believe it. I am so deeply disappointed in you," with all the accompanying facial cues and tone of voice, can all but crush a child. Being repetitively viewed as a disappointment to another, especially another who is so significant as is a parent, immerses the self in feeling inherently deficient.

Clearly, failure to respond appropriately to those who depend upon us can occur in a great variety of ways, some of which are so subtle as to go entirely unnoticed. Yet in every case they convey the sense that one is not quite good enough as a person. Let's turn to several other potent generators of shame.

Instances of disparagement comprise another means whereby shame can accrue. Here some form of belittlement takes place. A father comes home from work feeling heavily burdened by the pressures of the day. His daughter rushes up expectantly, having patiently awaited father's return for quite some time. She is eager to show father the first batch of cookies she had made all by herself. Proud of her new accomplishment, the girl excitedly wants father to admire her. But father's angry mood prevails and he snaps at her: "When are you going to grow up and stop asking me to look at everything you do?" Need more be said in order for us to appreciate the profound impact such a response has upon the young girl?

On occasion, disparagement results from parental comparison of the child with her friends or siblings. "Why can't you be like Johnny? Johnny doesn't cry." Or: "You're just a cry-baby." And in such a way, are we not teaching the child always to compare herself with peers *and to find herself deficient for the comparison?*

When blame is either fixed or transferred to another, some identifiable event typically has taken place which necessitates that transfer. Most often the event involves something having gone wrong, such as an accident, a breakage resulting from poor judgment, or a mistake. Imagine a young boy playing ball outside his home who, in his excitement, flings the ball through a neighbor's window. Certainly the boy is painfully aware of his responsibility yet is met with blame when father learns of the incident: "You stupid idiot, when are you going to learn how to throw straight and be careful? You're always so careless and clumsy. You should have known better than to play so close to that house." All this accomplishes is fixing the blame so squarely upon the boy's shoulders that he cannot find any way to walk out from under it with his head held high. Like rubbing salt in an open wound, the boy's nose is further rubbed in the mess he made. Blaming produces such intolerable shame that he may be forced even to deny responsibility for the precipitating event or find ways of excusing it. In the midst of shame, we need to salvage something in order to preserve our dignity and self-respect. When these are visibly called into question, the owning of honest responsibility is altogether averted.

Expressions of disgust or contempt communicate unambivalent rejection. The object of contempt is found disgusting and offensive. According to Silvan Tomkins, the sneer and the raised upper lip are facial signs of contempt. The look of contempt, particularly from someone who is significant, can be a most devastating inducer of shame. An overly critical attitude toward others is one way in which contempt becomes manifest interpersonally. Such a person becomes a perpetual critic, always finding something wrong, some fault with people or things. To have such a person for a parent guarantees continual subjection to shame.

Derisive laughter and ridicule are nowhere more prominent than among the child's own peer group. One's emerging alliances with the outer world are fragile though significant. To be mocked, ridiculed or laughed at is to be held in such contempt that one is not fit to belong.

Next we come to instances of open humiliation. There is no more humiliating experience than to have one's relative lack of power in relation to another continually rubbed in one's face. Children are forever forced to contend with others who are bigger and stronger. A familiar pecking order or dominance hierarchy develops along the lines of relative size, strength, and aggressiveness. Submitting to the neighborhood bully leaves one feeling defeated as a person and very much alone. But imagine a boy struggling with his own ambivalent feelings about whether to fight back and risk getting hurt, goaded on by the instigating onlookers shouting "Coward!" if he does not fight back. Imagine his profound inner turmoil at that moment. And, in the midst of this, his father sees what is happening and grabs the boy, hauling him aside, and angrily shouts at him: "If I ever see you getting hit first and you don't fight back, I'm going to give you the beating of your life! I'm going to make you fear my beatings worse than fighting back!" And what happens? Fighting back itself has now become bound by shame.

Not only does the boy not fight back, and so experiences the certain humiliation of cowardice before his peers, but he is subjected to recurring humiliation through beatings at the hands of his father for his refusal to fight back. At each turn, he is shamed. There is no more humiliating experience than to have another person who is clearly the stronger and more powerful take advantage of that power and give us a beating. The shame engendered, the deep abiding wound to the self, and the tremendous rage all but consume the boy. Desire for vengeance upon the humiliator burns to a fever. The once-loved father now is both feared and hated.

As this example shows, humiliation is a fertile breeding-ground for hatred and for revenge-seeking. This is one means by which the humiliated one can salvage something for his dignity. It may lie only in the knowledge that *he can't make me fight back*. And, indeed, no one could make the boy fight back, not the father's beatings and not the cowardice shown to his peers who are goading him on. It must seem a strange paradox that taking on the humiliation on both fronts can become a way, in this case, of preserving some shred of dignity in one's own eyes. To do otherwise is to give in to the power of others, to relinquish one's integrity, and in so doing to lose all respect for oneself. In such a situation, there is shame however one proceeds.

To round out the present discussion of the seeds of shame in later childhood, let us consider how performance expectations can be a source of shame. Parents who experience an inordinate need to have their child excel at a particular activity or skill will likely behave in ways that pressure the boy or girl to incessantly do more or better. When the parent sets the standard which the child must then live up to, performance expectations are thereby generated. Of course there are many areas of living, particularly regarding children and the family scene, where holding expectations of a child is vital. How to get along peaceably with others, whether peers or family members, is a value which parents pass on through expecting such behavior from their children. Expecting a reasonable degree of personal cleanliness is not undue. Requiring a child to respect the property of others, whether a sibling's or the neighbor's, is essential in rearing an individual who is capable of living well in community with others. Respecting privacy is another expectation that is reasonable and even necessary. In a basic sense, respecting the rights, the feelings, and the needs of others are standards of behavior which ought to be required. Through such expectations, the family becomes a key vehicle for the transmission of cultural values.

These are the kinds of expectations which promote growth. Appropriate expectations serve as necessary guides to behavior and are not disabling. Disabling expectations, on the other hand, have to do with pressure to excel or perform at a task, skill, or activity. Whenever such expectations are directly or inadvertently set upon us, binding self-consciousness can be induced because we immediately become aware of the real possibility of failing to meet those expectations. That very self-consciousness itself, that painful watching of oneself, is what is most disabling. When something is expected of us in this way, attaining the goal is made harder if not altogether impossible. It is only to the degree to which however we do is *good enough* that we become free to do our best and thereby maximize chances of success. This is an evident paradox certainly noted by existentialists such as Viktor Frankl as well as others. The intervening step is hypothesized to lie in the genesis of shame, for anticipating either success or failure can induce disabling self-consciousness and accompanying exposure fears, creating a vicious spiral.

Let us consider two examples, one drawn from the family and the other from the peer group, of how performance expectations can in fact disable learning. Imagine a situation in which father highly prizes sports yet happens to have two sons, one who is inclined similarly and the other who is not. If the father excessively encourages both boys towards sports, the second son is apt to experience pressure from father to excel at an activity he either does not like or is not well suited for. He is additionally likely to feel that something is wrong with him because he cannot measure up to father's expectations. Since his brother is able to do so, he can only feel that the failing must be his own. Each try is likely to engender further self-doubt and awareness of failure, feeding a self-consciousness in which increasingly the boy expects to fail again and again. Each attempt is complicated by that growing self-consciousness which interferes all the more. After sufficient experiences of failure, one solution is simply to retreat from sports altogether. In such an eventuality, the boy will likely feel confirmed to himself as a failure. He will have learned to think of himself as lesser compared with his peers or brother. And he will experience himself in all likelihood as a definite disappointment to his father.

Of course, if father is reassuring and is able to own his own part in the process, his need for the boy to enter sports and do well there, that sense of utter deficiency can most assuredly be lifted. If father can in this way share responsibility for the failure, the boy will no longer feel that it was all his own fault. Through such restoring of the bridge shame is transcended.

Performance expectations are not by any means confined to the family arena. The school setting and peer group increasingly come to share the focus as the growing child's world expands. Acceptance by peers is a universal striving. Admission to the neighborhood peer group or school clique may become particularly enamored by a child. In such an event, the expectations of others can unfortunately come to affect our good feelings about ourselves.

I do believe that nature endows us with talents and interests which distinguish us from one another. A boy who is innately impelled toward sports may well want to excel, *for himself,* because the activity is sufficiently pleasurable. But many of us have not been so inclined, either because of insecurity, or else lack of interest or somewhat poorer physical coordination. That sports has become an accepted American cultural institution, through which one also gains admission to the peer group, must be evident. I have met many men, myself included, who during childhood were among those last to be picked for the team. We were the awkward ones who had to be included because everyone had to play. At least, that was the rule at school or camp. Always we felt that intense pressure to excel, most especially the watching eyes of our teammates when our turn at bat came up. Our eyes turned inward in the midst of that inordinate pressure. Immediately, the reality of failure, of what it would mean, came upon us. We knew also the contemptuous looks we would get from our fellows if we struck out. We would be letting everyone on the team down, most of all ourselves. In the midst of extreme self-consciousness, our ability to do well is altogether disrupted. When that painful and binding watching of oneself absorbs us, there can be no pleasure either in playing or in learning. We walk away from the activity concerned most eager to escape, yet also dreading the next time. It is apparent that the peer group is able to function much as a significant other, capable of arousing shame, for each of us has yearned to feel a part thereof, to claim our rightful place and in so doing, to belong.

THE ADOLESCENT EXPERIENCE: IMPACT OF SHAME

The foregoing discussion of the peer group's role in the genesis of shame brings us to a consideration of adolescence. There are several key ideas to keep in mind through the ensuing discussion. First, adolescence, as any developmental epoch, is most usually experienced ambivalently. There are rewards and pleasures at hand or fantasized to come. We in this case can feel especially proud of our emerging womanliness or manliness and excited about what lies ahead. Yet each step forward implies a relinquishing of security in some measure. We are giving up some things as well as gaining others. Adolescence, perhaps as no other single developmental step, harbors one universal attribute: it is a time of especially heightened self-consciousness. Adolescence, then, is a critical period of significant vulnerability to shame.

A second useful idea to retain is that, perhaps in response to this heightened feeling of exposure, the adolescent is apt to turn inward. Privacy becomes the hallmark of his or her world. The self searches for some means to retreat from too much visibility. Thus, he or she hides as well whatever inner turmoil may be taking place.

Adolescence is not a negative experience, but it is an ambivalent experience which is at least partially submerged from view. As a time of heightened self-consciousness and exposure, it is a uniquely trying time for many. How we are responded to during this critical turn in development by those most significant to us, whether parents, siblings, peers, or teachers, will carry essential meaning as to our very worth or adequacy as newly becoming men and women.

The potentially disruptive impact of adolescence can be mitigated through the benevolent actions of others significant to us. Parents are the most likely guides for adolescents to turn to in learning to navigate into adulthood. An adolescent girl, whose father openly admires her emerging womanliness by saying, "You're growing into a fine young woman and I'm proud of you," will learn the joys of femininity and the ability as well to affirm her own value from within. For her, the passage through adolescence will be filled with many pleasurable moments which likely will counteract the effects of heightened self-consciousness that is also inevitable at this time.

Not all adolescents are equally fortunate. For many the passage is more turbulent, particularly if prior encounters with shame have been too frequent. Let's view adolescence from their vantage point and seek a deeper understanding of how disabling shame can be. In essence, let's view adolescence through the looking glass of shame.

The onset of adolescence brings about an especially trying time for an individual who is leaving behind the certainties of childhood, however unpleasant these might have been. It would seem that now one's own body is becoming an inescapable source of renewed encounters with the alienating affect. One's body has begun its ancestral journey of transformation, of relinquishing the boyishness or girlishness of youth. Prepared as one might be, the inevitable changes that are now to befall us come most suddenly and unexpectedly nonetheless.

However poor the physical body nature has provided us, we had still grown accustomed to it over the years. Even visible deformities, which in themselves must remain a poignant source of derision, of humiliation, of exposure of the self, pale before the universal experience of adolescence. It is as though our own body, which has stood us in good stead before, now suddenly begins to betray us. Imagine the immediacy of the sudden cracking of one's own voice in the midst of a class sing, bringing all eyes upon the self amid hushed giggles. Indeed to be exposed and trapped by one's own body. And then the growth of body hair, or the lack thereof, which brings the watching eyes of others if not their comments. The blossoming of breasts for newly becoming women cannot long escape notice or comparison by peers. And all those facial blemishes which cannot be hidden no matter how hard we try. No wonder we become so painfully aware of our presence. All of these bodily changes visibly call attention to the self and expose it to view for all to gape at. The agonizing awkwardness of adolescence bespeaks an all but consuming self-consciousness that now has come to pervade one's daily living.

Not only is the peer group crucial at this critical turn in development that we call adolescence, but the family likewise plays its own continuing role. How parents, siblings, and relatives respond to the changes besetting a particular individual counts mightily. Do they repeatedly tend to notice and *comment* excessively, in a finger-pointing manner, about the changes underway and in so doing generate the torment of self-consciousness? Or do they remember what it was like and, in kindness, let the troubled self have its cocoon as best he or she can in the only privacy there is, one's home? Or do they yet again make fun, tease, or behave derisively? Does an older brother repeatedly call attention to or otherwise demean a younger sister's breasts either as too small or too matronly and in so doing heap further shame upon her already present feelings of exposure? Or does a father suddenly, inexplicably, shrink away from a daughter's fond embrace, feeling her now getting too old? Even our parents have betrayed us! That is how it feels to the exposed self.

Beyond the family and peer group, we have also to keep in mind the school setting itself as another quite critical developmental setting. Teachers and the way they respond to us carry import for our essential dignity. A youngster may come to look to a teacher for needs quite unfulfilled at home. I know one fellow who met continual ridicule from a particular teacher whenever he spoke in her class. And the laughter from his peers drove home the shame all the more. It eventually came about that this bright fellow increasingly retreated from verbal interaction when in any class situation. That this event occurred during adolescence, a time of already heightened self-consciousness and exposure, made it all the more poignant.

Human relationships suffer under the strain of protracted shame. The climate of adolescence itself is one of heightened self-consciousness as we have just seen. The adolescent also has begun to navigate in increasingly uncharted waters as he searches to make contact with a girl and she searches for no less with a boy. Feelings of exposure most assuredly spread to our initial attempts at male-to-female relating. Many overcome the hurdle shame hands us in the form of self-consciousness. Many never do. One boy would agonize for hours over whether to put his arm around a girl, literally would sit there feeling paralyzed. He was unable to will his arm to move, so totally was he bound up by self-consciousness.

Why does the peer group carry such weight with us? Why is the family able to affect what ails us? Where comes their power? That is a question of profound significance, for with it rests an understanding of development itself. It is in the honest looking to others for our most essential human needs that we give over to those others that power of which I spoke. We are needing creatures to begin with. And that is a source of strength as well as a potential source of shame.

Few strivings are as compelling as is our need to identify with someone, to feel a part of something, to belong somewhere. Whether it is in relation to one significant other, or the family, or one's own peer group, we experience some vital need to belong. And it is precisely the identification need which most assuredly confers that special sense of belonging. So powerful is that striving that we might feel obliged to do most anything in order to secure our place. Yet equally powerful is the alienating affect. For shame can generate, can even altogether sever one's essential human ties, that we might either feel barred from entry forever or forced to renounce the very striving to belong itself and resignedly accept an alienated existence. No matter how strong one's inner yearning to belong, one's essential dignity as a fellow human being matters more.

IMPACT OF CULTURE[1]

Culture shapes personality in ways analogous to the family and peer group. Along with work and school, these settings are the instruments of culture, through which meanings, values, and taboos are transmitted. These settings become the principal arenas in which the motives of shame and honor publicly contend.

Culture is the fabric, the interpersonal bridge, bonding a people together. Through publicly celebrating its heroes, holidays, and rituals, through retelling its heritage and history, and through participating in its hopes and dreams, its conventions as well as taboos, people experience a sense of common purpose. A bond is forged. They come to feel identified with one another.

Culture is also the mold handed each new celebrant coming of age, a mold he or she must be cast into. It is as though we are handed a cultural script—the life-part we are expected to enact. There are three expected, central cultural scripts in contemporary American society which generate shame.

The first is the *success ethic*, which enjoins us to compete for success and to achieve by external standards of performance. The mythic figure of the self-made man or woman is a dominant image of the literature of our nation. We are stimulated to seek our

---

[1] This section is based on the following:

Kaufman, G., and Raphael, L. "Shame as Taboo in American Culture." In R. Browne (Ed.), *Forbidden Fruits: Taboos and Tabooism in Culture*. Bowling Green: Popular Press, 1984, pp. 57-66.

advantage over others through competition. We are taught to view achievement as the measure of our intrinsic worth or adequacy. We are further taught to strive after success and to measure it directly through our accomplishments. Hence, external performance becomes the measure of self-esteem. Striving for success can breed anxiety in the form of fear of failure because success is never entirely within our control. When success by any external standard becomes the measure of self-validation, then competition is inevitably fostered, generating hostility and fear. Failure to attain these goals produces loss of self-esteem and feelings of inferiority. This is shame.

Failing at any new enterprise will now activate shame. Simply being average must seem a curse. The injunction to compete for success inevitably strangles our capacity for caring and vulnerability.

A second cultural injunction is to be *independent and self-sufficient*. Deeply imbedded in our cultural consciousness are images of the pioneer, cowboy, and more recently, the detective. These archetypal figures mirror how to stand proudly alone, never needing anything, never depending on anyone. Needing becomes not a source of strength, but a clear sign of inadequacy. To need is to be inadequate, shameful. Crying and touching are expressions of personality which are heavily shamed in this culture: we are shamed for being human.

The final injunction is to be *popular and conform*. In a culture which esteems popularity and conformity, individuality is neither recognized nor valued. Being *different* from others becomes shameful. To avoid shame, one must avoid being different, or *seen* as different. The awareness of difference itself translates into feeling lesser, deficient.

These three cultural injunctions create conflicting scripts. It is virtually impossible to accomplish all three visions simultaneously: compete for success, be independent and self-sufficient, yet be popular and conform. These cultural scripts become additional sources of shame. Through shame, culture shapes personality.

Our society *is* a shame-based culture, but here, shame is *hidden*. There is shame about shame and so it remains under strict taboo.

Other cultures, for example, Eastern and Mediterranean, are organized more openly around shame and its counterpart, honor. What we need in our culture is to honor shame, and thereby redeem it.

FROM INTERPERSONAL SHAME TO
INTERNAL SHAME AND ITS EVENTUAL HEALING

We have explored various means, both direct and subtle, by which shame can be generated interpersonally. Shame is inevitable in my view precisely because we are human and therefore behave in ways that have unintended impact. When a particular interpersonal interaction occurs which ruptures that vital bridge linking individuals who have become significant to one another, this sets in motion a chain of events resulting in shame. We have so far dynamically linked shame to a failure to respond appropriately to another's need. Responding appropriately entails having the need understood and openly acknowledged whether or not it is gratified. Simple oversight, lack of sensitivity or even well-intentioned criticism from someone regarded as significant can convey the sense that one is not quite good enough as a person. Expressions of anger, particularly at the preverbal child, can be a primary inducer of shame; most especially, it is the failure to tend to the child's expressed need for reaffirmation of the relationship and hence, security, which leaves the child feeling most acutely trapped in shame. When our response to another who holds us in high regard involves disparagement, contempt, a direct transfer of blame, or humiliation, the consequent shame experienced at our hands is more intense, accompanied by rage bordering on hatred and, possibly, that burning longing for revenge as well.

The situations described are all instances of emotional severing between people in an ongoing relationship. It is this emotional severing which is dynamically most relevant for inducing shame interpersonally. The impact of shame increases accordingly when the relationship between the individuals concerned becomes one of central importance to them. The potential for disruptive consequences of shame is greatest in the childhood and adolescent years, especially so when shame is experienced in relation to those two people who are most important in the growing child's world, the parents.

This is the point we have reached thus far in regard to the development of shame. We have yet to consider how shame can come to lie at the core of the self, literally to embrace our essential identity. The most crucial setting involved in this internal development of shame is the family. For example, shame is generated in children usually about those aspects of self that the parent continues to experience shame for in himself or herself. If a father was rejected by his own dad and experiences being defective as a result, he will very likely and unconsciously behave in ways toward his son that repeat the pattern. Even if nothing overt is done, the father's sense of shame itself may transfer. If a mother felt unwanted by her parents, she may subtly prohibit her own son from getting close to his father; the interference induces shame and thereby reenacts the drama. In such ways, shame is recycled and passed on from generation to generation. We will take a closer look at these developmental phenomena in the following three chapters. From there we will move on to a consideration of shame's healing.

Even though the aftermath of shame can be severe, the way to a self-affirming identity lies in the deeply human capacity to be fully restored, in the knowledge that one individual can restore the interpersonal bridge with another however late it may be and in the awareness that human relationships are reparable. Through such restoring of the bridge, shame is transcended. The significant other who was involved in the original shame-inducing experiences need not be the one who must restore the bridge. Someone who later becomes significant, friend, colleague, or therapist, can become that person.

We carry with us always the deep emotional impact of shame, and yet when someone deeply valued risks his own exposure to become vulnerable and openly acknowledges his imperfect humanness, his part in making us feel shame, we are carried beyond shame. The growth impact of having someone take that risk with us is far greater than if he or she had never triggered off a shame experience in the first place. Severing the interpersonal bridge when it is followed by restoring that bridge is the healing process itself, the growth process. This is the process that helps someone move beyond shame toward a self-affirming identity.

2

The Internalization of Shame and the Origin of Identity

We have explored a number of ways available to human beings for inducing shame in one another. The fact that shame is a poignant experience of the self by the self and that shame is both alienating and isolating are not sufficient in themselves to explain the significance of shame as a central motive in human development and interpersonal relations. We must look beyond the interpersonal realm and seek an understanding of internal development in regard to shame. That understanding involves the additional concept of internalization.

The developmental theory of shame unfolding here is based on the internalization of shame as the next significant process dimension. It is precisely following the internalization of shame as a major source of one's identity that the self becomes able to both activate and experience shame without an inducing interpersonal event. The self is then vulnerable to shame irrespective of any external messages communicated from others. In effect, shame becomes autonomous when internalized and hence impervious to change.

In the process of internalization lies the significance of shame for identity. Shame internalization is a development that is both gradual and complex. In order to understand how it comes about we must look at the phenomenological meaning of internalization itself and, beyond it, to the larger process of identification from which it spawns.

IDENTIFICATION AS A HUMAN PROCESS: THE NEED TO IDENTIFY

We as adults struggling to maintain a secure place in a changing world must ask ourselves: "Who am I, *really*? What is core in life for the *me* inside? Where do I *belong*?" These ageless questions renew themselves and recur as life unfolds. So many distinct and varied social groups claim our loyalty, from family, religions, racial subgroups to national allegiance; from paths of knowledge such as science, the arts, to schools of meditation; from whatever sports we identify with to our skills, hobbies, and careers. Any idea, cause or field of endeavor can invite us to join, to participate with and identify with others, and to embrace a kindred spirit. Through believing in something enough to invest our time and efforts, we come to feel a part of that particular cause.

The need to belong to something larger than ourselves underlies many of these pursuits. We long to feel a vital part of some community of others, to have the security that comes through belonging to something larger than ourselves. It is through identification that ultimately we know rootedness.

Identification begins within the family. Learning how to become a person originates through identification, as we first identify and thereby have a beginning base from which to navigate the human world. This idea is pivotal to all that follows. Only later do we individuate by differentiating our own unique self. These two processes, identification and differentiation, alternate with one another as we go about the task of becoming a fully separate person.

Automatically and without any conscious awareness of its occurrence, the young child begins modeling himself or herself after one or both parents. No wish of the child is stronger than to be like the beloved or needed parent, as Tomkins also notes, and modeling is one primary vehicle through which such identification takes place. Modeling is observational learning. The impulse motivating that modeling is the need to identify with a significant other. It is the awareness of separateness which, in part, necessitates a striving to reidentify, to become one with. Phenomenologically, identification involves a merging with another, a partial giving up, if only for a brief moment, of one's separate self. Through observing how the parent behaves and functions, interpersonally as well as internally, the child is enabled to merge with that parent, borrow from him, and try out the behavior in the child's own style. Finally, if the adopted behavior proves valuable to the child, then she can make it her own.

Remember that old familiar, childhood injunction: "Do what I say, not what I do?" It represents the universal awareness that, more often than not, what gets learned is what is unconsciously, that is, *un-self-consciously* observed and attended to. Identification begins as a visual process but does not remain so. It becomes an imagery process which occurs wholly internally. What is first observed outside the self transfers into inner reality through visual imagery. Imagery provides the bridge from outer to inner and enables the child to experience himself as a part of father or a part of mother.

Modeling of parental behavior is one vehicle for identification, but alone, it is not sufficient. Most especially it is through open and close *communication* between parent and child that the much-needed experience of identification takes place. And the parent must *permit* the child to identify with him or her in order for positive identification to occur. Talking with a child about what is truly important to the parent—for example, about the way the parent functions as a person and handles various situations, his hopes, her dreams—is what enables the child to join either parent experientially through the child's own imagery and, in so doing, to *feel identified* with or a part of that parent. In this way the child learns about the parent from the inside, learns what it is like almost to be that other human being who is so important to the child. In a most significant way such an experience of identification at critical times provides needed support, strength, and healing for an evolving self.

We identify with our parents as well as older siblings or grandparents, with whomever plays a consistent role in the growing child's world or takes sufficient interest in her. As children, we identify in order to emulate those we admire, to feel *at-oneness* or belonging with these special ones, and to enhance our sense of inner power from so doing. If the people upon whom we depend as children prove worthy of our trust, not perfectly but humanly, we are likely to continue to identify with them and also want to be like them. Identification based on love and respect, that is, experiencing a significant other who primarily treats us in these ways, will enable us to learn to treat ourselves tenderly, lovingly and with respect for our own imperfect humanness.

But all children are not equally fortunate. In many families, it is yet shame, fear, or contempt which shape the parental climate. Yet even a child who lives in dread of endless beatings or other forms of humiliation will still identify with those two individuals who hold absolute power over his world; certainly, this is so for the first six years, until school begins and the child must move out of the exclusive family orbit. In this latter case, the resulting identification is not positive, but negative. Yet the question remains: why identify with a shaming or contemptuous parent? I think there are at least two reasons for this. The first refers to the condition of perceived helplessness of the child for surviving on his own, coupled with the very real power parents wield in the early years. A child may perhaps outwardly resist, yet inwardly learns to humiliate himself because he has no other model for becoming a person. Also, he is too helpless to leave the home and say good-bye to the only parents he knows.

Parental power to influence the young child's world and the child's own very real feelings of relative helplessness lay important conditions for identification, whether positive or negative. There is, however, a second wellspring for identification, namely, the child's desperate longing to love and to feel loved and thereby derive that precious sense of belonging. Whatever one's parents, still one needs to belong somewhere. Thus, love-based, fear-based, or shame-based identification will develop according to the pattern of parental caring for the child.

Identification is a human process. By this I mean it is an inevitable occurrence in human affairs, universally experienced, and life-long. We never outgrow the need to identify, though the need may become evermore differentiated as one proceeds through life. The child begins to identify first with those significant others in his or her immediate world. Gradually, the child's inner world expands to include a variety of heroic identification images. Fairy tales as well as more contemporary myths and television characters provide one source of such figures with whom the power-lacking child, that is, a child powerless in relation to adults and older children, can identify and thereby enhance his perceived strength and self-esteem. The need to identify intensifies at times of felt inner weakness. Yet the need is much broader than this, occurring in a variety of situations in which the self is not so much wounded as lacking direction or preparedness. To this we shall return later.

The wish to identify continues to differentiate. Same-gender identification predominates more and more of the time: father, older brothers, and peers for the boy; mother, older sisters, and peers for the girl. As the growing child's world expands, new possibilities for identification emerge, most notably, teachers in school.

When the new adult enters his or her chosen career, the need for an esteemed, more experienced individual with whom to identify reasserts itself with renewed force. It is through such identification with a mentor that the novice develops a secure base in that trade, career, or profession from which he or she can then proceed more and more autonomously .

The current flourishing of religious cults and guru movements represents other manifestations of the identification motive. Finding a way of life to believe in enables many to find meaning, purpose, and belonging in an impersonal world. Identification with a guru, a teacher in living, quiets that inner yearning to belong somewhere. And through belonging comes inner security and peace.

We have sketched in some of the most salient aspects of the identification process as I construe it in order to prepare the way for an understanding of internalization. We shall return to identification later in the context of developmental needs and see how the need to identify itself can become bound by shame.

INTERNALIZATION: AN OUTGROWTH OF IDENTIFICATION

Identity emerges haltingly out of the process of identification. Internalization is the important link by which identification leads to identity. Internalization involves three distinct aspects. We internalize specific affect-beliefs or attitudes about ourselves which come to lie at the very core of the self and thereby help to mold our emerging sense of identity. We also internalize the very ways in which we are treated by significant others and we learn to treat ourselves accordingly. This forms the beginning basis for our relationship with ourselves, another important dimension of identity. And we internalize *identifications* in the form of images—we take them inside us and make them our own. These identification images remain internal in the form of specific guiding images. Through internalization, the conscious experience of the self inside is shaped and a relationship with that self develops. This is identity.

We internalize, literally take inside, mainly through identification. Specific ways of thinking and feeling about ourselves are learned in relationship with significant others, parents most especially, but including anyone who becomes important to us. Having a parent honestly say, "Child, I am pleased and proud to have you for my son or daughter," will likely become internalized as an inner conviction of inherent worth. Alternatively, having a parent repeatedly call a boy "stupid" will certainly leave its imprint upon his impressionable psyche. The label conveys more than a simple admonition; it carries meaning as to the boy's deficient worth as a person. With sufficient repetition, he may learn to think of himself as a stupid person, thus creating a distorted sense of self. In such ways as these, the verbal messages communicated by significant others can become internalized as core affect-beliefs which help shape our sense of identity.

Internalizing core affect-beliefs is one aspect of internalization. To look at another, we internalize not only what is said about us, but the ways in which we are treated by significant others in the form of visual images of those interactions. If a girl is repeatedly met with blaming for errors of judgment, she will learn to blame herself when things go wrong, thus transferring the externally experienced pattern directly into her inner life. The internal image of the blaming parent provides the link from outer to inner and imagery mediates the transfer. Alternatively, if the child is instead required to repair whatever mess has occurred without being blamed, she will learn to be responsible for her own behavior, but not have to blame herself for mistakes. We learn to treat ourselves according to the way we are treated by those significant to us, thereby continuing internally the very same pattern we first experienced externally.

Interaction patterns with significant others, whether positive or negative, can become internalized in the form of images of those interactions because of the child's wish to identify with the parent, who is central in the child's world. Not only do we internalize specific ways of treating ourselves in this process, but we also and inevitably internalize *identification images* principally based on those individuals who are most vital for our survival, namely our parents. Again, these images can derive from an identification that is love- and respect-based or from an identification that is terror- and/or shame-based. These internal identification images function in a guiding capacity within the inner life, paralleling the external parental figures from which they derive. They serve as guiding images for the internal functioning of the self. Identification images can play an excessively controlling role in the inner life, encompassing more than the parent had ever intended to control. To the degree that such identifications are based on shame and contempt, the inner life itself becomes perpetually subject to shame.

Identification images are internalized through the identification process gradually over sufficient time. These images eventually comprise one component of identity. The images are mainly rooted in our unconscious, the originating source for them being experientially erased. Phenomenologically, an identification image eventually comes to be experienced as an *auditory voice* inside that remains distinct from the self's own voice. Usually the visual or imagery aspect of the image becomes unconscious, though on occasion it may erupt directly, even disturbingly into consciousness.

Internalization is a direct and natural outgrowth of identification. Visual imagery plays a major role in mediating the transfer from outer to inner. Let us now apply these ideas to the process of shame internalization in particular. There are three additional contributing sources of shame internalization. I am referring to three motivational systems—affects, drives, and needs—in which shame can generate and eventually bind whatever has become associated with shame. Let us take a closer look at these developmental phenomena.

DEVELOPMENT OF AFFECT-SHAME BINDS

As we seek a more differentiated and at the same time a more precise language of the self, it seems evident that there have been quite a number of distinct ways of slicing the "personality pie." Different theorists, by virtue of their being different perceivers of the common ground of human experience, have evolved very different systems for understanding human motivation and development. I wish to articulate the view that the human being experiences a *multiplicity of motivational systems*. The question is not which is *the* correct view of human motivation but, rather, what is the interaction among the various motivators that have been discerned? Asking the question in this latter fashion permits us to entertain a variety of distinct motivational systems without worry as to which is the right one. All are present, perhaps even to significantly varying degrees, in different individuals.

One important motivational system is the *affect system*. The principal theorist in this regard, Silvan Tomkins, has worked toward developing a formulation of the primary affects as well as a theory of human motivation based on affect. The list below summarizes Tomkins' formulation, in which nine innate affects are distinguished, labeled as to both low and high intensity of experience, and described in terms of their respective facial responses:

POSITIVE

1) Interest—Excitement: eyebrows down, track, look, listen
2) Enjoyment—Joy: smile, lips widened up and out

RESETTING

3) Surprise—Startle: eyebrows up, eye blink

NEGATIVE

4) Distress—Anguish: cry, arched eyebrow, mouth down, tears, rhythmic sobbing
5) Fear—Terror: eyes frozen open, pale, cold, sweaty, facial trembling, with hair erect
6) Anger—Rage: frown, clenched jaw, red face
7) Shame—Humiliation: eyes down, head down

8) Dissmell: upper lip raised
9) Disgust: lower lip lowered and protruded

This description of the innate affects serves, for Tomkins, as an introduction to the impact of shame, itself one of the innate affects, directly upon other affects. That impact is conceptualized by him in terms of *affect-shame binds*. Moreover, a contributing source of internalization in my view involves the development of specific or multiple affect-shame binds directly within the emerging personality.

Whenever the expression of a particular affect, whether it be anger, fear, even enjoyment, is followed by some parental response which induces shame, an internalized affect-shame bind can result. The parental response may be direct and intentionally shaming, or it may be unintentional. The impact is what matters. The development of an affect-shame bind then functions to control the later expression of the particular affect involved.

Fear-Shame Bind

Let's take a closer look at this process. Imagine a situation in which a child awakens from a nightmare and cries out in fright. Mother rushes in, asking what is wrong. The child screams, "I'm scared, I'm scared! There's a monster!" Mother abruptly silences the child's screams with, "Now stop that. Don't be silly. Big boys don't get scared of silly things like dreams." The effect upon the lad is that he has been shamed for being afraid. Perhaps this same boy, running away from a bully at school, is told by his Dad, "Don't be a coward! Real boys aren't afraid to fight." If this boy has sufficient experiences in which his scared or frightened feelings are met with shaming, he will learn that there is something wrong with him whenever he feels afraid. Feeling afraid has become shameful, bad. Situations which trigger fear will now also trigger shame. This indirect activation of shame has now become autonomous, thereby causing the expression of fear itself to become bound by shame. Thus, a particular affect can come to spontaneously activate shame without shame itself being directly induced.

Experiential Erasure and Repression

Through the development of such an affect-shame bind, shame is able to exercise a most powerful, however indirect, control over behavior. That control may not stop at the boundary of expression of affect. Feelings must first be internally experienced before they are expressed in some overt manner. The very *experiencing* of a particular feeling can also become silenced if the binding effects of shame spread to the internal, conscious registering of the shame-bound affect. At that moment when the self suddenly feels exposed, if only to itself, the awareness of the contents of consciousness (and of the triggering affect) can be erased experientially. When feeling exposed, the conscious self becomes blank, if only momentarily. Gradually the self can learn not even to be aware of experiencing a feeling which generates shame. For whenever that feeling but creeps into awareness, shame is spontaneously activated, and the feeling becomes bound, controlled and now silenced internally as well. In a most fundamental sense, I would offer that repression has its origin in the process of shame internalization. It is precisely the feeling of exposure inherent in shame, even when the shame activation process has become internalized, which causes this *experiential erasure.* This is one of the more pronounced effects exposure has upon the self.

Distress-Shame Bind

The expression of any affect, shame included, can meet with shaming in one form or another. Let's look at another example. One of the most prevalently shamed affects, at least in our society, is the cry of distress. As children leave babyhood, there are increasing injunctions placed upon them not to cry. Parents may resort to any number of overtly shame-inducing strategies to silence a child's tears. The pressure is especially intense upon male children: "Big boys don't cry"; "You're nothing but a cry-baby"; "Take it like a man, with a stiff upper lip," etc. Such tactics evidently generate a distress-shame bind such that whenever the child experiences sadness or hurt, shame is spontaneously activated as well. And attached to the experiencing of hurt will be the inevitable feeling that something is wrong with the self for feeling it in the first place. Feeling hurt itself becomes shameful, a clear sign of deficiency. Thus, whenever that self in adulthood encounters natural situations which trigger hurt, sadness, or grief (all of these being manifestations of the affect of distress), that self also will feel deficient.

Fear- and distress-shame binds are two examples of how internalization of shame can accrue. Any affect that meets with sufficient shaming can develop into an affect-shame bind. What is central to the development of such an affect-shame bind is how the expression of particular affects is responded to by significant others. If all affects meet with shaming, a total affect-shame bind can result such that the expression of affect per se becomes bound and controlled by shame. If at every turn the child is met with shame, this only hastens the realization that one is, at bottom, inherently shameful as a person.

DEVELOPMENT OF DRIVE-SHAME BINDS

One of the most prevalent theories for understanding human motivation has been conceptualized in terms of the *drive system*. That has been represented in psychoanalytic theory, for example, by sexuality. And I do not mean to imply that there are no social and/or learned components to sexuality, for certainly there are. Yet I think we can comfortably agree upon a biological or physiological component to sexuality that has most conveniently come to be known as the sexual drive. Whether and to what extent there are also other physiologically based drives is not the principal issue before us.

Rather, I would like to develop the drive system particularly in relation to shame. Of all the physiologically based drives, the one most significant in its association with shame is sexuality. Exploratory genital touching, masturbatory activities, sexual curiosity, childhood sexual play, and adolescent sexual strivings are ready targets for any number of shame-inducing responses on the part of either parents or others who play a significant role in the growing child's world. A recurring pattern of parental responses which either call too much attention to the behavior in question, thereby engendering overconcern and self-consciousness, or otherwise directly shame the child for it, can eventuate in a sex-shame bind much as affect-shame binds are created.

Masturbation is a prime example of such behavior, since its occurrence in childhood is so widespread. Parents who feel uncomfortable when their child touches his or her own genitals may quickly react with anger, disapproval, or worse, disgust. Global comments such as "That's bad," or "Don't ever touch yourself *there*," begin the association between sexuality and shame. If a parent metes out shame or disgust every time a young boy is observed to masturbate, then the boy not only will learn to hide that behavior from the parent but will also begin to feel shameful about it. The shame that in this way gradually becomes linked to sexuality, and hence internalized, will likely continue well into adolescence, eventually finding expression in what has more commonly been labeled guilt. I know one boy who grew up in such a family. As adolescence dawned, his urge to masturbate became so insistent that he felt powerless to control it in spite of years of repeated shaming. He had learned to hide better, but the behavior went on in secret. He would try to contain himself yet inevitably he would succumb. Then an incredible sense of sinfulness, of utter disgust for self, would overwhelm him. He would pray each night to God for forgiveness and promise never to masturbate again. Yet try as he might, the inevitable would happen and the cycle repeated itself, further engulfing his sexuality with shame.

There are any number of ways, both subtle and overt, in which one can learn that sexuality per se is shameful. To the degree that sexuality becomes associated with and hence bound and controlled by shame, the individual concerned is faced with an intolerable dilemma: how to come to terms with a vital part of the self that is seen as inherently bad.

Even when sexuality itself has not become shame-bound to any significant extent, the effects of shame, particularly in the form of self-consciousness, can nevertheless spread to our sexual life in both adolescence and adulthood. Typically in our society, we learn at an early age to live up to externally imposed standards of performance. Recall from the preceding chapter how such performance expectations can so induce self-consciousness as to altogether disrupt learning.

In the course of later development, individuals may come to experience their sexual life either as a testing ground for their adequacy or else as an arena in which performance expectations otherwise abound. Our sexual response is a most natural one. Whenever performance enters the scene, we become overly watchful of ourselves, scrutinizing our own bodily reactions such that spontaneous sexual responses are disrupted. If we feel a need to perform sexually with another, then the pressure consequently experienced internally to live up to those expectations of ourselves will in turn mask any possible sexual pleasure. We must allow ourselves the freedom to have or not have sexual impulses at any given time. And we must allow those impulses to follow whatever course they will, neither having to conform to any pattern nor to measure up to a particular standard. If we expect of ourselves to *have to have* an erection, or orgasm, or to last any particular length of time, or whatever, then we will be attempting to bring this about. A part of us will be detached from the ongoing bodily experience, watching from within our own bodily reactions. We will be scrutinizing ourselves rather than experiencing one another. This very self-consciousness itself is what is so disabling because it interrupts all spontaneous, natural movement.

As we begin to realize that our bodily responses are failing to measure up to whatever standard we have set for ourselves, our sense of exposure deepens. The very holding of performance expectations readily implies failure to live up to those expectations. In this eventuality, failure to measure up to any particular standard of sexual performance unfortunately carries meaning as to our sense of inherent adequacy as men and women. It is only when our sexual life is free of expectations and, hence, self-consciousness, that our inner sense of adequacy can remain separate from whatever transpires in the bedroom. It is then that sexual pleasure flows naturally.

DEVELOPMENT OF NEED-SHAME BINDS

Neither such physiologically based drives as sexuality nor the primary affects are sufficient in my view to comprise a sustaining motivational understanding of human development. Sexuality plays a role, even an important one, in human relationships. Anxiety and shame function as significant motivators. And the struggle for identity, I contend, suggests another motivational construct, one which shall surface again and again in these pages. Yet we must look beyond all of these and seek an understanding of motivated development in relationship terms. Here we once more weave back into the interpersonal realm.

Let us explore the area of interpersonal needs. The experience of forming and maintaining a mutually satisfying relationship with a significant other is central to human maturation. The concept implicit in this view has been expressed by Sullivan, Horney, Kell, Fairbairn, and Guntrip, to name but a few theorists. Their observations of the processes involved in human growth must be further explored in order to unfold more clearly a third motivational construct: the *need system*. Insofar as interpersonally based needs comprise a significant source of motivation, the experiencing of shame directly in relation to those needs is a prime source of internalization.

As we proceed, we must keep two related, though separate ends in mind: a differentiation of developmental, interpersonally based needs *and* a consideration of failures in relation to developmental needs such that those needs become bound and controlled by shame.

TOWARD A FORMULATION OF DEVELOPMENTAL NEEDS

The task ahead is one of teasing apart in some clear fashion those distinguishable aspects of a complex organization, the need system, while, at the same time, neither oversimplifying that complexity nor sacrificing clarity. As we shall see, many of the needs to be discussed already have been touched upon earlier.

Need for Relationship

Forming, having, and maintaining a mutually satisfying relationship with a significant other is perhaps the most fundamental interpersonal need of all. Biological birth does not of itself confer a relationship among the family participants. The realities of the child's physical dependence upon the parents for survival do not win over the child's emotional loyalties until an emotional bond begins to grow. It is the active establishing of emotional ties between child and parent from which that trusting bond develops.

Both parent and child experience certain feelings, needs, and expectations in relation to the other. A willingness and desire to enter the child's experiential world conveys to the child the parent's interest in having a relationship. And ultimately the child will come to make similar overtures to the parent. Such a condition of mutuality conveys to each party that the relationship is real, honest, and mutually valued. Even more, the child comes to feel that the relationship is truly wanted by that significant other. Neither the fact of biological birth itself, nor the knowledge that a parent abstractly wants children are sufficient to satisfy our most fundamental of needs, the need for relationship.

Through such a relationship, one feels genuinely understood, secure in the knowledge that one is loved as a person in one's own right (Fairbairn) and wanted for oneself (Kell). Such an experience of being in relationship to a significant other communicates, as nothing else can, that one is indeed special to that significant other. And when one is wanted and so experientially knows with some certainty that one is special, the existence of other relationships involving that significant other pose little if any real threat.

We are born of two parents and each child needs different things from those two significant individuals. One thing that the child needs with each parent is a distinct relationship, a relationship which enables the child to feel *wanted* by that parent.

When a child fails to experience that a relationship with him or her as a separate individual is wanted, shame most often results. It is the parent's actions rather than words, by virtue of their impact upon him, which *convince* a child that he either matters and counts as a person in his own right, or that he really isn't wanted. Let us look at how shame can generate in a poor parent-child relationship. Rejection of the child, when present, may be clear and open, ambivalent and hidden, entirely unconscious, or defended against by overpossessiveness and overprotectiveness. Such rejection can arise when either one or both parents did not want the child at all or really wanted a child of the other gender. Resentment toward the child will find secret expression and the child will feel that he does not belong despite parental verbal assurances to the contrary. And it is the child who will feel to blame.

Shame can also be rooted in a parent looking to the child to make up for the parent's deficiencies or to live out the parent's dreams as though the child were but an extension of the self of the parent. Or again, the parent may directly look to the child literally to be parent to the parent; in this case, the natural flow of the parent being there primarily for the child is reversed such that the child must now tend to the parent's needs instead. Still again, the parent may repeatedly convey to the child that he or she is never to need anything emotionally from the parent; this communicates in no uncertain terms that the child should have been born an adult and so must relinquish childhood without ever having had it.[1]

In order for a real, mutual relationship between child and parent to develop properly, certain conditions are necessary. The child must be consciously wanted and the parent must be able to be there emotionally for the child, to meet his or her core needs and not the reverse. Certainly the child will need to relinquish center stage and learn to both respect and care about the needs and feelings of the parent. But the flow of the parent being there for the child, not perfectly but humanly, nevertheless must remain intact. When these conditions are missing and the relationship patterns described above instead hold sway, the child becomes entangled in a web of profound uncertainty. The conditions for basic security are absent and the

---

[1] I am indebted to Dr. Sue Jennings for an understanding of some of these matters.

child will come to feel unwanted in some fundamental sense. If the pattern of rejection persists sufficiently over time, the child will come to feel that he or she is lacking in some essential way: "Since my parents are infallible, after all they clothe me and feed me and tell me they love me, it must be I who is deficient. The failing is my own."

Need for Touching/Holding

The human infant's requirement for tactile as well as other forms of sensory stimulation has become an accepted fact. The tactile sense, that is, the human skin as a sensory organ, suggests to Ashley Montagu a fundamental, biologically based need, the need for human touching. While the need for touching is physiologically tied, I chose to include it here rather than in the prior section on drive-shame binds for reasons which I shall develop.

The purely physiological component of the need for touching does not communicate what I shall contend to be its more significant, developmental *meaning*. Tactile stimulation during the first year or so of life is certainly necessary if the infant is to mature in a healthy fashion. Ever so gradually, beliefs and feelings about oneself begin to emerge out of such experiences of physical contact. It is the kind and quality of holding which form the earliest sense of self and lay the groundwork for a later secure, self-affirming identity.

As the child grows, the need for holding itself differentiates, being required less often and in response to increasingly specific activators. Physical touching and holding is one of our principal ways of expressing affection or tenderness. At certain times it may be some need for an experience of bodily contact or bodily warmth per se which motivates a child's wanting to be held. At other times, physical holding is the child's natural request in response to emotional need or distress. For example, occasions of physical injury constitute one kind of precipitator of the need for holding. Hurting oneself, crying in distress, and then needing some kind of physical contact with a parent or significant other is a typically observed pattern. As development proceeds, the source of distress or pain gradually removes itself from the purely physical domain and increasingly encompasses the internal and/or interpersonal domains. When emotional hurts, in addition to physical ones, motivate the child to seek out *physical* comforting, verbally expressed reassurance may not be sufficient to reaffirm the child's inner well-being. At times such as this, holding communicates not so much affection as protection and security—the basis for trust.

While day-to-day expressions of affection through touching or hugging are vital, those rarer, special embraces at significant moments carry equally enduring impact. At these times, the self is feeling distraught, saddened, or otherwise in pain and somehow begins to communicate this emotional fact. Communicating that physical contact is what is needed is done either actively (verbally, reaching out, etc.) or through unconscious transmission or interpersonal transfer of the need. These are the moments in our emotional lives that represent what I have come to call the *need for holding*.

We have seen earlier in the context of parental anger as a shame-inducing mechanism that those occasions when anger is expressed toward a child, particularly a preverbal child, can at times generate shame through severing the interpersonal bridge. We saw how parental failure to restore that bridge following expressions of anger could intensify the rupture and leave the child feeling trapped in shame. In addition, failure to respond to requests for holding in the midst of parental anger can lead to direct association of the need for physical contact with shame and perhaps to eventual repression or experiential erasure of the need altogether.

Let's consider further how an event as common in so many families as physical touching is, can become inadvertently shame-bound through a parent's unintended impact. At least in the very early years, a child is often provided opportunities for physical contact, touching and holding, though unfortunately this may be later withdrawn. But whether a parent senses the child's need for reaffirming either the ruptured relationship or his own inner security, and directly provides for that reaffirmation of self through a spontaneous though much-needed embrace, is quite another matter.

The recognition that another person is needing to be held comes to us through some form of active, though not necessarily verbal, transmission of the need. Alternatively, that inner, perhaps ambivalent yearning for holding may remain entirely inside and unspoken, even to the self needing it. Thus, the wish may never get transmitted actively to any other person.

Parents or others who are significant will at times understand the child's need and so provide for it. But often enough while the need is experienced vaguely within the child, the parent fails to recognize and to understand that need. When the need for holding is not responded to appropriately, that is, fails to be understood, this unleashes that familiar chain of events which produces shame. The need begins to convert into a bad feeling and the child comes to feel that either the self or the need is bad in some fundamental way. In such a manner, the need for holding can become bound and later controlled by shame.

In our culture, males in particular are taught not to touch one another. I can remember being told, "Boys don't hug or kiss," when I reached to embrace my older brother. A young lad, accustomed to hugging his dad, will feel betrayed when one day that dearly valued father suddenly and unexpectedly shies away from the boy's touch, feeling him now too old to embrace. And no less a wound is experienced by a young girl, enamored of her newly emerging femininity, if her father lets her know that there is now something wrong with their embracing or with her sitting on his lap as she had always done before. Not only may her need for physical holding become bound by shame in such an eventuality, but the reason for her being pushed away is *felt* to reside in her newly emerging sexuality. Father's shrinking back from her touch can shame the girl's sexuality even when that desire for touching is not motivated by anything remotely sexual.

Parental discomfort with physical contact will readily transfer to a child or adolescent and, eventually, that child or adolescent will stop whatever is making the parent so uncomfortable or obviously embarrassed. Thus, a significant part of the self, the need for holding, can become bound and silenced through shame.

Because of its multiplicity of meaning, human touching or holding constitutes a developmental need which at critical times is essential for development to proceed on course. And physical contact in the form of touching or holding, while certainly pleasurable, is *not* inherently sexual. The widespread societal confusion of sexuality with physical holding has contributed one of the most significant sources of shame about a natural, universally experienced human need. Touching is a sensory experience and, hence, a pleasurable one. But so is *listening* to fine music, *seeing* a captivating movie, *tasting* a delicate meal, *smelling* a fresh rose, etc. These comprise our sensory equipment. And the skin is one of our sensory organs. Sexuality, which in my view refers specifically to the physiological sexual drive or to genital contact and/or genital activities, must be differentiated from the need for physical contact. Certainly the two motivational dimensions will shade into one another. But touching which serves sexual ends is to be distinguished from touching which communicates affection and from holding which is needed to restore trust and security, to reaffirm one's own well-being.

As we draw our discussion of touching to a close, one last thing must be said. Physical holding is one of the means through which a separating individual can return to replenish some of his or her emotional stores, then to move out once more into the world.

Need for Identification

The need to identify, the wish to be like the deeply valued parent, is the motive which enables the parent to transmit, and the child to acquire, a personal culture. Parental mannerisms, styles of speech, ways of handling situations, certain ways of walking or even holding the body may become particularly enamored by a child and unconsciously adopted as though the child were acquiring a part of the parent or practicing to be like the parent. Whoever becomes significant to the child, be it parent, sibling, relative, or friend, becomes important enough to arouse the need to identify.

The first step in the identification process is observation. The child has to be able to observe what will later be taken on. However unconscious the entire process may be, observation is critical to identification. Earlier, I referred to this visual component of identification. Let's explore it a bit further now.

Visual communication from one person to another is a problematic situation for most of us. According to Tomkins, sustained eye contact is a most intense form of interpersonal communication. Mutual looking can very early become bound by shame when the child is shamed both for looking too directly into the eyes of a stranger *and* for being shy in the presence of a stranger. While it makes little sense to speak of a need to look, such instances of visual observation of others and of the sustained meeting of eyes may well represent one manifestation of what I am calling the need for identification.

Shame associated with the visual process and particularly with mutual looking is one of the ways in which identification itself can be interfered with. It is as though through the eyes we can see into one another, perhaps even experientially enter the other's skin and so come to know him or her from the inside. Like open windows, the eyes bid us enter. And when eyes meet, the bidding is a mutual one. The meeting of eyes usually is very brief; only rarely do we sustain that meeting for longer than a moment, for the sheer intensity of the experience of mutual looking most often becomes too much to bear.

When the duration of eye contact passes beyond a critical point, the level of intensity of the experience triggers the feeling of exposure. While briefer instances of mutual looking may indeed permit some degree of affective communication to occur, such as visual merging or identification, a point comes when the self turns away from that merging with another and focuses attention upon itself instead. That point, whether it comes as a result of the critical density of the affective experience or some other factor, is a highly individual matter. Shyness, or what is more accurately understood as shame either in the presence of or at approaching strangers, will affect an individual's capacity for sustaining eye contact. And the same individual will avoid the direct meeting of eyes under some circumstances, and encourage eye contact at other times. Sustained eye contact is a powerful nonverbal experience.

While identification is rooted in the visual process, the need to identify is broader than mutual looking. Identification carries essential meaning as to where one belongs. I am speaking of rootedness, connectedness, and a sense of communality with others.

Whenever the self is in need of direction or preparedness for coping with situations that are sufficiently uncertain or threatening, having an external model available to guide oneself by maintains inner security while enabling the self to navigate the unknown. Certainly, many times precisely what is needed is to be permitted to struggle on one's own, and even to fail. There is important learning in struggle, in making mistakes and in failure. But there are times when sharing with another how he or she handled a particular situation enables us to feel prepared for it, whether or not we actually choose to follow that course. Through such close communication with someone significant, a sense of belonging grows.

Childhood and adolescence, as preparation for adulthood, are times when preparedness and direction are especially urgent. Knowing how another human being lives and functions on the inside— how he or she handles the vicissitudes of life, copes with its joys and its frustrations, faces critical choices, meets failure and defeat as well as challenge and success—is what especially enables us to feel prepared for life. And at each critical turn in development, such as adolescence, marriage, parenthood, entering a career or profession, or facing old age and death, the need for preparedness, for an external model which then can serve as an internal guide for the self, reemerges with renewed vigor.

It is the availability of appropriate individuals with whom we can identify, individuals who also permit us to do so, which quiets that inner yearning. By directly providing support for the self, identification encourages growth, returning one once more into the world feeling restored and, hence, more able to cope on one's own. Identification is one of those vital sources from which identity springs forth.

A boy learns what it means to be a man from his father and a girl learns what it means to be a woman from her mother. These are the principal models for the development of the gender component of identity, masculinity and femininity. It is the close and open communication between parent and child which most thoroughly fosters that identification by enabling the boy to feel that special bond with father which lays no uncertain claim to his maleness and the girl to feel a similar attachment with mother, one which lays equally essential claim to her femaleness.

Some parental modeling inevitably will occur, and more so if the parent is sufficiently rewarding to be with. In spite of such initial, positive identifying with a parent, events can so turn around that identification becomes interfered with or blocked entirely.

There are critical situations in the course of a particular individual's life which may not seem all that singular at the time but nevertheless have a most pronounced effect in altering that course for good or ill. Take our earlier example of the father who attempted to beat his son into fighting back. One consequence of that critical time was that the boy slowly began to reject his father as someone with whom he sought to identify. A certain amount of identification occurred anyway, but this involved ways in which the lad learned to shame and humiliate himself. He no longer sought out father at those crucial times when he needed either preparedness, direction, or aid for his wounded self.

When a child adopts some unwelcome parental quirk, mannerism, or behavior yet is met with, "Don't do that," from that or the other parent, the child is thrown into an impossible situation. Either parent can interfere with the child's identification efforts by simply admonishing her not to be like the admired parent. When the child responds with something like, "But you do it," the forthcoming reply usually is, "Do what I say, not what I do." This is another manner in which the child's identification efforts can become associated with shame.

And a child may not be permitted truly to come to know one or the other of his parents. Either the child is kept at a distance, or close communication occurs only for the parent's need, never in response to the child's.

Still again, the child may be able to identify but learns rather quickly that such occasions of experiential merging are followed by the parent's attempts to hold onto or otherwise control the child. Identification is a fluctuating need, usually followed rather directly by needing to separate. When separation is interfered with or shamed, the child may have to renounce identification altogether, resisting it to avoid being engulfed and trapped. In such an eventuality, the need goes underground and becomes highly ambivalent. Part of the self may desperately long for it while another part just as strongly fears it. In such an insoluble dilemma lie the seeds of later distorted relationships with others.

In all that has been said so far, I have focused principally on the initial life situation all of us experience, the family. And the family accounts for some eighteen years of our lives. But the identification need continues well after we have attained an independent life for ourselves. To the degree that the need was responded to sufficiently—and differentiation was equally supported, as we shall see shortly—the emerging new adult is able to navigate through life more-or-less autonomously and is able to ferret out others with whom to identify as, for example, when entering a trade, career or profession.

But the need continues and periodically will press for expression, whether this be in relation to specific persons such as parents or mentors, or in relation to particular groups. Throughout life individuals seemingly gravitate to one another along whatever lines permit that kind of bonding implied in identification. A sense of kindred spirit, of common purpose, brings together those of us who can identify with one another through the medium of whatever seemingly unites us. In such a fashion, loyalties to groups evolve and begin to move us. We identify with a religion, a way of life, or a cause. Perhaps it is a political party that wins our loyalty, or a football team. And whether it is a racial group or a nation which sways us, loyalties can evolve into allegiances. And we may even be forced by the unforeseen events of life to choose between different loyalties and different allegiances.

So dear is the need, however unconscious, to belong to something or someone, to feel identified with something *larger than ourselves*. Whether it is a group, a cause, or an idea which we feel a part of, so strong can be that bond that we might take up arms and go to war with one another in its name. Thus it happens that human beings, who share a common bond by virtue of belonging to one and the same species, will differentiate and fragment along subgroup identification lines which then predominate over that larger identification with the whole, that communality we all embrace together. For so much easier is it to feel identified with a particular cause, religion or even nation than with humanity as a whole. Additionally, at every turn the equally pressing need to differentiate, to separate into distinctly different parts, pulls at us. And even as human subgroups begin to unite and so to merge with one another, though still holding fast to their differentiated identities, we have yet to make that final leap, a leap to identification with our natural environment, a merging with nature of which we as a species are but one member among many.

Whether or not identification with a particular significant other becomes blocked, the more diffuse expression of the need through identification with varying groups and subgroups usually remains a possible alternative. If nowhere else, at least one can feel a part of some group or cause or idea and, in this way, derive that precious sense of belonging *somewhere*.

Need for Differentiation

If identification confers that special feeling of belonging, then differentiation embraces no less a striving, for separateness and for mastery. This is the instrument by which individuation comes about. Every individual needs to differentiate his or her own unique self, to discard those attitudes and practices acquired from others which either do not suit or have served their purpose and are no longer wanted, and to develop those qualities which are most congruent with the real self inside. To differentiate is to say, "This is me—I am different." Strivings for autonomy and independence emerge from this fundamental need that begins to manifest itself with the dawn of the locomotive capacity. When an infant makes the first movement away from mother, separation is already underway. This early beginning, separation from mother, is followed later by establishing separate relationships with each parent, and finally by separation from the family. Separation culminates, if development proceeds on course, in attaining a separate identity.

It is the active discovery of one's uniqueness and differentness as a person which enables one to know with some certainty, "This is who I am." Through the knowledge of those things about us which make us different from others not only do we come to know who we are, but also and equally important, we come to know who we are *not*. An open recognition and acceptance of who we are not is essential to experiencing ourselves as fully separate individuals.

Let us take a closer look at the separation process and then follow with a discussion of mastery. Separation is as central to the progress of human development as identification. These represent the twin poles of our nature. The quest for separateness takes many forms. When parents teach children a task, the child often does it differently. That change occurs because each of us strives to find our own unique way, to discover our differentness. Holding ideas or beliefs that are at variance with a parent's is an expression of separation. Choosing a different career or life style, as well as departing from parents' religion or values, represent other variants of the motive. Deciding for oneself about marriage or having children, even if these depart from parental practices, are continuing expressions of the need to differentiate, to become a separate person in one's own right. And separation may lead one to move away from the family orbit entirely. Separation from the family happens physically as well as emotionally on many different levels. Fully taking the reins of one's own life is what is most vital.

But the internal push to separate does not occur in isolation. Competence building is necessary to support the child's separation efforts. This is where separation and mastery interface one with the other. A child who has not learned how to be a competent worker will unlikely feel secure enough to venture forth alone into the world. Likewise, a child who has not learned how to maintain satisfying human relationships through gaining interpersonal competence cannot well afford to separate. In order to separate from one's family, one needs to feel secure enough inside and competent enough outside to live life on one's own. One learns this gradually through taking increasing responsibility for oneself in the world, particularly during adolescence. It is this developmental epoch in which the striving to differentiate, both to separate and acquire mastery, is perhaps most insistent.

Increasing mastery over one's own life walks hand-in-hand with becoming a fully separate person. Mastery initially manifests itself through the young child's desire to exercise new functions as maturation progresses, to explore the environment, to acquire language, and to gain control over bodily functions. The acquisition of mastery embraces both developing mastery over internal functioning, bodily as well as psychic, and developing competence in the outer environment. The latter finally matures into the striving for productive and meaningful work, the search for some aspect of the environment whose mastery provides inherent pleasure.

Let us turn to a consideration of shame's disruptive impact upon both separation and mastery strivings. Separation can be resisted at any level of manifestation. Overprotectiveness and overpossessiveness are two means by which this can occur. Moving away from mother or later the family can be resisted by parents. A child can be shamed for having certain values, ideas or preferences if these are seen as different in a negative way from the parents'. And finally when legal adulthood is attained, our parents can forget to relinquish their power, their right to take charge over us. Excessive parental control combined with a parental climate in which a child feels powerless as well as trapped, together are a seedbed for shame.

Interference with the child's natural and spontaneous efforts to differentiate can engender shame about a most vital part of the self. If separation is resisted or forbidden by a parent, a child may become openly defiant in order to preserve autonomy. Or the child may hide his efforts from the parent. Or still again, the child may outwardly submit to such enforced dependence on the parent yet inwardly withdraw into a secret world inside, a place where the parent cannot follow. And mixtures of these most often occur. What the child thereby has learned is that there is something wrong, vitally wrong, with wanting to be separate or different.

I know one young boy who continually voiced his ideas and often these were different. His considerably older brother would take issue with the boy and deliver the "party line," telling the way it "really" was. When the younger boy persisted in disagreeing, the older, who had fifteen years on the boy, finally shut him up with: "Well, you're just too young to know what you're talking about. When you grow up, you'll see that I'm right." Throughout the heated interchange the parents would sit silently, never defending the boy's right to be different. By their silence they supported the older brother's position. This was a unique family constellation; the fifteen-year spread between the boys' ages enabled older brother to function as an additional parent. What happened for the boy is that gradually he learned to keep his ideas to himself and to feel something wrong with wanting to be different.

The passing on of religious or other cultural practices remains paramount in most families. It becomes critical that the child believe, for instance, in whatever divinity the parent believes in. Keeping to these traditions passes on the culture from one generation to the next. Parents too often want to pass on this *meaning* unchanged. One must believe as one's parent does and never question the appropriateness of their beliefs for ourselves. Many children are shamed for wanting to consider or follow a religious path or way of life different from their parents'. One day last year, my six-year-old son was making decorations for Chanukah, a tradition of meaning in our family. Without looking up at me, he asked, "Dad, when I grow up will I be Jewish?" I answered, somewhat taken aback, "Well, I guess so, son, if you want to be." He thought a moment, his hand busily working the crayon; then he piped up, "Can I be Christian?" I scratched my head and chuckled, "Sure, if you want to. When you get to be grown up, son, you can be whatever you want to be." In this simple form, we give expression to our differentness, our need to pick and choose what suits us in life, to find our own unique way: *this is me, I am my own self.*

Shame can also fall upon the child's early efforts to develop mastery. One of the most pronounced arenas for shame inducement lies in so-called "toilet training." So often the battle of wills which generates inevitably ends in humiliation for the child who is no match, either physically or psychologically, for the stronger parent. That observation prompted Erikson to view this time as a critical one for the genesis of shame. The traditional psychoanalytic view of the inevitable anal phase has been rejected by Fairbairn, in whose view the anal phase is a developmental artifact, created precisely by obsessive-compulsive mothering. I would agree with both theorists, though I would hasten to point out that shame can originate at any point in the life cycle, beginning as early as four to seven months of age when the infant has begun to display stranger-anxiety. The point at which Tomkins dates the possible onset of shame is birth. The infant stranger-anxiety scene itself can now be reinterpreted as a phenomenon that is primarily governed by shame, and not by fear as previously supposed.

Let me cite an example of shame relating to bodily mastery which highlights shame's potential for disruption as well as its appropriate handling. The incident occurred with one of my sons some years back. He was learning to control his bladder during the night and to be able to go without diapers, which for him meant a real accomplishment. One morning I passed by his bedroom just as he was getting up. He looked at his bed which was obviously wet. Immediately, he put his head down on the bed and wept bitterly, covering his face and not looking at me. I was perplexed at first. Then I asked him, "Are you feeling disappointed in yourself because you wet the bed?" After a short pause, he nodded his agreement though still hiding his face and crying hard. I then said to him, "That's okay, son, you don't have to be all grown up all at once." Immediately his tears dried up, he looked up at me, we hugged, and then he finished getting dressed.

There would have been no way for him to verbalize what I deduced to have been an experience of shame brought on, I have to assume, by his failure to measure up to his own expectations of himself. This was an instance certainly of internally induced shame but through my reassuring response, he was able to radically reduce his own expectations of himself and thereby no longer have to feel bad about failure. Had I instead responded to him with further ridicule, real disgust or evident disappointment, I would have only intensified his shame rather than enabling him to learn how to cope more effectively with that most poignant experience of disappointment in self.

Whether it is in regard to exercising new functions, exploring the environment, acquiring language, or gaining control over bodily functions, shame can become a barrier to gaining mastery. The child may be responded to with contempt or disparagement when bladder or bowel control fails. If a significant other continually corrects a child's speech, he may become acutely self-conscious about talking and retreat from verbal interaction. Over-correction will induce self-consciousness and disrupt the learning of any skill. Stuttering, for example, has its origin in the early fusion of shame with language acquisition. Much depends on the particular child, his native resources, and temperament, but we shall return to this issue later.

The salient point is that differentiation, whether expressed through separation or mastery, is vulnerable to shame. One can emerge feeling either strong or weak, autonomous or dependent, competent or inadequate in the world. The failure to actively encourage and support differentiation, as well as a tendency to punish, shame, or otherwise interfere with it, is most apt to foster a dependent adaptation to life.

There is no more trying, more stormy task in life than parenting. Bringing a new human being into this world, then nurturing this emerging self into an adult who is capable of living his or her own life competently, with dignity and affirmation, is a challenge which knows no bounds. Parents invest eighteen years of themselves in care-taking which, if it is done right, culminates in letting go. To give so fully of oneself to this unfolding new person only to one day open that family door, watch with respect mixed with sadness as this newly becoming adult steps forth alone, and then set aside the robes of parenthood, requires a painful greatness.

There are no longer in our culture identifiable rites of passage into adulthood. At age eighteen (unless we vote to change it) children become legally adult. Yet in so many families parents continue to hold the reins in their children's lives for whatever reasons. These "legal" adults have not as yet claimed their rightful adulthood. They have not separated from their family. What would be useful in my way of thinking would be a ceremony in the family upon each child's eighteenth birthday. Father and mother would gather with the family and say something like this: "Son, daughter, now you are an adult in the eyes of our land and in our eyes as well. We have given you life that you may discover your own destiny, your own path in this world.

We have tried to teach you the things we believe in and hold dear: respect for all living things, honesty with oneself above all else, and the courage to be who one truly is. We have also taught you how to live in community with others and most of all to live responsibly. For eighteen years we have had final say over many things in your life. Now we give over to you all the power to live your life the way that's right for you. Make all the mistakes we inevitably will, but do try to take something useful from each one. Of course, we'll be around if you need something. And come home only when *you* want to. What we gave to you we gave freely. Finally, along with this freedom comes the responsibility to use it well."

Need to Nurture

We come now to that kind of interpersonal interchange in which the child is not so much in need of receiving something emotionally as giving it to another. The observation began with Mueller and Kell, who describe this need to nurture. Implicit here is that after having been given to, the child will eventually *want* to give something back to a parent, whether it is affection, a hug or a gift. How that hug or gift is received by the significant other concerned is most crucial to whether the child comes to feel that his love is accepted as good. And this was the other critical observation made by Fairbairn: not only must the child *feel* loved as a person in her own right (need for relationship in my view), but the child must also *feel* that her love is accepted as good. In different language, these theorists have pointed to the saliency of the need to nurture.

How the child is received determines whether the need to nurture is validated and accepted or becomes associated with and bound by shame. For example, a mother may be feeling bad one day. Her daughter, sensing mother's distress, comes over to offer a hug or some comforting words. All mother need do is receive the girl's offering respectfully. However, if mother feels ashamed of appearing so weak in front of her own child and rejects the girl's approach, the girl will learn that there is something bad about wanting to give to mother. That is the likely outcome unless mother can later openly and honestly acknowledge her own discomfort, thereby owning her own part in what had occurred; this would restore the interpersonal bridge.

Need for Affirmation

We are nearing the close of our exploration of developmental needs. This last I have come to call a need for affirmation. In a singular vein, this is the valuing need and the restoring need. Life is at best an uncertain prospect, for adults as well as children. Events can unexpectedly call into question our adequacy, our very belief in ourselves. Internal security is never entirely beyond the reach of threat. Throughout our lives we all, from time to time, experience moments of self-doubt. Nor should it be otherwise. For it is in the facing of those moments that we learn to build the essential inner resources that enable us to withstand the storm more solidly next time. Each of us needs to feel that who we are, the person inside, is worthwhile and valued. It is through having someone significant provide that affirmation of self for us that we can gradually, and over time, learn how to give it to ourselves. Through building this inner source of valuing, we cease being wholly dependent on the evaluations of others for our own sense of self-worth and esteem.

Related to affirmation is a basic valuing of our uniqueness and our differentness. Those inherent qualities which set us apart from others must be recognized, acknowledged, and openly valued. Through having our own unique differences valued by significant others, we begin to value them in ourselves. And we come to have a sense of our own value in the world.

We are born different in many fundamental ways. Temperament is one critical difference which can be observed from birth on, to give one example. Though environment can influence and alter what is native to us, a basic predisposition to be either introverted or extroverted probably is biologically given, and needs to be respected. The quiet, more introverted child, for example, must be accepted as such, not admonished to be more socially outgoing.

Certainly encouragement is needed, but so is respect. Such a child must be aided to find especial value in his introvertedness, which is one of the qualities that makes him unique in the world. The same is true of the unique configuration of talents and interests that evolves in the growing child.

Let us now look at how shame may develop in a child from a failure to affirm some inherent aspect of the self. Returning to our example of temperament, in terms of parental expectations, a particular child may simply have been born the wrong temperament for the sex. Although cultural expectations have begun to broaden, quiet, more introverted boys and aggressive girls have traditionally fared less well in our culture. When a child's native temperament disappoints a parent or someone else who is significant, the ground is laid for the genesis of shame. That child cannot help but experience this sense of being a disappointment, and feel deficient for being the cause of it. Parental behavior can also have unintended rejecting impact upon the child through communicating failure to meet parental expectations even when parental attitudes are not inherently rejecting.

Affirmation of self is vital, but just as vital is affirmation of a relationship. When a rupture in an important relationship has either actually occurred or has only been feared, there follows a natural, spontaneous attempt to reaffirm or restore that relationship. When that attempt is not understood by the significant other concerned, and affirmation is not forthcoming, one feels emotionally cut-off in the relationship and shame inevitably is confirmed.

For all of us, when affirmation is *not* forthcoming at vulnerable moments, an awareness of difference between self and other can translate into a comparison, what Tomkins has called the "invidious comparison." That comparison is one of good versus bad, better versus worse, and so on. Rather than valuing the difference between self and other, either we then feel obliged to wipe it out or we try to be all things, even things not appropriate to or congruent with the self inside of us. Beliefs, values, and practices that may be appropriate for one person transfer to another without that individual ever considering their appropriateness for himself. This happens through a sequence of internal processes that go something like, "She thinks it's important to have lots of friends. I don't have lots of friends. Maybe I should."

A client of mine is a school teacher. She came in the other day feeling bad about herself. The circumstance was this. My client has made it a practice of making birthday cards for the children in her class and then leaving the card on the desk for the child to find. Another teacher was telling my client about how she handled birthday acknowledgments. This other teacher bought cards and mailed them to the children, and then added that the children always told her how much they liked this. Well, my client became immediately aware of the *difference* in their ways of handling the situation and then thought to herself, "Gee, my kids don't tell me anything when they get their cards. Maybe I'm doing it all wrong. Maybe I should do it her way." Because she had never received the needed affirmation of self and valuing of her differences from a parent, my client never learned how to affirm herself from within. Thus, she remains vulnerable to interpersonal contagion, that transferring of feelings, beliefs and practices from one person to another.

There is one other situation involving a need for affirmation which probably needs some mention. I am referring to affirmation of emerging sexuality by the parent of the other gender. Puberty unleashes a host of physiological as well as psychological changes. In order to develop relationships with boys, relationships which eventually are to include sexuality, a girl will first need to *practice* a bit on her dad. Likewise, the boy with his mother. This is what enables each child to then go out and build a complete relationship with a member of the other gender with confidence of satisfaction. Such practicing may take the form of flirtation, coquettishness, etc. What is needed is for the parent of the other gender to simply *accept* the boy's or girl's practicing and to *admire* his emerging masculinity or her emerging femininity. Both Bill Kell and John Money have observed this, but John Money has termed this "complementarity," saying that a girl needs both to identify with mother as well as have her femininity complemented by father who, in so doing, teaches her the joys of femininity. In my view, such "complementarity" is a form of affirmation of the child's or adolescent's emerging manliness or womanliness. To admire is to openly acknowledge and value this vital part of the self. When that parent fails in some way, either through open disparagement or shrinking back from the adolescent's practicing efforts, shame can generate swiftly and disrupt the integration of sexuality and the later capacity for sexual pleasure.

THE SOURCES OF INTERNALIZATION: AN INTEGRATION

The foregoing discourse has been necessary in order to develop most fully the motivational *need system*, as this arises interpersonally and developmentally. The development of specific need-shame binds comprises a primary means by which internalization of shame can come about. Hopefully, I have made clear that internalization, as an outgrowth of identification, can be both positive and negative. Here I differ from Fairbairn and Guntrip who treat internalization primarily in terms of internalizing "*bad* objects." In my view, we internalize good as well as bad identification images. Identification and internalization are inevitable human processes from which identity gradually emerges.

The affect system, drive system, and need system are three motivational arenas in which shame can generate and eventually control whatever has become directly associated with shame. We have seen how the experiencing or expression of particular affects can become bound by shame. To the degree that this occurs, an essential part of the self, conscious knowledge of and free access to one's feelings, becomes distorted. Physiologically based drives likewise can become shame-bound and no longer freely accessible to the self. And our most fundamental interpersonal needs, needs which are directly tied to the very progress of human growth, either may be understood and responded to appropriately or else may become doorways to deprivation and to shame. The development of affect-shame, drive-shame, and need-shame binds are three important contributors to internalization.

Additionally, I would like to offer the hypothesis that periods of significant or protracted emotional pain increase susceptibility to internalization by making the self uniquely vulnerable. All defenses are lowered at such moments. In particular, both the external verbal messages communicated and other affects induced in the individual during moments of deep pain can become internalized as core affect-beliefs.

I should like to recall our earlier discussion of internalization proper as involving three quite distinct aspects. First, we internalize specific affect-beliefs or feeling-laden attitudes about ourselves. These come to lie at the very core of the self and thereby help shape our emerging sense of who we are. Second, we internalize the actual ways in which we are treated by significant others. We learn to treat ourselves accordingly, forming the beginning basis for our *inner relationship with ourselves.* And third, we internalize identifications in the form of internal images. These identification images play a very significant role in the inner life. They function in a guiding capacity, serving as guides to internal living as well as external behavior.

I trust we have seen that through internalization, the conscious experience of the self inside is shaped and a relationship with that self develops. Together, these embrace our emerging identity.

LANGUAGE AND IMAGERY: THE LINK BETWEEN SHAME AND IDENTITY [2]

Isolated shame experiences become magnified and fused via imagery and language. Scenes of shame become interconnected, and thereby magnified. "I feel shame" becomes transformed, given new meaning: "I *am* shameful, deficient in some vital way as a human being." Shame has become internalized. It is no longer one affect

---

[2] This section is based on the following:

Tomkins, S. S. "Script theory: Differential Magnification of Affects." *Nebraska Symposium on Motivation,* 1979, *26,* 201-236.

Kaufman, G., and Raphael, L. "Relating to the Self: Changing Inner Dialogue." *Psychological Reports,* 1984, *54,* 239-250.

Kaufman, G., and Raphael, L. "Shame: A Perspective on Jewish Identity." *Journal of Psychology and Judaism,* 1987, *11,* 30-40.

among many, but instead comes to lie at the core of the self.

Through language, we come to interpret separate shame experiences as signifying essential meanings about the self. We feel there is now something vitally wrong with us as a person. We feel diseased. In this way, shame becomes bound up with our developing identity. Shame and identity do not become linked until the capacity to translate those shame experiences into words has matured; then we link those words together, creating meanings about the self.

Scenes of shame become linked partially via language, but they also become fused directly. Consider Martha, a young woman who entered therapy to find out whether she was indeed crazy, as her father had always said. She related the following incident which occurred when she was sixteen. She had stayed out late at a party and her parents had been up worrying when she finally arrived home. She remembers sitting at the kitchen table talking to her mother when her father rushed down the stairs, scissors in hand, and promptly cut off her hair. Imagine the scene: intense humiliation. Weeks later, she reported an incident which immediately preceded the haircutting scene. On the way home from the party, a male acquaintance raped her. Martha had experienced two distinct shame experiences, both at the hands of a male, each involving bodily violation. Her shame, rage and distrust of men became magnified because those two isolated scenes were suddenly fused together. Tomkins theorizes that such a magnified set of scenes then creates a *script*, a language-action pattern for predicting and controlling a magnified set of scenes. These are strategies for escaping from and avoiding shame which we will examine in the next chapter.

THE OUTCOME OF INTERNALIZATION :
ITS EFFECTS UPON THE SELF

Internalization of shame means that the affect of shame is no longer merely one affect or feeling among many which become activated at various times and then pass on. Rather, internalized shame is now experienced as a deep abiding sense of being defective, never quite good enough as a person. It forms the foundation around which other feelings about the self will be experienced. This affect-belief lies at the core of the self and gradually recedes from consciousness. In this way, shame becomes basic to the sense of identity. While the underlying affect is the same, the conscious experience of internalized shame differs widely. For example, feelings of inadequacy, rejection or self-doubt, feeling guilt-ridden or unlovable as a person, and pervasive loneliness are all conscious or semiconscious expressions of internalized shame.

Internalization also means that the self can now autonomously activate and experience shame in isolation. Conscious awareness of limitations, failures, or simply awareness of not achieving a prescribed goal can activate shame. There need no longer be any interpersonal shame-inducing event. One client who felt terribly ambivalent about ending his marriage experienced acute shame when he approached a clerk to ask for a divorce application. That occasion forced him to expose his failure which activated his internalized sense of shame, irrespective of the clerk's courtesy towards him.

The varieties and depth of shame, a shameful identity in the form of an underlying sense of defectiveness, and autonomous shame activation by the self are consequences which stem from shame internalization. There is a fourth consequence, one which ensures that these three continue to reinforce one another so that shame becomes ever more solidified within the emerging identity. I have termed this phenomenon the *internal shame spiral*. A triggering event occurs. Perhaps it is trying to get close to someone and feeling rebuffed. Or the event could be a critical remark from a friend. It could even be simply not being sought after or invited out. Either the event is in actuality shame-inducing (involving a current significant other breaking the interpersonal bridge) or the event autonomously activates shame wholly from within. Either way, when a person suddenly is enmeshed in shame, the eyes turn inward and the experience becomes totally internal, frequently with visual imagery present. The shame feelings and thoughts flow in a circle, endlessly triggering each other. The precipitating event is relived internally over and over, causing the sense of shame to deepen, to absorb other neutral experiences that happened before as well as those that may come later, until finally the self is engulfed. In this way, shame becomes paralyzing. This internal shame spiral is experienced phenomenologically either as "tail-spinning" or "snowballing." Each occurrence of the shame spiral can go on to include a reliving of previous shame precipitating events which thereby solidifies shame further within the personality and spreads shame to many different people, situations, behaviors, and parts of the self.

Shame rarely remains a wholly conscious process. When shame does remain conscious, the sequence of internal events can happen so rapidly as to blind clear recognition of those events by either self or others. Gradually, defending strategies evolve to enable the self to escape from and avoid paralyzing shame, particularly if intense exposure fears develop as well.

Fear of exposure is one of the secondary reactions to shame. It can, however, become intensified when the child's natural attempts to reaffirm the ruptured parental relationship are somehow shamed again. This can happen directly or inadvertently, through parental withdrawal or through a refusal to relate. Exposure fear then operates to further encapsulate shame, hide it from view, and finally mask shame from consciousness. All too frequently, only the fear remains consciously accessible.

After internalization, exposure itself takes on a much more devastating meaning. Exposure now means exposure of one's inherent defectiveness as a human being. To be seen is to be seen as irreparably and unspeakably bad.

Additionally, shame itself functions partially and secondarily as a defense against awareness of and reexperiencing the deprivation associated with unmet developmental needs, by encapsulating the concomitant hurt and pain. When need-shame binds become paramount as a source of internalization, one or more fundamental needs has not been responded to as required in order for development to proceed. Such a developmental failure brings on a most painful deprivation, this being a complex affect comprising some combination of such basic affects as distress, rage, fear, and shame. The deprivation accompanying unmet needs initially will likely press for some kind of interpersonal expression. When a child attempts such expression and no understanding response is forthcoming from the significant other concerned, the experience is felt as intolerable. Eventually, the young personality may be forced to regain inner control by silencing the awareness of deprivation itself.

After shame becomes internalized, a new shame experience, whether induced interpersonally or activated autonomously, must be defended against, compensated for, or transferred interpersonally because exposure both to others and to oneself has become intolerable.

SHAME AND THE NEED FOR IDENTITY

Identity is that internal integrator which evolves out of experience, organizes the various beliefs, images, and attitudes which guide us day-to-day, and carries forward the goals, hopes and visions to which we aspire. Identity integrates experience while at the same time mediating how we choose to behave, both internally with ourselves (inner reality) and interpersonally with others (outer reality). Identity is that essential core of who we are as individuals, the conscious experience of the *self* inside. By embracing these three things, who I was, who I am, and who I can be, identity provides the experience of continuity of self over time.

The changes which have produced our technological society have in turn created new challenges for the individual seeking to develop a secure identity in the wake of such accelerating conditions as rate of technological and societal change, societal mobility, bureaucracy, depersonalization, alienation, and felt powerlessness. The search for a stable identity, which is the means by which we navigate the storm of life, becomes ever more urgent and at the same time more embattled. The need for a sense of identity dissolves into a struggle to find out "who I am" and "where I belong"—the discovery of one's differentness as a person as well as of where and how one can identify with others. The search for identity encompasses both sides of that struggle, differentiation and identification.

Identity haltingly emerges as a conscious integration of the self, embracing needs as well as tasks. These tasks are developmental in nature and reflect a fundamental process, that of becoming a fully separate person. Although the tasks are varied—including separation from mother, acquisition of language, increasing mastery over one's own life through gaining control over bodily functions and developing competence in the environment, forming peer relationships, developing intimacy, integrating sexuality, separating from one's family, finding productive work, for some, marriage and parenthood, handling old age, and, finally, coping with death—an underlying process emerges. The central task of the life-work can be construed as one of evolving a uniquely personal identity that gives inherent meaning to one's life, provides direction and purpose to one's work, and enables one's *self* to retain a sense of inner worth and valuing in the face of all those vicissitudes of life with which we must contend, not the least of which are anxiety, suffering, and the lack of absolute control over our own lives. It is this last which guarantees a perpetual vulnerability to shame.

Some experiencing of defeat, failure, or rejection is inescapable in life. It is this fundamental reality which makes of shame a universal, inevitable occurrence as well as a potential obstacle in the development of a secure, self-affirming identity. And, yet, some degree of shame is necessary precisely in order for identity even to evolve. Shame is not so much to be avoided as coped with. What is needed is an understanding of shame and how best to cope with it, of its dynamic role in human development, and of how profound can be its aftermath.

3
Defending Strategies Against Shame: The Beginning of Adaptation Toward Outer Reality

We have traveled along diverse paths to reach the point in the development of shame and identity when defending strategies become necessary for continued emotional survival. There is no uniform point, generally arrived at, when individuals learn to defend. There is such latitude in human affairs that cautions us to speak with some certainty only about those things we can observe rather consistently. Innate factors such as particular native resources, temperament and a predisposition to be either introverted or extroverted constitute one class of variables which dramatically weights the outcome of adaptation toward the human environment, making generalization shaky at best. Such factors as temperament will even influence the specific kind of defenses which arise. For example, an extroverted child who by nature is already more expressive is more apt to utilize expressed rage as a defense than is an introverted child. The latter is more apt to resort to internal withdrawal in the face of any threat to self. Again, we speak of tendencies selectively encouraged by genetically based factors that nevertheless remain open to modification through learned experience in the family or else in the wider environment.

Another class of variables influencing the selection of defenses concerns the particular patterns of affect, drive, and need socialization within a given family. The way in which the expression of affects, drives, and needs, as I have defined these earlier, is handled in a specific family also makes available ready means of defense.

Likewise, the dynamics of the particular family as a social group counts heavily in the selective sorting out of whatever useful means of adaptation may be at hand.

Adaptation is what defenses are all about. Defenses are learned because they are the best means available to the child for survival. Defending strategies are adaptive and have survival value. That is the natural reason they come about. If they were not necessary or did not work at all, we would be most unlikely to develop them

Depending upon the nature of the supporting human environment in which the child matures, defenses can either remain flexible and positive or else can become too rigidly relied upon and, hence, internalized as armaments for the self. Let me cite an example of positive defending which stands in marked contrast to the kind of defenses which arise in reaction to shame internalization. When my young son first began kindergarten, he would at times come home in tears because older children mockingly teased him, calling him "kindergarten baby." This clearly left him feeling wounded and hurt, perhaps even shamed. We talked about this and I tried to help him understand in simple terms that the reason these boys called him names was because they *saw* how much it hurt him. Then I offered him a *defense*. I said, "Whenever someone calls you 'kindergarten baby,' look him straight in the eye, and with a great big smile, say 'Yup, you're right, I am one.'" Well, nothing more was said about such incidents for some time. Much later, he casually remarked one day that he was teaching his fellows how to deal with similar name-calling.

This incident is but one example illustrating the usefulness of learned defenses in aiding us to navigate the interpersonal realm. Defenses that remain consciously accessible and flexible are positive. Defenses which are learned, on the other hand, to ward off excessive shame experienced directly within the family are quite another matter.

Thus it is that a point comes—and it can come at differing ages for some as compared to others, but in any event it comes nonetheless—when the self feels acutely threatened and we seek ways to protect against such threats. The ways found may not be the best one could utilize, but they do assist us in maintaining inner security in some measure. Even when shame has not become internalized to any significant extent, the need to cope with inevitable recurrences of that affective experience remains paramount. But it is the internalization of shame which activates that especially acute need for defending. The human environment has failed somehow. And so the self must take on the task of defending the self. This is the beginning of adaptation toward outer reality, the interpersonal realm. What happens interpersonally becomes the model for how we treat and relate to ourselves internally; this we will address in the next chapter. Adaptation is not so neatly divided into categories of interpersonal and internal. Rather, this separation is more for communication purposes than to suggest that it necessarily happens so in actuality, for development continually criss-crosses, as it were, from outer to inner and back again. In order to see adaptation more lucidly, I think it necessary to treat one side of it and then follow with the other.

INTERPERSONAL TRANSFER OF EXPERIENCED SHAME

Particularly following internalization, that psychological event which makes shame so intolerable, the self begins to develop *strategies of defense* against experiencing shame and *strategies for the interpersonal transfer* of experienced shame. Together, these dual modes comprise a general process of defense which encompasses both protecting against shame and dealing with it once shame has become activated. Strategies of defense are essentially forward-looking; they aim at protecting the self against further exposure and further experiences of shame. Strategies of transfer, in contrast, are aroused only after some shame has begun to be felt. Such strategies of transfer aim at making someone else feel shame in order to reduce our own shame. For example, if I feel humiliated, I can reduce this affect by blaming someone else. The blaming directly transfers shame to that other person, enabling me to feel better about myself.

This interpersonal transfer of shame usually follows the lines of the familiar pecking order, or dominance hierarchy which emerges in social groups. Whether it is in the *family*, the *peer group*, the *school setting* or the *work setting* a dominance hierarchy will have emerged based on either actual or perceived power. Shame will transfer right down the line, from the stronger to the weaker. Yet the weaker in one setting may emerge as quite the stronger in another setting. Thus it happens that father comes home humiliated at the hands of a superior at work and transfers shame to his older son, who does likewise to the younger son, who in turn goes out among his own peers to find someone weaker whom he can humiliate. And if none can be found, perhaps he'll kick the dog! The family, school, peer and work settings represent critical, developmental settings in which shame can and does transfer interpersonally.

In addition to the active transfer of shame, the affect of shame itself often unconsciously transfers from one person to another without any action being necessary to effect that transfer. The observation that feelings transfer interpersonally without much conscious aware-ness of its occurrence is not a new one. Such observers as Sullivan, Kell, and Tomkins have said as much when they described how affects can transfer via affect contagion, empathy, or identification. This occurrence is not what I am referring to when discussing strategies for the transfer of shame. These latter are active strategies, that is, something very direct is done by the individual to reduce bad feelings at the expense of another's good feelings. However, in the active transfer of shame, conscious awareness of the activity which effects the transfer, of the intent behind it, even of its impact, all are usually lacking

The interpersonal transfer of experienced shame constitutes a generalized, not specific, strategy for coping with shame. By this I mean that the exact means by which the transfer happens can vary widely. Any action which either induces shame directly in someone else by virtue of our being significant to that other person *or* activates that individual's own, already present sense of shame can function as a means of transfer.

When environmental experience selects out some particular action or set of actions, and rewards these as more useful to the defending self so that they become rather consistently relied upon in the face of shame, then we may speak of a defending strategy as having arisen developmentally. A particular means has been found which is natural to the self, and thus easily available. And what is more, it works. The action is sufficiently effective, hence adaptive, to become a useful armoring for a wounded self. In such a manner, specific defending strategies arise and enable the individual concerned to survive intolerable shame. Let's take a closer look at the several most prominent strategies that so far can be identified and differentiated. As we proceed, keep in mind that the primary aim of each strategy is protection of the self, protection against shame.

RAGE

We encountered rage earlier in the discussion of the basic shame-inducing process. Rage is one of those more spontaneous, naturally occurring reactions often observed to follow shame. Its presence serves a much-needed, self-protective function by both insulating the self against exposure and by actively keeping others away. An extroverted child will be more likely to express some of the rage at being shamed while an introverted child will tend to keep the rage inside, and hence more hidden from the view of others. Whether held inside or expressed more openly, rage serves the purposes of defending. It may also, secondarily, transfer shame to another.

If rage emerges as a strategy of defense, what we will see is an individual who holds onto rage as a characteristic style. This manifests itself either in hostility towards others or bitterness. Although this hostility or bitterness arises as a defense to protect the self against further experiences of shame, it becomes disconnected from its originating source and becomes a generalized reaction directed toward almost anyone who may approach. This description of rage as a strategy of defense is akin to what Kell and Burow referred to when they spoke of *feeling states* as distinct from *feelings*. What has happened, in my view, is that along with shame, rage as a defending strategy has become internalized as well; hence, it is no longer one affect or feeling among many which all become activated and then pass on. Rage is actively held onto and thereby prolonged, whether expressed or only felt inside.

There is no more certain poison for the self than internalizing rage and thereby fomenting bitterness within the self. Bitterness can kill, can so wither the self inside the person that it becomes like dead wood, dried up, old and withered. Coming in contact with an embittered individual usually will leave us with a bad feeling.

Rage can build to the point of sheer hatred and, when accompanying the striving for power as a second strategy, may produce longings for taking revenge upon whomever humiliates us. Still one must remember that it arose as a means of protecting the self, of defending against excessive shame.

CONTEMPT

Contempt, unlike rage, is not a naturally occurring affective reaction to shame. Thus, other factors must be sought in order to account for its emergence as a prominent strategy of defense. That it does so function must be stated emphatically. The most essential requirement in the internal development of contempt as a defense against shame is experience with a parent already skillful in the modeling of contempt. An overtly contemptuous parent will enable a child, lacking in ready means of protection, to acquire through identification what the parent uses so effectively.

Contempt may be experienced directly at the hands of the parent. In such a case, the child experiences himself as offensive to the parent and feels rejected in no uncertain terms. Contempt is an affect blend, a learned combination of anger and dissmell, which distances the self from whatever arouses that contempt. In Tomkins' view, there is least consciousness of self in contempt and very intense consciousness of the object which is experienced as disgusting. Shame is an ambivalent experience because the self still longs for reunion with the self or significant other. Hence, it is deeply disturbing. In contempt, the object, be it self or other, is completely rejected.

Parental contempt may also be modeled for the child in relation to other people. That modeling can happen when a parent is observed by a child to respond contemptuously toward a sibling, the other parent, or strangers. How a parent is observed to cope with particular threats to the parent's own self can serve as the model for the child's adoption of similar defending strategies when the child feels threatened. To the degree that contempt for others is resorted to by a parent, either in word or deed, a child becomes vulnerable to also acquiring this as a generalized strategy.

In the development of contempt as a characterological defending style, we have the seeds of a judgmental, fault-finding, or condescending attitude in later human relationships. To the degree that others are looked down upon, found lacking, or seen as somehow lesser or inferior beings, a once-wounded self becomes more securely insulated against further shame, but only at the expense of distorted relationships with others.

STRIVING FOR POWER

While rage keeps others away and contempt both distances the self from others and elevates the self above others, the striving for power is a direct attempt to compensate for the sense of defectiveness which underlies internalized shame. In selecting for power, the individual sets about gaining maximum control either over others or over himself in whatever situations are encountered. To the degree that one is successful in gaining power, particularly over others, one becomes increasingly less vulnerable to further shame. This is so because shame usually travels down the dominance hierarchy. An individual who both makes this observation and has the necessary resources to acquire it may eventually decide to strive for power as a way of life.

There are many ways in which power-seeking manifests itself. One obvious means is through directly climbing up the "pecking order" that emerges in all social groups. An individual who reaches a position of real power over others has become less vulnerable to having shame activated. Such an individual is also well situated for transferring blame to others should shame somehow become activated. The president of a company or group certainly has potential power over subordinates depending on his need for control and the checks and balances inherent in that particular group's social structure.

A parent likewise has very real power to influence the lives of his or her children for good or ill. And teachers in secondary school as well as professors in college have power over the academic if not emotional lives of their students. In these instances, power is inherent to one's role or position.

While power clearly enters into all social groups through jockeying for position, what may be less apparent is how power becomes an inevitable undercurrent, if not an explicit process, within every human relationship. Whenever we care what others think of us, we have given over to those others some degree of power to affect how we feel about ourselves. Whenever we openly admire someone and hence more willingly surrender to their guidance or influence, we have also surrendered power. Whenever we permit ourselves the vulnerability of needing something emotionally from someone regarded as significant, we inevitably give that special person also a measure of power which can either be respected or abused. In these instances, power is relinquished interpersonally, however inadvertently, rather than acquired directly through one's position or role. Yet the power given is no less real, no less capable of being misused.

Individuals who strive for power as a way of life strive to maximize their power in relation to others. They will do so through their position or role and will even seek out those of us who are perhaps weaker or less secure, and hence are more easily influenced. Power-seeking individuals prefer to gain control in relation to others and also remain in control when in any interpersonal situation or human relationship. To share the power is precisely what they are unable to do. Sharing the power in a relationship would mean stopping at the point of obtaining equal power in relation to others. Striving for power over others allows only the self to feel powerful, in control or in charge.

Power becomes the means to insulate against further shame. Power can also become the means to compensate for shame internalized earlier in life. To the degree that one can now feel powerful in relation to others, through gaining power over them, one has reversed roles from the way it was in early life. As already noted, such an individual might indeed stop at the point of obtaining *equal* power in relation to others, which is certainly adaptive. On the other hand, an individual may continue to strive for power as a generalized strategy which knows no bounds. To the degree that such a person lacks other adaptive means of coping with such recurring threats to the self as shame, power-seeking must inevitably be resorted to in the face of threat. For defenses are rarely if ever so effective that they completely exclude all felt *experience* of threat.

The power strategy may or may not include longings for vengeance and the active seeking of revenge. But it does encompass instances in which security is to be won through control and self-esteem is to be amassed through power. When power-seeking predominates, and native endowment coupled with a ripe environment select for it, the potential for destructiveness in human affairs also may know no bounds.

STRIVING FOR PERFECTION

Instead of striving for power, an individual may quest after perfection. This, like power-seeking, is a striving against shame and attempts to compensate for an underlying sense of defectiveness. If I can become perfect, no longer am I so vulnerable to shame. No less a keen observer of the human condition than Karen Horney recognized the disastrous effects attendant upon an individual's seeking to become perfect rather than to realize himself. The source of that striving, in my view, is rooted in internalized shame.

The quest for perfection itself is self-limiting and hopelessly doomed both to fail and to plunge the individual back into the very mire of defectiveness from which he so longed to escape. One can never attain that perfection, and awareness of failure to do so reawakens that already-present sense of shame. It is as though one sees the only means of escaping from the prison that is shame is erasing all signs that might point to its presence. Thus it is that an individual already burdened by a deep, abiding sense of defectiveness will strive to erase every blemish of the self and experiences an inordinate pressure to excel in an ever-widening circle of activities. Since one already knows that one is inherently not good enough as a person, nothing one does is ever seen as sufficient, adequate, or good enough. No matter how well one actually does, it could have been better. And so such an individual strives incessantly to perfect herself. And each occasion of that striving only communicates how much she has fallen short of the mark. It still could have been better.

A perfectionist never has developed an *internal* sense of how much is good enough. Instead, he or she views only the external performance and judges it against some externally derived standard, a standard which never is attained. How might an individual develop perfectionism as a generalized strategy for coping with shame? Such a posture toward the world is learned and, somewhere, there was a model. Imagine the following familial pattern. Every time a young boy comes home from school and tells his esteemed father how well he has done on an exam, father's reply goes something like this. If the boy brought home a B, father says, "Well, it wasn't a B +." When the boy brings home the B +, father replies, "Well, it wasn't an A." And when the boy at long last attains even that goal, father answers, "Well, but it wasn't an A+." Never does the boy obtain the much-needed reward for his labors, *satisfaction with self*, either from his father or from himself.

One day the boy thinks he has at long last outwitted the father. Even when he scores a 100 out of a maximum of 100 on an exam, thus obtaining a theoretically "perfect" score, father says, "But it wasn't a 105!" Always, the carrot is held before his nose but never given to him. The day of outwitting father came when the maximum score on a particular exam was 110 points and the boy achieved that coveted 105. At long last he could now proudly announce his victory. He had done it. Father could say nothing more. And father was indeed thrown when the boy announced his score of 105. Quickly, father recovered, asking "But what was the highest score possible?" "110," answered the boy. "Aha!" said father with a smile, "It wasn't a 110!" And the boy's momentary pride in himself was snatched out from under him, leaving him more confused, in doubt, and in shame.

Whenever parental love, acceptance, or pride become dependent upon a child's performance in the world, the seeds of perfectionism are being sown. The above example illustrates one way in which an individual learns, literally is taught, always to strive onward, never to feel a sense of inner satisfaction at accomplishing something. No matter what one tries or how well it is done, it is never enough. Somehow one is always left feeling lacking or deficient. All one can do to reduce the reawakened sense of shame is to throw oneself once more into activity designed to perfect the self that is so obviously, so painfully defective. Thus it may come about that an individual embarks upon the hopeless treadmill of perfectionism, desperately seeking to escape agonizing shame yet forever doomed to be plunged back.

For such an individual, shamefulness requires that awareness of difference between self and other becomes automatically translated into a comparison of good versus bad, better versus worse. An individual already carrying shame reacts to such awareness of difference by engaging actively, though wholly internally, in a form of comparison making, comparing himself to the other who is seen as different in some essential way. Rather than valuing the difference, such an individual feels threatened by it. Hence, in perfectionism, one attempts to be all things rather than simply who one is. The perfectionist has yet to learn that only when we can stop trying to be all things do we ever become free to be who we are.

When perfectionism is paramount, that comparison of self with other inevitably ends in the self feeling the lesser for the comparison. On the other hand, when contempt as a defending strategy predominates, the internal comparison making ends in a reversal such that the self emerges feeling enhanced at the expense of devaluing the other. And each strategy, perfectionism and contempt, may be learned and employed by the same individual, but either at different times or in different situations. More often than not, several defending strategies are found functioning together.

In comparison making lie the seeds of inadequacy-motivated competitiveness. Here, competition is not so much directed at being the best one can be, which is certainly growth-directed, but rather at outdoing others so that one can thereby feel enhanced. Competing to be better than others can become a generalized strategy for acquiring good feelings about oneself. Almost the only way to collect self-esteem is through remaining vigilant in maintaining one's decided edge over others. When competing to see who is the better is the learned means for restoring oneself, a practice widely fostered in our society, human relationships must suffer. A competitive environment, whether in the family, peer group, or work setting, seriously interferes with, if not altogether disrupts, having real and honest human relationships.

There is, of course, a third outcome possible when some awareness of difference has occurred. Neither the self nor the other need emerge as the lesser if awareness of difference can remain just that, a difference to be both owned and valued. Such an eventuality comes about through having had our own differences valued by significant others. When our differentness is not acknowledged, that is, when our need to differentiate fails to be understood *and* when that differentness is not affirmed, some form of devaluing comparison making is inevitable whether directed toward self or other.

Engaging in comparison making also becomes an internal means by which the self can continue, in the present, to generate shame without any external assistance. When comparison making itself has become a generalized pattern, it emerges as a specific way of relating to oneself, however unsatisfying it may be. It is a way of continuing in inner reality, the realm of the self, the pattern first encountered in outer reality, the interpersonal realm. And the pattern, though originating in the past, is currently maintained actively in the present and thereby continues to perpetuate shame in the face of even the most positive of new experiences. That is, unless the pattern itself is interrupted, relinquished, and replaced with a new, more satisfying way of having a relationship with oneself. Though as a society we have begun to recognize the complexity in attaining meaningful and satisfying relationships with others, we have hardly understood how to go about having a similar relationship with ourselves.

THE TRANSFER OF BLAME

When a child is met sufficiently often with blame for things that go wrong or is able to observe a significant other highly adept at fixing blame, the conditions are laid for the eventual adoption of a similar defending strategy through identification. In a blame-oriented environment, attention is focused not upon how to repair the mess that has occurred but on whose fault it was, on who is to blame. Let's create a situation to amplify what is involved in the fixing or transfer of blame.

Imagine that a family has embarked on vacation in their car. Late in the day, the car runs out of gas. Such a mishap is likely to produce feelings of frustration, perhaps of helplessness, even of rage. Underneath, the self of the driver may furthermore feel some shame, some disappointment in self, at not having averted the mishap. In a blaming family, the dialogue might go something like this.

FATHER:[driver] God damn it! The *gas gauge must be* broken.
　　　　　　　Why didn't *you* tell me it's been off?
MOTHER:　　What do you mean, *me* tell you?
FATHER:　　Well you drive the damn car most of the time,
　　　　　　　don't you?
MOTHER:　　But *you're* the driver. Why didn't *you* stop
　　　　　　　for gas at the last exit? You *should have*
　　　　　　　known it would run out soon.
FATHER:　　What do you mean *I* should have known it?
　　　　　　　Why didn't *you* tell me to get off ?

And thus the dialogue rages on, and on, and on. Each transfer of blame prompts the other party involved to engage similarly. One learns to blame in order to counter blame received from others. Blaming breeds blaming in retaliation. Rather than accept the event for what it is and seek to right the matter, one focuses interest upon who can be found responsible for it. If fault can be fixed and responsibility transferred, the self is freed of any suggestion of culpability. One has preserved one's belief that one has done nothing wrong. One remains pure, perhaps even righteous, in the face of the mishap.

But an individual need only transfer blame if the precipitating event has somehow activated, however subliminally, that person's own shame. It may be only in the dim awareness: "I blew it. I should not have done what I did. I should have known better." When an individual is unable to accept such inevitable instances of his imperfect humanness, be they of mistaken judgment or whatever, and that individual has either directly experienced or observed successful blaming from a significant other, he will very likely model and eventually adopt a similar posture toward the world: when things go wrong, find fault somewhere else.

When blaming generalizes as a strategy, we have the familiar pattern of "scapegoating." Someone else is searched for to bear the blame for the mistakes of others.

And when blaming becomes sufficiently directed outside oneself, that is, externalized, we may see an individual who perceives the source of all that goes wrong to lie outside the self, and, paradoxically, beyond internal control. And though that individual resents the resulting feeling of powerlessness, a powerlessness to affect and change what ails him, he never recognizes that he has colluded in the very process of creating that powerlessness. By perpetually seeing fault to lie externally to himself, he is inadvertently teaching himself to experience the control over events as wholly external to himself as well. It is not that full control ever is available to us as human beings, but we do have control over how we face life, how we handle what comes our way or happens to us, and how we internally experience ourselves. While the blaming individual escapes culpability for wrongdoing or mistakes and hence avoids shame, he reaps a harvest of discontent derived from perceived powerlessness. If the source of what goes wrong in life becomes external to the self, one has also relinquished the power to affect or alter what happens.

When the transfer of blame becomes a defending strategy, it means that occurrences of shame have become so intolerable to the self that their source must always be transferred elsewhere. In such a manner, transferring or externalizing blame can function as a defense against internalization itself. Internalizing means "taking inside" and externalizing blame can so bar the gates as to prevent anything from coming inside and disquieting the self. An externalizing temperament (extroversion), in addition to experience with a blaming model, will select for the adoption of externalizing blame as a strategy.

In following the development of a blaming strategy or posture, we have yet to understand how it comes about that a particular individual will react with blaming when *someone else* has committed the unpardonable offense of making a mistake. While it is an easily taken step to go from experience with a blaming parent to internalizing such a posture through identification, it is much less clear why a parent reacts with blame to the mistakes of a child in the first place. After all, while I may have learned to blame others whenever I make mistakes, it is less apparent why I should behave similarly when my son makes a mistake of judgment. That a strategy learned in the one situation would simply generalize to the other does not offer a sufficient explanation in my view, though indeed it is plausible. I will suggest that a child is certainly a significant other to his or her own parent. Much may hang, for the parent, on the outcome or fruits of parenting vis-a-vis the parent's own sense of adequacy. Because of that unfortunate fact, a child is able to stimulate, even to induce shame directly in a parent. The parent-child relationship is a most reciprocal one.

I should also like to recall an earlier comment relevant to our present discussion, namely, that shame as a feeling can transfer interpersonally through empathy or identification. I will further suggest that to the degree that a parent *overidentifies* with a child, the parent may himself experience shame when the child has committed a wrongdoing, used mistaken judgment, or failed somehow. And, further, if that parent has learned to defend himself against shame through blaming, that very blaming activity will inevitably be called out by his child's mistakes because either the parent's own internal shame has been awakened or he has begun to experience shame anew through identification. In such a case the child, who is seen by the parent as but an extension of the parent, is seen as blemished. If the child is blemished so must the parent be, for the two are one and blaming becomes the means to deal with the threat to the parent's self created by the child's mistakes, the blaming being directed at the child as though he were merely an offending part of the self of the parent.

The external transfer of blame can come to function as a defense against experiencing shame through empathy or identification, against anything which activates one's own internalized shame, and against internalization itself. As a generalized strategy it proves highly resistant to being relinquished and replaced by other, more adaptive means of coping.

And some mention must also be made of the fact that an individual may learn to blame himself, to internalize rather than externalize blame, as a way of avoiding blame from significant others. Such a person learns that if he is quick enough to blame himself, a parent's blaming will subside or be altogether avoided. It is as though the child makes an implicit contract with the parent: I will do the blaming so you will not have to. In this way the intolerable blaming, which induces shame in the child, is placed under the child's own, internal control. It becomes internalized such that the child's inner life is forever subject to spontaneous self-blame.

The punishment that is in such a manner inflicted by the self upon the self is one of the two sources of what has more traditionally been labeled as guilt. The other source is, in Tomkins' view, internalized contempt. Self-blame and self-contempt must further be distinguished from *immorality shame;* here guilt is simply one variant of shame. When blaming or contempt, either singly or in combination, become internalized secondarily to shame, the seeds are planted for an over-burdened, guilt-ridden conscience and the way is prepared for the splitting of the self into two parts, one of which becomes the offender while the other becomes judgmental, punitive, even persecutory. These developmental phenomena will be discussed in depth in the next chapter.

INTERNAL WITHDRAWAL

The last of our generalized strategies for meeting such exigencies of life as are created by internalized shame is internal withdrawal. Susceptibility to utilizing withdrawal as a defense is increased when the native temperament of the individual includes an introverted stance. Such an individual is already more likely *to live inside the self* than in the outer world. By this I mean that more often than not, interest resides not in external people or things so much as in the inner life itself. Carl Jung has made it evident to us that pure types are lacking by and large, and that some mixture of introversion with extroversion is more often the rule. While an introverted person is already more apt to withdraw inward as a fundamental way of life, experience will powerfully influence how entrenched that introvertedness becomes.

The pivotal idea here is that there are genetically based predispositions, temperament being one, which readily lend themselves to function as defending strategies when environmental experience so necessitates. A more extroverted person certainly may develop internal withdrawal as a defense just as an introverted person might. But the extroverted person will still live out in the world more comfortably and more of the time. In fact, in each of us, to some degree living inside oneself usually alternates naturally with living out in the world, if the cycle is not interfered with. The introvert lives more often and more of the time inside while the extrovert does the opposite. Again, these are just predispositional tendencies and each temperament type goes through its own cycles.

Now, when faced with excessive shame in significant human relationships, an introverted child will very likely fall back on internal withdrawal as a means for coping. What happens is that the self withdraws deeper inside itself to escape the agony of exposure or the loss of the possibility of reunion. Let me develop this with an example. One introverted boy would retreat inside himself whenever he met rejection from peers. He would then actively engage in internal fantasy and imagery designed by him to restore his good feelings about himself. He did not feel free to openly approach his parents for that kind of reaffirmation since it was at their hands that he encountered shame in the first place, leaving such wounds in his self and unrestored ruptures in the relationship as to forbid any approach. Instead, he retreated inward to fantasy creations of his own making, literally inventing an internal fantasy world to which he could retreat, in order to provide himself with the much-needed parenting that was so lacking in his life.

But fantasy was only partially successful in providing him with this "substitute parenting." While he could envision himself as a hero, placing in danger but then saving and rescuing the peer who in reality had rejected him, and thereby in fantasy win him for a friend, the boy never learned how to cope more effectively in the interpersonal realm. He could only retreat to his internal world and there fantasize himself as of royal birth and with magical powers. This he did whenever his self felt wounded. The boy invented and then relied upon the illusion of a misunderstood yet secret greatness within him whenever he felt cast off or unwanted in the world, an illusion which in his fantasies would suddenly stand revealed, be unmistakably recognized by those others, elevate him in their eyes, and thereby redeem him.

In this way, internal withdrawal, together with active fantasy, functioned in a defending as well as compensating manner for him. But the lad never learned how to free himself from feeling unspeakably and irreparably defective as a person. And, fortunately for him, he knew the difference between that inner fantasy world inside of him and the outer world of people and things, though he would occasionally slip from one to the other without knowing it. And, equally fortunately, he never told anyone about his secret inner world.

DEFENDING AS AN ADAPTATION
TOWARD OUTER REALITY

Defending strategies such as contempt, blaming, rage, or perfectionism are acquired principally in an attempt to cope with externally based sources of shame. These strategies become means of defending oneself in, and thereby adapting oneself to, outer reality. Such strategies are first learned in significant interpersonal relationships where they are needed as armaments for the self. They gradually become an acquired part of the self, to be called out in the face of new encounters with shame as the self continues to navigate the interpersonal realm. These defending strategies may remain externally directed so that only threat or danger which is externally triggered will arouse the defense and call it to action. In such an event the defense, though an acquired part of the self, remains outwardly directed. The defense is aimed at others who threaten us.

Alternatively, certain defenses may later become directed inward and aimed at the very self of the defending individual. For instance, rage, contempt, and blame can be so turned against the self. Whereas previously the defense had functioned in outer reality, being directed at others, now the defense comes to function just as much if not more so in inner reality where it is internally directed at specific parts of the self. This is the beginning of adaptation in inner reality.

In drawing to a close our excursion through the development of defenses, I trust that certain ideas have been made clear: that defending strategies evolve to enable the self to escape from and avoid paralyzing shame; that following internalization of shame within the personality, each succeeding shame experience must be defended against, compensated for, or transferred interpersonally because exposure has become so acutely intolerable; that defenses are themselves adaptive and arise because they have survival value; that we adapt, always, the very best ways possible given who we are and the situation we find ourselves in at a given time; that the several strategies described are not unitary strategies but rather, they become expressed in most unique and varied ways, with several often learned and functioning together.

Rigid defending strategies will in turn produce distorted relationships with others, creating new pressures. These evolving problems in living more often than not have their origin in failures within significant human relationships. The kind of failure which is most critical here involves some severing of the interpersonal bridge so that trusting once more those we depended upon has become blocked. Failure in a relationship can be transcended when the one depended upon can honestly own her part in activating shame, her imperfect humanness, *and* can enable the other to *feel* genuinely understood. In this way trust, and hence the relationship, become eventually restored. Through such restoring of this vital, interpersonal bridge, which provides the needed experience of identification, shame is indeed transcended.

4

The Disowning of Self: The Beginning
of Adaptation in Inner Reality

Shame is able to play its significant role in the development of human problems in living through its effect upon the growing individual's emerging identity. And identity not only integrates experience but it also, and equally importantly, mediates how we behave both internally with ourselves (inner reality) and interpersonally with others (outer reality). Always, we are simultaneously living in these two worlds. And that inner world—the realm of feelings and thoughts, of images and fantasies, and of the unconscious—is no less real than is the outer. Both are central to becoming an integrated, productive human being able to cope effectively enough with the unforeseen exigencies which life hands us. Likewise, in developing a satisfying inner relationship with ourselves, the inner and outer worlds converge.

THE SELF'S RELATIONSHIP WITH THE SELF

Interpersonal learning in the family becomes the model for the gradually unfolding relationship which the self comes to have with the self. It is this current though internal relationship with ourselves which enables interpersonally derived dynamics to transfer into the inner life and there to become installed as internal dynamics, no longer connected with their interpersonal origins. Though conflicts originate interpersonally, with anxiety or shame being generated first in significant human relationships, they become internalized and eventually unconscious, leaving us disconnected from our essential human origins. What better antidote to the sense of despair or futility that accompanies so many of us through life than to discover that the internal strife waged against disowned parts of the self inside of us had origins *outside* ourselves.

This day-to-day, here-and-now relationship with ourselves, however lacking in full conscious awareness it may be, is the means by which conflicts originating in the past continue into and are kept active in the present. Through the moment-to-moment activities actively engaged in wholly inside our skins, we perpetuate the very patterns, first learned a long time ago, which paradoxically prove so dysfunctional to our current lives. Thus it is that the school teacher I spoke of continues to actively engage in comparison making when faced with awareness of difference, yet never understands how it comes about that she ends up feeling inadequate, deficient, or depressed. The activity engaged in, comparison making, has become an internalized part of her identity, a way in which she actively relates to herself *in the present*. This conception of the self's active relationship with the self is one of the important dimensions of identity.

DEVELOPMENTAL ROOTS OF DISOWNING: A REVIEW

Achieving a secure identity is essential for individuals in order to accomplish the natural sequence of developmental tasks so necessary to becoming a fully separate person. When sufficient shame generates early in life through developmental failures, the growth process is disrupted, perhaps even blocked, and a secure, self-affirming identity fails to emerge. The first two process dimensions in the developmental sequence along which shame and identity evolve are shame inducement and shame internalization. Shame inducement is the process by which shame originates directly out of interpersonal interactions in significant human relationships. Shame internalization refers to the process by which shame comes to lie at the very core of the self, and hence one's identity, and shame activation becomes an autonomous function of the self. There is no clear break between these two developmental events. Shame inducement does not suddenly stop and then give way to shame internalization. Rather, these are overlapping processes which can recur throughout life.

Following the spaced onset of these first two processes, means of defense begin to be tried out and, if sufficiently useful, develop into strategies of defense. Now we have a third developmental process also overlapping with the first two. This is the point we have reached thus far in our exploration.

The important link between shame internalization and the formation of a shame-based identity lies in a process by which the self within the growing person begins to actively disown parts of itself, thereby creating splits within the self. The consequent internal strife waged against disowned parts of the self becomes the foundation for all later pathological developments.

Like its forerunners, internalization and defending strategies, the disowning of self also is rooted in the identification process. It is the parental disowning of a part of the child, or a part of the parent, I might add, which becomes the model for the self's engaging in like action. In such a manner does the internalized splitting of the self arise.

This fourth process dimension in the developmental sequence, the disowning of self, also is rooted in shame internalization. While the self is learning through experimentation with various means of defense to ward off or avoid entirely further encounters with shame in outer reality, thereby acquiring ready means of protection, there is still an urgency to come to terms with the shame already internal to the self. While effective barriers to the outer or interpersonal world are in preparation, how is the self to cope with the "enemy within?" Is this metaphor not reflective of what happens when the self has come to feel unspeakably and irreparably defective? To continue experiencing oneself in such a fashion is beyond comprehension. Some means must be found to right the matter within the self, to somehow restore the balance of things so that at least the conscious self, from whom one can never escape, is freed of the intolerable, paralyzing effects of shame. In a most fundamental sense, repression or experiential erasure and the splitting of the self into owned and disowned parts have their origins in the process of shame internalization.

While rooted in parental disowning, and hence in identification with the disowning parent, the active disowning of self is an attempt by the self to cope with internalized shame. Thus it is that adaptation in inner reality comes about.

DISOWNING OF SELF: AFFECTS, NEEDS, AND DRIVES

Because we learn to treat ourselves precisely the way we either experienced or observed significant others to do, we learn to shame ourselves, hold ourselves in contempt, blame ourselves, hate ourselves, terrorize ourselves, and even to disown a part of ourselves that had been rejected and consistently enough cast away by a parent, whether intentionally or inadvertently. Such internal actions as these can additionally be mediated through the parent's internal representative, the *identification image*, which serves as the watchdog of the inner life, the gatekeeper of the unconscious, the self-appointed guardian scrutinizing all that happens inside the self and dispensing shame, contempt, hatred or fear as warranted. Because the self already feels deficient, what choice has the self but to agree with the pronouncements forthcoming from the parent's internal representative? Hence, we learn to speak to ourselves, to say the very things subvocally to ourselves which our parents originally said to us. If these were disparaging or aroused doubt, then we learn to do similarly inside. And if we were treated in critical, judgmental, belittling, or otherwise disrespectful ways, what other model have we on which to base our beginning relationship with ourselves *and* with which to combat the parent's internal representative?

But the disowning of self is *not* inevitable. A particular child may have had an inherently destructive relationship with one parent, and even internalize such a parent, yet may have a strong, positive self-enhancing relationship with the other parent and thereby reduce or avoid emotional crippling. Or it might be a valued grandfather who plays that role. If the child finds some other individual who is respecting and enhancing *and* is able to have a consistent relationship with that individual, the disowning of self can be significantly diminished in its effects or perhaps altogether averted.

Following internalization, the self faces two dilemmas. First, some means must be found to restore the balance, to come to terms with inherent defectiveness. Second, the parent's internal representative, the self's guiding identification image, must be coped with directly if that image is based primarily on shame or contempt. When the identification image derives from interactions with a significant other which are based primarily on love, respect, and open valuing for the self, that internal image poses no threat to the self and functions as a useful inner ally whenever unforeseen events so dictate.

Whatever is recognized by the self of the child as having led to or caused the state of affairs he now finds himself in becomes the target of adaptation in inner reality. Again, it is the *impact* of parental behavior upon the child, not whether it was intended thus, which counts here. Unintended rejecting impact is nevertheless experienced as rejecting. A sufficient number of shame experiences in a significant relationship may prompt a sudden realization that, "There is something wrong with *me!*"

At some point in his or her young life, a child comes to recognize, literally to "see," what it is about him or her which causes that much-needed significant other to behave thus. It is as though the child half-consciously begins to search for, "What about me is so vitally wrong?" Once his eyes are opened, as it were, he will find what is wrong about him. If there is any pattern at all to a parent's behavior, a child will discover it.

When shame internalization has derived from any of the following circumstances—the child never having been really wanted, having been born the wrong gender, the parent's looking to the child to make up for the parent's deficiencies or to literally be parent to the parent or wanting the child never to need anything emotionally from the parent, or the child's having the wrong temperament—an inherent part of the child's self has been intentionally or inadvertently rejected. Whether it is sexuality as a member of the drive system, or one or more of the primary affects which represent the affect system, or any of the fundamental developmental needs which comprise the need system, an inherent part of the self (drives, affects, or needs) has become bad, deficient, and rejected in the process of shame internalization. In effect, the parent, even without knowing it, has begun to model for the child how he ought to behave, in this case, how he *ought* to disown those parts of himself that the parent has disowned.

Again, observational learning is just as potent in this regard as is direct experiencing. The child need simply observe consistently enough how a parent disowns some part of the *parent's* self. When a child confronts a parent with an emotional truth about the parent, such as the parent being angry, yet is met with discomfort, perhaps embarrassment, or open denial of the child's perception, the parent is modeling the disowning of self. It is this active process of disowning of self which leads to the splitting of the self into parts that are owned and parts that are disowned, akin to what Sullivan had hold of when he described the "Me" versus the "Not-Me" or "Bad-Me."

Needs, feelings, drives: these are three distinguishable yet interrelated parts of the self which also function as motivators. These three are vulnerable to disowning and to the distortions of the self which disowning creates. Disowning can be directed at the entire range of feelings or at either one or several. Likewise with needs. A specific need, or the entire experience of *needing* itself, may be disowned. Thus it happens that we may see an individual lacking either in awareness or expression of basic affect and wonder why he has no access to his feelings or we might see an individual who presents a righteously self-sufficient stance to the world, seemingly contemptuous of those weaker ones among us who depend on others or express needs. In each case, a vital part of the self has been actively silenced and disowned, thereby creating a split within the self, and all in an attempt to cope with the perceived locus of the shame which has grown so intolerable through internalization.

If it is clear that disowning robs us of inner wholeness, the essential integrity of the self, it may be less apparent that disowning, through the creation of splits within the self, is also the origin of inner psychic pain, a pain inflicted wholly upon ourselves. Disowning of self creates a split within the self which gradually widens over the years, eventually fully isolating that disowned part of the self. The acceptable parts remain conscious while the disowned part withdraws itself deeper into the unconscious, though never completely so. Always, there are faint murmurings of it that can be painfully felt. Any degree of conscious awareness of what has been intentionally cast adrift brings on the most acute inner pain.

SPLITTING OF THE SELF: AN OUTGROWTH OF DISOWNING

The disowning process can be pursued relentlessly by the self in order to erase whatever has so given rise to intolerable defectiveness (for it must reside within the self since parents are, after all, infallible). Disowning may also be relentless in an effort to assuage a harsh, punitive identification image, the parent's internal representative. And disowning may be relentlessly pursued as a learned way of relating to oneself. These three outcomes of internalization guide the next process, the disowning of self.

When that disowning is relentless or begins at too early an age, or there lacks any positive counterbalancing experience with other significant humans, then disowning can eventuate in such a profound splitting of the self that independent, split-off parts may emerge. Let's proceed by way of example.

One client, Sandy, felt rejected as a child by her mother whenever she became anxious or frightened. Mother had either ignored her fears or reassured her in a condescending manner which only left her feeling more humiliated. Mother never aided Sandy in learning to cope with the sources of her fear.

During one session in the course of therapy, together Sandy and I began to understand how her growth had become blocked. Interestingly, this session followed a visit home to see her parents and grandmother (mother's mother). One piece of the puzzle related directly to grandmother. As a child, Sandy spent a lot of time with her grandmother. The grandmother repeatedly told her frightening stories which filled Sandy with dread and terror, causing nightmares. This we had known. But what I had not seen before was how controlling grandmother was: she attempted to manipulate others through terrorizing. Always before, the image of grandmother was of a terri*fied* old lady; now the image which emerged was of a terri*fying* person. For the first time, during this visit, Sandy saw how her grandmother sought to manipulate everyone around her by making them anxious.

Since Sandy spent so much of her childhood with grandmother, I wondered out loud, perhaps grandmother was a source of Sandy's terror as a child. And her persecutory fears were the internal images of grandmother that Sandy internalized as a child, through identification. Grandmother literally created the hostile world Sandy began to experience, for everything was dangerous or destructive to grandmother. Everything posed a threat to life or safety; that was her way of stopping Sandy from doing whatever grandmother did not like. Sandy remembered how often she came running to her mother terrified, even refusing to go back to her grandmother. Yet mother could never give her the support Sandy needed since mother herself could never stand up to grandmother. And when the nightly nightmares started up and Sandy went to mother for comfort, mother *refused* to wake up! Thus, Sandy literally was helpless in a hostile world, a world of internal persecutors, images internalized out of interacting with grandmother. Later, those images became projected outside in the form of fears.

But why did mother refuse to wake up? That was a refusal to mother Sandy when she most needed it. Even more important, why did she ignore Sandy's complaints and send her back into the terrifying situation? I reasoned out loud that if this was what happened to Sandy, it must also have happened to mother when mother was a child. And it had. Sandy recalled that mother used to tell her how afraid she herself was as a child. But suddenly, mother had seemingly gotten over it.

No, I speculated, mother had *rejected* that part of herself. She had rejected the frightened little girl within her as well. So mother had no choice but to reject Sandy also when Sandy became that frightened little girl. Grandmother induced terror and mother induced shame through rejection of the frightened child. Thus, the two affects, shame and fear, had become linked together, internally spiraling toward panic. And Sandy continued the internalized pattern: she also rejected that frightened little girl within her and expected others in her current life to do likewise whenever that helpless, frightened little girl showed herself. In such ways shame is recycled and passed on from generation to generation.

We literally are taught to disown those parts of the self inside of us which are disowned by significant others. In Sandy's case, being anxious was rejected and so she learned to disown and reject that part of herself. The insecure, frightened little girl within her became bad, shameful, thereby causing the growth process to become blocked. Whenever we must disown and dissociate a part of the self, rather than own and integrate it, further growth of identity is interrupted.

For Sandy, we were able to differentiate and make conscious the internal images within her which had plagued her all her life: the persecutory, terrorizing grandmother; the rejecting, shaming mother; and her own image of herself as a helpless, frightened, inadequate little girl. Now, there was room for the self inside to grow, a self now learning to love and respect instead of continuing to reject the frightened child within her, a self that can begin to experience herself as womanly, competent, and valued from within. In this way, the self which had originally become split through the internalization of shame begins the work of reintegrating, of becoming whole.

Let's consider a second example. In the case of Martha, there had been such contempt shown for the girl by her mother whenever she needed anything emotionally from mother that Martha learned to continue this internalized relationship with herself. She began to feel loathing and disgust for the needy little girl inside of her. As a grown woman, she felt reasonably okay only as long as that weak, disgusting part of her did not show itself. But whenever it but approached conscious awareness, let alone interpersonal expression, Martha meted out swift punishment to herself including physical self-abuse. This was her way of trying to destroy the needy little girl inside of her, the part of her so painfully disowned by her mother.

The splitting was so pronounced that not only was there a weak, insecure little girl disowned and split off, there was also a persecutory part of the self functioning more-or-less independently which literally sought to destroy that little girl part. There were times when a more-or-less integrated Martha dissolved, leaving visible two, more infantile partial selves, the one child-like and needy and the other harsh, punitive, and persecutory. During one critical session, her personality briefly disintegrated and a brutal dialogue between these two partial selves ensued.

That session was a critical one because I was able to intervene. Intuitively, I knew I needed to act and I felt our relationship was strong enough. I insisted that she, metaphorically speaking, now pick that little girl up, hold her in her arms, and love her. Martha immediately convulsed into sobbing pain. And she emerged much more integrated and on the path toward owning the needing child within her as an inherent part of her self.

Another example. This client, Jane, lived with a blaming, fault-finding, intrusive, domineering father, and a mother who was literally no more than an extension of her husband. Thus, she was no real person in her own right, separate from her husband. For Jane to get close to her mother meant literally becoming "stuck" there, much as mother was stuck inside her husband in Jane's perception. Jane avoided all closeness with mother but had an older sister with whom she could experience some of the needed identification. No integrated, whole self ever developed. Instead, she described her inner life as comprising three distinctly different partial selves. She herself was in the middle, while "personality A" was on her right, and "personality B" was on her left. She referred to these as "A" and "B" and said she was never without their presence. Well, after many months, it gradually became clear that "A" was the little girl inside of her, the little girl who had feelings and needs, the lost child part of her. And "B" felt to her like her sister, the only person she had ever had even the faintest of positive relationships with.

Clearly, when disowning and splitting eventuate in more-or-less separate, independent partial selves within one and the same individual, events have indeed taken a most unfortunate turn. Nothing is so precious to the self as its own integrity.

One final example before we move on. A young boy, perhaps eight years old at the time, had been stealing money, but only from his mother and older brother. One day he suspiciously came in with a new purchase. His mother and father began to inquire as to where he had gotten it. They did not believe him when he said it was really an old gun of his which he had just now found in his room. He was caught and he panicked: "What would they do to him!" He made them promise not to beat him or punish him before he would tell them the truth. He pleaded with them, begged them, and thus humiliated himself. They agreed. Then he told how he had been taking the money from mother's purse and from brother. The parents were devastated. "How *could* you? Didn't you know we'd give you anything you wanted?" said his father, acutely disappointed in his son. With that, father abruptly turned away and walked out of the house. Mother said little yet such a look of contempt and disgust crossed her face that a beating could scarcely have inflicted a greater wound to his self.

From that point on, the boy sought to make amends, to reform, and to atone. He stopped stealing and in fact never stole again. And he spontaneously began a daily confessional of every wicked thought or feeling which passed through him. If he had done something mean or only felt like it, he confessed. Whether concerning anger, which he had already learned was a forbidden affect, or sexuality, the boy confessed it to his mother *and* to his father. Whenever he masturbated, which had caught his parents' wrath before, he felt he now had to confess this first to mother and then to father. Doing so to one parent was somehow not enough; he had to put himself through the ordeal twice. That was his seemingly self-imposed punishment. And the parents did nothing when he confessed except to convey each time a look of increasing disappointment.

Gradually, the confessing became more and more painful to the boy; the look of disappointment which he received grew more and more severe. Over the course of several months, the daily confessing became agonizing to the point of being intolerable. In this way, he was continually, daily, resubjecting himself to further shame and humiliation. After all, he had secured his parents' promise not to punish him. Without knowing it, he had taken that punishment upon himself.

And on and on it went. His parents never seemed about to put a stop to it. No one seemed ready to say to him, "Okay, you have punished yourself enough." It came as a thunderbolt upon him: "This will go on forever! They're never going to stop my confessing." With that intolerable realization, the boy immediately ceased his ritual of confession. And what's more, from that day on he never again let anyone see what went on inside of him. Most literally, he shut out the world and his parents with it. Never would he trust again or reveal his innermost self to another human being. And he kept that promise to himself for another fourteen years, until he began therapy. And throughout that time, all that the world ever saw was a superficial, social mask. The real self, and most especially the needing part of him, withdrew even deeper inside in order to avoid the intolerable agony of exposure.

INTERNALIZED RELATIONSHIP BETWEEN SPLIT-OFF PARTS OF THE SELF

We have dealt at length with how disowning comes about and how it becomes manifest. All of the complex factors in this process have not been discerned. I do not presume either a finished or a complete understanding of all that is involved here. And individual experience is so unique, so rich and varied, that we must guard against ever presuming to know all the answers to the complexity of human development. What I have presented is what I feel sufficient certainty about, based upon my own experience, my observations, and upon what others also have observed.

What seems to happen when parts of the self become disowned and eventually split off is that defending strategies employed in outer reality now transfer into inner reality and are *actively* used by one part of the self directly against another. Thus, this internalized relationship between parts of the self may comprise any or all of the following: contempt and judgment, outright persecution, terror, shaming, or isolation of that part even deeper within the self (what I have termed internal withdrawal). The use of such defenses within the inner life wreaks havoc with the self and becomes the source both of internal strife and *internalized insecurity*. The internal use of those defenses actively perpetuates and maintains the splitting of the self. This is the real source of that feeling of perceived inner weakness. It is not only the presence of a shameful, split-off part, but most especially the active disowning of such an inherent, vital part of the self which both creates and maintains the internal insecurity underlying inner weakness.

Disowning of self robs us not only of integrity but of inner security as well. And through the current, internalized relationship between split-off parts of the self, conflicts and dynamics which originated in the past are continued into the present and actively maintained.

INTERNAL RELATIONSHIP WITH IDENTIFICATION IMAGES

In addition to the active disowning of parts of the self and the more serious actual splitting of the self which can ensue, the inner life also comprises one or more internal identification images. The self must contend not only with those parts of the self which have been disowned or actually split off, but just as certainly with the parent's internal representative. A part of each parent or significant other becomes internalized and thereby installed in inner reality to serve in a guiding capacity for inner as well as outer living. In this manner, the outer relationship with the parent becomes transferred into the inner life. The self continues to relate to and contend with the parent within just as it must do so with the significant other external to the self.

More often than not, the power of the identification image begins to emerge more clearly following actual separation from the family. While the self is still consistently engaged in a relationship with a significant other, the internal relationship between the self and the identification image, though present, remains obscure. When separation has been effected, the vacuum created thereby is filled internally by the identification image. After all, never do we wholly outgrow our need for parents, for belonging somewhere. When we relinquish that need as we inevitably must through separation, a ready replacement is found internally. That is, unless or until a new significant other comes upon the scene, a person with whom the self can develop that much-needed but hopefully more satisfying *real* relationship, a person able to wean the self away from its internal, self-limiting identification images as well.

THE RELATIONSHIP BETWEEN
INTERNALIZATION AND PROJECTION

The parentally derived identification images internalized through the identification process comprise one unconscious-conscious component of identity. The images are mainly rooted in our unconscious—the originating source for them being experientially erased—yet frequently either erupt directly into consciousness or disturb our internal functioning.

When we later find a person who somehow reminds us of the original significant other with whom we have unconsciously identified, we engage in a new process aimed at restoring the failure in the original relationship. After all, it was a failure which induced shame, the internalization of which permitted, along with it, the internalization of an identification image. The new process is projection: we project onto this other person in our current lives feelings and reactions learned in the original situation without any question of appropriateness or accuracy entering our minds. When an image becomes activated through a current interaction which somehow reminds us of it, we suddenly behave *as if* we were back in this original situation. All of the feelings experienced and beliefs learned in relation to both self and other in the original situation become attached to the image, internalized, but now reactivated and relived. Underlying this projection or transferring of past reactions is the activation, and then projection, of the internalized identification image itself onto this other person. The latter in fact probably precedes the projection of feelings and reactions, but usually remains mostly at an unconscious level.

I would thus offer the hypothesized conclusion that an internalized identification image underlies many instances of projection. Whenever we see projection occurring, we must look beyond it to the unconscious identification image underlying it. What is in my view actually being projected is the internal relationship between the self and the internalized parental identification image. Through internalization, the once external drama plays out internally, and internal unfinished situations transfer back into current human relationships.

THE CONVERSION PROCESS

While struggling to cope with the internal world inside the self, some means must be found to quiet the parts of the self that have been disowned. One way to accomplish this is to convert what is forbidden or shameful into something either more acceptable or else more tolerable. The two most critical forms of conversion which I have widely observed are *affect conversion* and *need conversion.*

In affect conversion, a troubling feeling such as anger is blocked from conscious awareness but also converted into another more tolerable affect, such as distress or guilt. Let's imagine the following situation. A six-year-old boy has become extremely enraged toward his mother. The mother has disowned anger for herself and reacts with feeling threatened. She begins to cry in front of the boy and says the following: "One day you will come home and I won't be here. I will have gone off and died!" What happens is that the boy rushes to mother's side, begs her not to leave him, and promises to be good. Not only will separation anxiety, even abandonment terror, swiftly generate, but the boy's awareness of his anger will of necessity be lost. That anger will inevitably convert into guilt, for how could any decent person cause his own mother to go off and die! This is certainly an extreme example of what can happen when parents react with *hurt* to a child's natural expression of anger.

In need conversion, any of the fundamental developmental needs may be blocked from conscious awareness, but then the *experience of needing something* becomes converted into something else. For example, a young boy who learns never to need anything emotionally from his parents because doing so is not safe is faced with a dilemma whenever he feels young, needy, or otherwise insecure. If masturbating has been his principal source of good feelings, even though it be bodily pleasure, he may resort to masturbation in order to restore good feelings about self at times when he is experiencing needs quite unrelated to sexuality.

It is an observed phenomenon that individuals do not grow in straight lines. Thus, progression forever alternates with regression. There are significant moments when one feels insecure, younger, or needy, this being the best phenomenological description of that inner experience, and so most in need of parenting. But if needing has been shamed and hence blocked, and there is nowhere else to turn, a child may resort to masturbation. In such a way, experiences of feeling needy become associated with the sexual drive, eventuating in a conversion of emotional needing into genital sexuality. Later, whenever insecurity is aroused or a need begins to surface, this inner event becomes registered consciously only in explicitly sexual guise. Such an individual may then look to sex to meet needs that sex cannot really provide.

Conversion of needs and/or affects into one or another form of bodily or somatic expression may certainly be a third form of conversion which parallels the other two. In all likelihood, there must also be predisposing genetically based factors such as particular organ weakness along with modeled experience with a somaticizing parent and/or some reward for bodily illness in order to support somatic conversion.

SHAME-BASED IDENTITY

The process of disowning of self and the even more burdensome actual splitting of the self to which disowning may give rise round out our picture of the development of shame. The self has now completely taken on the capability of perpetuating shame indefinitely. Certainly, some aspects of self or areas of internal functioning may escape the binding effects of shame. These may even become much-needed sources of good feelings about the self, to be relied upon at moments when excessive shame engulfs the self. Though conscious awareness may often be experienced as positive for an individual emerging from the turmoils of adolescence, certain vulnerabilities to shame may yet be present. For that inner quiet within conscious awareness may have been won at the price of silencing some disowned part of the self. The more effective that adaptation is, the greater is one's apparent inner peace. Yet unexpected events can so disrupt the functioning of the self and bring on a new encounter with shame that inner well-being can no longer be so easily regained. Meeting head-on with defeats, failures, and rejections, particularly when these events are sudden or unexpected, is one principal source of fresh encounters with shame as one proceeds through life. To the degree that an individual never has learned how to cope with shame *without internalizing that affect*, the real likelihood of renewed or additional shame internalization emerges. In such an eventuality, an individual's sense of shame may only intensify or deepen further.

Yet events which seemingly seek to call our selves into question, these ever-recurring crises for the self, really pose only challenges to be faced, for good or for ill. It is in the honest facing of those tests of self that we most especially find out of what stuff we are made. For it is in *how* we face those inevitable defeats, those necessary failures, those painful rejections—not whether they were deserved—which matters most in my way of thinking. An individual may emerge from such crises, such confrontations with self as shame hands us, either more solid and secure in his personhood or more uncertain, self-doubting, and confirmed in defectiveness. Always, there remains the possibility, if not the potential, for growth if one but takes the risk. And growth is at best a risky prospect. No one can ever claim with anything even approaching certainty to know what the outcome might be. Thus, the uncertainties of life are what provide us with the possibilities for restoring ourselves and for growth.

Yet, just as likely are the possibilities for the solidification of shame further within the emerging identity of an individual. And that is the final step in the developmental sequence, when one's essential identity becomes based on shame. In such an event, defeats, failures, or rejections need no longer be actual, but only perceived as such. Simple awareness of a limitation may be sufficient to count as a mortal wounding of the self, a new confirmation of inherent defectiveness. Such an individual may experience himself as an inherent failure as a human being. Mistakes, which ought to be expected in the course of daily functioning, become occasions of agonizing self-torture. And when disowned parts of the self make themselves felt or, what may be even worse, their presence is somehow sensed or seen by another, the self may inflict unrelenting suffering upon the self. And that internal shame spiral is unleashed which can all but consume the self.

The internal shame process has become painful, punishing and enduring beyond what the simple feeling of shame might produce. The internalization of shame has produced an identity, a way of relating to oneself, which absorbs, maintains, and spreads shame ever further. And the internalized relationship between owned and disowned parts of the self re-creates directly within the inner life the very same shame-inducing qualities which were first encountered in interpersonal living. That internalized relationship becomes expressed and maintained through the active use of defenses directly against disowned parts of the self.

THE OUTCOMES OF DEVELOPMENT IN REGARD TO SHAME

The outcomes of development are varied indeed. A more-or-less unified self may be present which must contend with either an enhancing or a harsh and punitive internal identification image. Or, a significant part of the self has been disowned, the needing child part, for example, with which the self must contend along with that identification image. Or, the self has become split into two or more partial selves, for example, the one punishing or even persecutory and the other insecure and needing; again, present along with these is one or more identification images which can be judgmental or contemptuous. And a particular individual may either possess partial knowledge of or entirely lack conscious awareness of the varied personages so engaged in the internal drama taking place within the inner life. That inner life can all but be absorbed in the internal dialogue an individual now must live with.

Neither disowning nor splitting are necessarily inevitable occurrences. A given individual may emerge into adulthood with a reasonably intact, unified self able to cope rather effectively; with a precarious, more vulnerable self lacking in essential inner resources needed for continued coping with such threats to self as shame; with a self divided and at war with itself; or with either a fragmented self or a self vulnerable to such disintegration into two or more partial selves.

SHAME-BASED IDENTITY SYNDROMES: A VIEW OF THE SCHIZOID, PARANOID, AND DEPRESSIVE POSTURES

Distinct varieties of shame syndromes may be a likely developmental possibility. A host of factors will interact leading to such an eventuality. Innate temperament differences, particular patterns of affect and need socialization, the unique dynamics of the family interaction, the developing strategies of defense against shame, along with whatever continued, modifying interaction occurs with the wider environment are the most prominent factors identified so far. Tomkins has already argued for the significance of shame as one vital factor in the development of depression, the paranoid posture, and paranoid schizophrenia. I have independently come to a similar conception, though it was arrived at somewhat differently.

I found Tomkins' notion of a "posture" toward the world a useful one in furthering the delineation of varieties of shame-based identities. Equally useful is the view of innate temperament differences, under which I subsume introversion-extroversion. Combining these two notions, I have been slowly crystallizing the view that some individuals may develop either a schizoid, paranoid, or depressive posture toward the world.

When an individual with a given introverted nature is forced to contend with excessive shame, excessive beyond current capacity to cope or due to some failure of the supporting interpersonal environment, that individual is likely to fall back upon his own natural tendency to withdraw inside as a useful means of adaptation. When that adaptation is pushed to the hilt, the individual develops a *schizoid posture* toward the world. Human relationships become highly ambivalent, leading to an oscillating pattern of going in and out of relationships. Or else relationships with others are avoided or abandoned for a time altogether. Such a person is able to behave thus because his basic introverted temperament already is predominantly focused inwardly: interest already lies primarily within the self.

An extroverted individual cannot so easily abandon human interaction even in the face of the most pronounced onslaughts of shame.

For such an individual, interest resides primarily outside the self. And for such an individual whose temperament already is an externalizing one to begin with, internalization itself may well be slower to come about. An expressive, externalizing, extroverted temperament is also more given to naturally occurring oscillations of mood. A tendency to cycloid mood swings combined with an extroverted nature (these being perhaps two somewhat distinct aspects of temperament) make the adoption of a schizoid posture highly unlikely. But such a combination, when reaching the extreme, may well emerge in a *depressive posture*. For such an individual, recurring bouts with depressive episodes is a most likely eventuality.

The depressive episode is a condition in which shame, disappointment in self, has become sufficiently prolonged as to be experienced as a continuing mood. Through internalization, the self has learned how to hold onto shame, to draw it out over time. The rage accompanying shame may either be directed externally or inwardly depending on prior learning. When an individual has additionally learned to direct that rage inwardly against the self, this becomes a second means of perpetuating, of literally reproducing, the very shame which then further protracts the depressive mood. And a self-sustaining cycle has been created which, if uninterrupted, will continue ad infinitum. It must also be noted that the *internal activities* engaged in by the self which eventuate in what the individual experiences as depression vary widely from person to person. That set of activities constitutes a particular individual's internalized process for reproducing shame, the very relationship which the self has learned to have with the self. And it continues despite how unsatisfying it is because it has become an integral part of that individual's identity.

For the individual who has been pushed to the schizoid posture, the presence of shame is no less disruptive. Yet it manifests not in an externally visible, depressive mood, but in withdrawal ever deeper inside the self. Such an individual is indeed hard to know. For at the slightest onset of exposure, he hides all the more. And conscious awareness may even be abdicated by an integrated self, leaving a host of personages present to wage internal strife, from disowned parts of the self to partial selves to identification images. And all that the outer world may ever see is that acceptable social mask, so convincingly disguising the inner turmoil.

The schizoid and depressive postures are two basic orientations toward living which can emerge developmentally. The *paranoid posture* is a third fundamental stance which an individual may be pushed to adopt in an effort to adapt to the exigencies of shame. I shall contend that either temperament type, introvert or extrovert, may additionally develop paranoid defenses in order to cope with excessive shame. In such an event, the individual becomes vigilant and watchful, always waiting for the humiliation, betrayal, or blaming he knows is coming. Such a person who has adopted a paranoid posture has learned to excessively personalize experience by misinterpreting innocent events as personally malevolent, to remain vigilant or forever on guard in response, and to transfer blame from the self elsewhere.

It is the utilization of the transfer of blame as a generalized strategy for adaptation to the human world which is the heart of the paranoid posture. As Harry Stack Sullivan also observed, but described in somewhat different language, the self of the paranoid feels hopelessly defective (stemming from internalized shame, in my view) and arrives at a solution to this dilemma through identification with a parent who behaved similarly toward the world. Experience with a parent who is rather adept at the transfer of blame for mistakes or failures provides a model for the self's engaging in like action. If this transferring of blame continues to generalize as a strategy for coping with the unforeseen exigencies of life, then a paranoid posture is in the making.

When the source of one's own inner deficiency can be blamed elsewhere, the self becomes momentarily freed at least of the *conscious* awareness of shame. Wrongdoings, mistakes, and other instances of personal failure cannot be honestly owned by the paranoid-prone individual and so must be disowned but then *transferred* from the self to others. With each partially successful transfer of blame for his own deficiencies, the galloping paranoid begins to *break with sincerity* with himself and may come to invent a malevolent belief system. This growing *misinterpretation of events,* as Sullivan first described it, provides confirmatory "proof" for the paranoid's original posture, thereby creating a fully self-sustaining system. This emerging belief system may ultimately integrate the conscious self of the paranoid around a self-righteous "holy war" if he then decides to persecute his perceived persecutors. In this eventuality the paranoid believes he has found his true calling in life which in turn provides him, though in a distorted way, with that vital sense of meaning for which we all search.

While the paranoid relies on the wholesale transfer of blame as a defending strategy, the schizoid individual utilizes internal withdrawal as his principal means of adaptation. Mixtures of these two postures inevitably abound, as pure types are nowhere prominent. Furthermore, individuals will vary widely in the degree to which either posture develops or how entrenched it may eventually become. Likewise, temperamentally cycloid, extroverted individuals encountering excessive shame within the family—for example, at the hands of a father who is given to pervasively transfer blame— will most likely develop a depressive posture along with paranoid defenses. The central thesis unfolding here is that innate temperament, along with family experience, as well as later modifying experience with the wider environment, together shape our emerging forms of adaptation to life.

UNDERSTANDING SHYNESS, EMBARRASSMENT, AND GUILT: TOWARD A NEW LANGUAGE OF SYMBOLIZATION

As we approach the close of our theoretical presentation concerning the dynamics and development of shame, we must consider how language itself can alter our perception, and ultimately our understanding, of inner states. Language provides us with tools of mastery when confronting the inner life. In conferring a *name* to a particular inner event, the linguistic symbol confers a measure of understanding from which conscious control in turn evolves. In all our language, societally we have for the most part never evolved accurate symbolizations for the phenomenological experience of shame. In part this has been due to the wordless nature of the affect concerned, and to the speech-binding effects of exposure itself. Another reason is that humans typically hide their own shame and avoid approaching anyone else's.

As language unfolds developmentally, our tools for symbolizing inner experience become richer and more complex. Subtle nuances of meaning are at once grasped through different linguistic symbols, the use of which may in turn mask an underlying unity that stretches through what *feel like* quite distinct experiences. In the course of converting an inner state such as affect into an interpersonally communicative process, the particular symbols or words used to grasp hold of that inner state may also act upon it to alter its very perception.

Phenomenology becomes intricately bound up with language whenever we stand upon the threshold of the self's inner life. But if we are ever to gain mastery, that emergent sense of inner efficacy from which springs wisdom, then we must hone our language so that the words used to describe inner states keep close to the ground of being. If we are to gain that conscious control over shame, we must first sift through whatever symbols have been acquired as representations of inner experience to extract their unifying roots.

The only means by which we have been able to catch hold of some singular aspect of shame or its effects upon the self has been through linguistic symbols such as embarrassment, shyness, self-consciousness, shame, inferiority, inadequacy, and guilt. Self-consciousness at talking before a large group, shame at failing to measure up to one's basic expectations of oneself, feeling embarrassed at having come inappropriately dressed to an important social gathering, shyness in the presence of a stranger, and guilt for an immorality or transgression are phenomenologically felt as distinctly different experiences. Yet the underlying *affect* in each experience is the same, as Silvan Tomkins convincingly argues. This is the affect termed shame, the root of which is the feeling of exposure of the self either in a painful or diminished sense.

With the concept of shame, we bring together in an integrative way diverse qualities of a central human experience whose significance generally has neither been well recognized nor its impact on development adequately understood. And, furthermore, shame is closer to the felt *meaning* conveyed in the experience. For these reasons, it makes sense to speak of shame as the integrative concept. Clearly, the word shame is being used here quite differently from contemporary usage.

Shyness: Shame in the Presence of a Stranger

Many of us experience shyness when faced with the prospect of approaching a stranger. The immediate feeling may be one of either self-consciousness or embarrassment. We may stammer inside, not knowing quite what to say. We may even feel altogether speechless and urgently seek a way to escape or hide, though a part of us secretly longs to reach out directly to that other person. Yet we feel too self-conscious to even move on that urge and, feeling bound-up, now feel trapped. In response to that inner conflict, we hang our head, avert our eyes, and let the moment slip away.

Contained in the experience of shyness is the feeling of shame, of exposure of oneself. It is this feeling of exposure which characterizes the essential nature of shame. To feel shame is to be seen. Our eyes suddenly turn inward and our attention unexpectedly focuses wholly upon ourselves. Suddenly, we are watching ourselves, scrutinizing the minutest detail of our being. This excruciating observation of the self generates the torment of self-consciousness which in turn creates that binding and paralyzing effect upon the self.

Shyness is to be understood, in my way of thinking, as shame either in the presence of or at approaching strangers. The presence of the stranger sets off the feeling of exposure which results in what many of us have come to call shyness. What *really* is being thus exposed you might wonder? Imagine ignoring one's impulse to turn away. Imagine going ahead in spite of feeling shy and actually approaching that stranger: *What would I say? I'd look foolish, stupid, clumsy even. I wouldn't know what to do. I'd die inside.* It is the very self inside of us which feels exposed in shame.

Before moving on, let's consider the implications of such a view for how best to grow beyond the barrier shame sets us in the form of shyness. This will highlight the developmental relevance of the particular conception of shame unfolding here. First of all we must give ourselves learning time, time to make mistakes as we go about the task of learning something new. And learning how to approach strangers is a skill that can be learned if we are willing to practice. Permission to fail is part of it. Permission to look foolish, even dumb, both to ourselves and to those others as well.

Then we must *practice*, practice going up to strangers and *expect* to fail some of the time. Expect that it won't work out and let failing be okay. We must learn to be gentle with ourselves. We must learn to treat ourselves kindly and lovingly and with forgiveness for our most imperfect humanness. It doesn't have to work out each time or necessarily even most of the time. And it's okay if we blow it all the time. It's also okay to be just plain shy. Only when *however we are* becomes good enough do we ever become really free to be our best.

Next, we must learn how to reverse that internal shame process. When our eyes become focused internally upon ourselves, we must learn to exert real conscious effort to focus all of our attention once again back outside. Becoming visually and/or physically involved in the world is one way of accomplishing that reversal. An example of this would be to become absorbed in the sights and sounds of the world around us. Focusing upon any such sensory experience, whether visual or physical, can enable the self to accomplish that much-needed refocusing of attention. Even talking to oneself about the things one sees or hears or touches can aid the self in letting go of shame. If we are able to refocus our attention once more outside ourselves, the feeling of exposure, of shame, itself will pass. And in this way we are able to gain increasing control over the binding effects shame is able to have upon us.

Another way of accomplishing this necessary refocusing of attention is by observing just what kind of person this stranger is *instead of* worrying about what the stranger thinks of us. When we are considering how *we* feel about another, whether it is someone we like, respect or might want to get to know, we are in a position of *equal power* in relation to the other. On the other hand, when our attention is instead focused entirely upon ourselves, upon how well or badly we are coming off or how the other sizes us up, this inner stance leaves us feeling rather *powerless* and hence more vulnerable to shame. With sufficient practice and determination we can learn how to switch from a relatively powerless position to one of more equal power in relation to others.

Each time we can reverse the process, each time we can go ahead and approach a stranger, however well or badly it goes, we gain increasing freedom to do it again and again and again. For the feeling of exposure begins to lose some of the paralyzing hold it has had upon us. And strangers are no longer as apt to trigger that binding feeling in the first place.

Of course, there will always be times when shyness recurs, times when we are once again vulnerable to shame. That is to be expected throughout life. And those are times when we ought to be tender with ourselves, neither critical nor punitive.

In these ways, we can learn to better tolerate shame in whatever form, shyness being one, and to be much less fearful of its recurrence. For we have also learned how best to cope with it when it does come upon us and, most especially, how to let go of that binding feeling of exposure.

Embarrassment

The kernel of embarrassment can be viewed as being seen in some vital way as socially inappropriate. This can certainly happen in various ways. Imagine yourself at an important social gathering. Suddenly, you spill your drink and all eyes turn your way. Immediately, your eyes turn inward upon yourself. You feel exposed amid the watchful eyes of others. You feel clumsy, foolish, even self-conscious. The feeling may be brief or lasting depending on how the self has learned to handle shame.

Another incident comes to mind which is all too frequent. We encounter someone we've either met previously or who remembers us, but we cannot recall the person's name. We pretend that we do remember and would feel an acute pang of shame to honestly admit our faulty memory to the other. If you are not convinced, next time this happens to you, go ahead and ask the other his or her name and see if you do not feel something like self-consciousness or exposure.

Embarrassment is *not* a different affect or feeling, but has come to stand for particular instances in which suddenly we feel socially ill-at-ease, self-conscious, or exposed. Phenomenologically, the affect present is nonetheless the affect of shame.

Guilt: Self-Contempt and Self-Blame

Now that we have considered the origin of defenses directed both at the outer world of people and things and that inner world inside the self, we can address one of the larger questions confronting a theory of development based on the interplay among shame, identification, and the self. The question referred to concerns our understanding of guilt as it relates to shame. Much that has been written concerning shame has sought to compare or contrast it with the experience of guilt. Piers and Singer, Lewis, Erikson, and most other theorists and writers back to Alexander continued the prevalent dichotomy between shame and guilt. An attempt to look at cultures as either guilt-oriented or shame-oriented has recently culminated in attempting to classify individuals as either shame-prone or guilt-prone.

This has been the traditionally accepted view of things that no one really questioned. Some years ago, however, I discovered Silvan Tomkins' ambitious work on developing a model for an affect theory of motivation. Tomkins offered a more precise language to differentiate the basic affects that could be identified and clearly distinguished from one another.

Tomkins then made the critical observation that shyness in the presence of a stranger, shame at a failure and guilt for a transgression or immorality were, *at the level of affect*, phenomenologically one and the same affect. Different components in the three experiences along with shame are what make them feel so distinctly different. Here, guilt can be understood as feeling disappointed in oneself for violating an important internal value or code of behavior. Shame over a failure also feels like a disappointment in self. But here no value has been violated; one has simply failed to cope with a challenge. The meaning of the two experiences is as different as feeling inadequate is from feeling immoral. But in each experience, one still feels bad as a person: the head hangs low.

When we are concerned with this dimensional quality of inner experience, it makes little difference to distinguish shame from guilt. The *affect* is still the same in each, and the affect is the principal component of the overall experience. However, inner experience is not only the realm of affect but of identifications and defenses, also of impulses, fantasy, and the unconscious. The critical differentiation is not between shame and guilt but between *shame as affect* and *internalized shame.* It is this developmental event which becomes the precursor for the development of defenses aimed inside as well as outside and, later, the actual disowning of parts of the self.

When contempt and blame become adopted as general strategies, they can be aimed at any object which arouses contempt or blame, even a part of the self. Tomkins broke with tradition in suggesting that much that has been traditionally labeled as guilt is, on closer inspection, internalized contempt. Intuitively, I knew he was right. Contempt is a learned affect blend of anger conjoined with dissmell; hence, the facial sneer of contempt is produced by the upper lip raised on *one* side of the face via dissmell. An overtly contemptuous parent models the expression of distancing dissmell plus punitive anger in the form of loathing and violent rejection of the offensive object. A child growing up in such a climate will likely internalize such a parent through identification. The internal image of the contemptuous, fault-finding, brutally critical parent becomes the model for the self's engaging in like action. Here is a likely dialogue within the self: "Oh God, there's something wrong with me. So disgusting. I can't stand myself. Look how fat *you* are. *You're* ridiculous." A part of the self identifies with the parent and begins to treat other parts of the self with contempt. Such an individual reacts with spontaneous self-contempt as well whenever shame is aroused.

This is one source of what has more usually been called guilt. Internalized blame or self-blame is the other source. A blaming parent is one who must put the blame for things gone wrong *somewhere.* Discovering exactly whose fault it was is the only thing that matters. The villain must be cornered, the guilty party found. When confronted with an instance of mistaken judgment, or discovering that one has been made a fool of, some individuals can, however painfully, own the event honestly, while others must transfer blame for the failing from the self elsewhere. The self reacts to any arousing of shame secondarily by blaming someone else. A child of such a parent will likely internalize an image of the blaming parent. Either the internal identification image dispenses blame within the inner life or one part of the self disowns another and blame *directed inward* maintains the split.

With a great many individuals, whenever I have pressed them to describe to me the actual internal actions (subvocalizations) which they then labeled as guilt, in every case what emerged was either some form of self-contempt or self-blame, unless, of course, it was the first-mentioned disappointment in self that really is not to be distinguished from shame at all except in the content of what the shame was about. Violation of an internally prized value in living, such as not taking something that belongs to another, or honesty in significant human relationships, can certainly lead to a most poignant affective experience of disappointment in self. When self-contempt or self-blame is additionally introduced into the inner life of the self, unrelenting punishment becomes inflicted by the self upon the self. The pain is protracted and prolonged beyond what the simple affect of shame might produce.

One implication of such a view is that the term guilt has been used to symbolize experiences which are more accurately understood through newer concepts. I refer, of course, to self-contempt and self-blame. What is left over, that is, disappointment in self, can readily be called guilt, provided that one remembers we are nevertheless dealing with the underlying affect of shame, but in response to a class of activators understood as moral. Guilt now becomes a descriptive symbol referring to one particular manifestation of the affect termed shame, much as self-consciousness, embarrassment, and shyness are other such forms, each also encompassing its own special activators of shame. Guilt refers to shame which is about clearly moral matters, a poignant disappointment in self owing to a sudden break with one's own most cherished values in living.

The affective experiences now differentiated and identified as self-contempt or self-blame refer to defending strategies operating within the inner life of the self, but unfortunately also aimed directly against the self. These constitute a wholly different order of inner events when compared to the basic affect of shame in whatever form.

Just as we have confronted the question of guilt, so might we say a word beyond. The disowning of self, coupled with the use of self-contempt and self-blame, offers an alternative way, and from my point of view a more useful way, of conceptualizing the development of the so-called punitive superego. The internalization of parental identification images likewise makes much more sense to me to speak of than does Fairbairn's concept of the internal bad object. I agree entirely with the referent but prefer a different symbolization for it. For Fairbairn, internalization leads to the splitting of the ego into one part that is persecutory and the other libidinal. Tomkins describes a similar bifurcation of the self through the internalization of parental contempt such that the self becomes split in two, with one part sitting as judge while the other becomes the offender. The once-external drama now is reenacted wholly within the self. I have suggested that such actual splitting of the self as occurs is an outgrowth of a broader process, the disowning of self. The internalization of contempt, that is, contempt turned against the self, is only one means by which splits within the self can and do arise. And splitting is neither an inevitable nor an irreversible event as Fairbairn suggests.

If the language being evolved in these pages is an unfamiliar one, I think it ultimately a more useful one. I have sought a language that is precise, yet a language that keeps close to actual inner experience. It may be evident that many commonly accepted symbols are nowhere present here. Freud's id, ego, and superego are glaringly absent, though parallels can be sensed, as are those symbols of other theorists who have looked through their own special microscope at the human experience. As we continue to verify as well as refine our symbols for a language of the self, understanding ultimately grows. From understanding comes eventual mastery.

DIRECTIONS FOR FURTHER WORK

The foregoing discussion of language and guilt, along with the preceding discussion of the schizoid, paranoid, and depressive postures as varieties of shame-based identity syndromes represent one view of those phenomena. Alternative conceptions or explanations of these as well as of other phenomena presented here can certainly be held. Admittedly, all of the factors which converge in developing along one line or another have not been discerned. But this is the direction my work with shame and identity has taken me, and even further, has pointed me toward for future exploration.

I have offered the views presented here because they have shown themselves useful as a way of understanding human development and interpersonal relationships, useful too in furthering the therapeutic enterprise. Today's accepted beliefs must inevitably yield before tomorrow's new ideas, new discoveries, new explanations— that ever-widening circle of understanding we call knowledge. Yet it is yesterday's conceptions which somehow point the way to tomorrow's discoveries and these in turn cause us to modify, verify, and discard what were yesterday's accepted beliefs. And thus it goes on.

With this chapter, we have reached a stopping-point in unfolding what I have come to view as a developmental theory of shame and identity. The psychology presented in these pages may not fit each and every individual's experience. It does, however, make understandable the life experience of a significant portion of the population which I have encountered in my professional work. Though neither finished nor completed, we have reached the end of what can be articulated with some certainty. And as new information inevitably comes in, the theory itself must change to accommodate it.

I have presented, I hope with sufficient clarity, my understanding of shame, its development, and my view of the significance of shame for our emerging identity. How clear I have been to my unseen reader I can only wonder. How well I have succeeded in engaging my reader with me directly in the exploration I cannot know. And whether what I have written has value for another must remain a question.

PART II
Toward a
Framework for Psychotherapy

5
Restoring the Interpersonal Bridge: From Shame to a Self-Affirming Identity

The process of therapy is so much an individual matter, so in need of fitting the particular therapist as well as client, that the art and science of the thing remain always just a bit elusive before the inquiring eye. It must also be said that many paths travel along the way of growth. There can hardly be one right way about anything concerning human affairs. Our very nature would forbid it. The very strength of the need impelling us toward differentiation, toward separateness, differentness, and mastery, demands us to change what is given, to find our own unique way.

This book has been written out of such a view. The approach to therapy unfolding here has been a direct outgrowth of my work with shame, identification, and identity. There are a number of key dimensions which need attention in the therapeutic endeavor. We will first explore the nature of the therapeutic relationship. From there we will move into a discussion of how shame needs to be actively approached in therapy and thereby made more consciously accessible. Next we will consider how to reverse the developmental sequence, in this way returning internalized shame to its interpersonal origins. From this point we will move in two directions, focusing on the current inner functioning of the self and current interpersonal functioning. These key therapeutic dimensions will then be illustrated in the closing section through a detailed recounting of a particular case.

THE THERAPEUTIC RELATIONSHIP: GENERAL VIEWS

At the outset, I should like to simply put forth the slow-in-coming beliefs which shape the kind of therapeutic relationship I now seek to form with my clients and that I consider essential in order for growth to come about. In the initial sessions, I try to get some picture of current conflicts, underlying dynamics, and the quality of early significant human relationships. We also see if we can work together since the decision is a mutual one. And, most importantly, I begin to establish mutual trust with my client, the beginning of that interpersonal bridge which spans the gulf between strangers and embarks us on a collaborative path toward self-discovery.

A willingness to both look inside oneself and to share that knowledge is essential for self-discovery to occur. And self-discovery is the foundation of personality growth or behavioral change. That willingness to search within, to see what is there and to share it, occurs best in an atmosphere of security, embracing mutual trust, caring, and respect.

The relationship between therapist and client must be a real one. Each must come to know the other as a real, very human person. And the relationship must be honest. In these ways the therapist will increasingly gain the client's confidence and the client will permit the therapist increasingly to enter his or her experiential world inside. The power to gain entry resides solely with the client, the one depending. It is in letting the therapist become important to him, whether expressed in beginning to look to the therapist for something or to need something very directly from him, that the client bids the therapist enter. Once let in, not only can the therapist provide some healing for a wounded self, but he can also literally "see" the current inner functioning or life of the self. Through this the therapist can guide toward change.

For that letting in to continue, the client must also begin to matter some to the therapist. And for the necessary restoring to occur, their relationship must be real, honest, and mutually wanted.

Security within a relationship fosters growth. The heightened anxiety attendant upon self-exploration, that confronting of one's dynamic conflicts, can be experienced, understood, and finally mastered only within a secure relationship. It is the active approaching of those conflicts by therapist and client together which engenders that anxiety; this mutual confrontation of conflict in turn further deepens their relationship.

Dependence upon the therapist will often follow. And depending can be permitted without its being encouraged. It is the permitting of dependence and identification as these become needed by a client which provides essential support, strength, and healing for a wounded or precarious self. Letting oneself be known at moments when the self of a client is in such distress permits the needed restoring experience of identification to come about. One does not *do* anything to bring it about. One simply permits it to happen of itself.

And while we permit such dependence and identification as our client might actually need, always we encourage and foster the eventual differentiation of the self. By siding with differentiation we lend our therapeutic weight to eventual separation, to gaining increasing mastery.

One of the recurring failings in development which I have widely observed is a lack of preparation for adulthood. The kind of preparation so many young people have seemingly missed stems from not being able to know how another human being, particularly one older and presumably wiser, actually behaves and lives on the inside. Many individuals have been deprived of seeing how one or both parents literally functioned as people. This is a failure of identification. They have seen the final product, for instance, the decisions made, but so rarely have they known what went on inside of a parent, how a parent responds internally to threat and copes with it. Nor have they seen how the parent copes with challenges and success, for these too can be frightening to us, as well as sources of pride.

There is such complexity to living and to being a human being that a young person needs some model for how it all happens in order to have a base from which to begin navigating the human world with ever-increasing autonomy. Of course our client may not have been deprived of identification at all. In fact, one young man I worked with suffered from having identified with a father who continually expressed his own failings as a person. Because his father continually felt himself a failure, this young man learned to do similarly with himself.

In addition to permitting identification experiences to happen, the internalizing of the therapist as a new, internal parental identification image works to free the inner life of the hold upon it of past identification images. Such a change is painstakingly slow to come about. It comes piecemeal, never all at once. And there is always backsliding.

Progression forever oscillates with regression as development proceeds, which brings us to our next consideration. Some regression is either inevitable or essential as part of the therapeutic process. While some *permission to be young* is something I am willing to provide, I will seek to contain or manage the regression as both Kell and Winnicott have described. Since I work with a functional, young adult population by deliberate choice, I need to keep a client able to function in outer reality as a blossoming or active adult. I try to manage the regression by permitting no more than can be integrated. At times a client will regress experientially and believe himself to have actually lost all capacity to cope on his own. I have to remind my client that, "Yes, indeed, he may feel that bad, but I have no doubts whatever about his *ability* to cope." Besides, I am not in the business of providing twenty-four-hour care. I am enabled to permit such regression as is needed because I know that I have no needs to keep a client regressed. In fact, I prefer them when they're more able to cope effectively on their own.

In providing permission to be young, often I am faced with clients needing to be held physically. At times, a client will ask rather directly for it. Or, I might sense the need without its having been voiced. For a long time, I had been uncertain as to how to respond. I have since come to a conviction concerning the therapeutic value of holding. There are both young and adult meanings to the need. Physical touch, whether by an arm around a shoulder, a handshake, or a hug can have a range of meanings, from affection and closeness to support and nurturance to protection and security.

Holding is a basic human need which can restore security at our most primitive level. And there are moments in the course of therapy when this is what a client needs. A client will need to feel restored at his or her most primitive level in order to begin to grow beyond it. Providing for such primary developmental needs can furthermore dissolve whatever binding effects of shame are yet surrounding the need, thereby freeing both its access to consciousness and eventual reintegration within the self.

I usually prefer a client's asking for holding directly since the client is apt to reject it if I offer it before he or she asks. This flipping of ambivalence about the need is more than just an occasional occurrence. I have learned with such clients simply to wait out the ambivalence. Other clients who have been too deprived of holding and terrorized into inner rigidity may likely need a therapist to take the initiative here. So it matters whether it is anxiety and perhaps even terror or instead ambivalence which is blocking further development. In almost every case I have also observed an intense sense of shame surrounding the need itself which, in turn, makes growth so very slow going. One must feel one's way with each and every client to find the path that feels right, fits both therapist and client and, what is more, works.

Releasing the need, which is an inherent part of the self, from the binding effects of shame is an important therapeutic accomplishment. For along with freeing the capacity for touch and holding, one begins to free the capacity for both the receiving and the giving of love.

There will be times when a client experiences some need to give to *me* or to respond to some need of *mine*. It may come in needing some assurance that I do in fact have needs of my own. Or it may come as some *gift*, perhaps a treasure made or found; whether as a piece of finely cut glass, a poem, or a photograph, this is a gift of self from one appreciative human being to another. Or, yet again, it may come at crucial moments in the life of a therapist. Not long ago, I had to cope with a real disaster: my home, along with many others, had been damaged in a major flood. When I called clients to cancel all appointments for a week in order to restore my home to livable conditions, I was surprised at the offers of assistance that came. And I was in no position to turn down anyone wanting to help.

We all have needs to nurture others; that is one source of the motivation leading some of us to pick careers of helping others. Thus, a client who has received something useful from a valued therapist will often grow to have special feelings about him. Whether it is the feelings themselves which are expressed or the direct offer of a gift, how I receive that offer carries impact at such a moment when the self of a client has become vulnerable. A client may eventually come to need from a therapist any of the things once looked for from the parent who, for whatever complex and perhaps unknowable reasons, failed the client's trust.

The therapeutic relationship is the dynamic arena where conflicts generate and get lived out. Through the balancing of therapist availability for identification with the active supporting of client differentiation, becoming one's own person in the world comes about. Eventual separation certainly happens, but this is distinct from necessarily ending the relationship my client has with me. Clients will sometimes come back to say hello, to let me know how and what they are doing. Or, they may even *need* again. The commitment of availability which I am willing to make to some clients can be a continuing one. And once more they go off into the world feeling better able to cope on their own. In a most fundamental sense, together we have enabled a new identity to begin to grow, one which is more freeing, more satisfying, and more competent. A kind of identity regrowth is in process.

RESTORING THE INTERPERSONAL BRIDGE

How are we to facilitate the growth process? How can we enable an individual to work through a core belief of not being good enough as a person, to emerge from an imprisoning identity infused with doubt, shame, and fear to one that is freeing? Attempts at either ignoring these core beliefs, convincing him otherwise, or trying to rid the person of them backfire. Such attempts deny the reality of those feelings and thereby engender shame about having them in the first place.

If denial of the validity of shame feelings is not helpful (saying "There's nothing wrong with you"), then what is? What needs to happen in approaching a person who carries much shame is an open validation of those feelings. Shame has to be actively approached, not avoided or denied.

This much had made sense to me as I came to understand the basic shame-inducing process. I had found Bill Kell's idea of an interpersonal bridge so incredibly useful that I adopted it. Restoring the bridge, as Bill and I had talked about it, translated to mean approaching the shame.

Let me illustrate. One young man who came to me for therapy, Tony, repeatedly referred to himself as stupid. Several times he would say, "Deep down I know I'm really stupid." He seemed utterly convinced of the truth of that belief, and he always hung his head when he said it. I finally said to him, "You are stupid." He looked at me quizzically for a moment, wondering if I really believed he was stupid or if I was understanding that his core belief was real for him. Then he said, realizing my meaning, "All my life, people have been telling me I'm not stupid when I knew I was. You're the first person not to do that." In effect I was saying to him, "Yes, I see your shame, your feelings of stupidness and worthlessness, and I'm neither afraid nor ashamed to approach." In this way, I began restoring the interpersonal bridge.

REVERSING THE DEVELOPMENTAL SEQUENCE

Now let us turn specifically to the resolution of internalized shame in psychotherapy. As long as shame remains internalized and autonomous, real change is prevented. New experiences with others, however positive, fail to alter one's basic sense of self unless the developmental sequence also is reversed. Such a reversal process is slow and painful because intense fear of exposure and strategies of defense prevent access by the self or others to that most vulnerable core of the self. Within the therapeutic relationship, internalized shame needs to be returned to its interpersonal origins. The self that feels irreparably and unspeakably defective needs to feel whole, worthwhile, and valued from within. If shame originates from an interpersonal severing process, resolution must involve a restoring process. If internalization develops from identification, from need-shame and affect-shame binds, and from periods of deep emotional pain which increase susceptibility to internalization, then disinternalization must involve the offering of a new identification model, the dissolution of affect-shame and need-shame binds, and an experiencing of the emotional pain associated with defectiveness within the therapeutic process itself, *provided* that new affect-beliefs about the self can also become internalized.

At the outset of therapy, internalized shame is rarely accessible to consciousness. Those manifestations which are conscious are uniquely varied. Feeling inadequate, inferior, or worthless, and fears of rejection are some examples. One client always believed she was a stupid person. Another client feels like a failure interpersonally. Another feels angry at the whole world. Another has withdrawn himself into a cocoon of loneliness and defiantly refuses to come out. Distress and pain may not even be evident since defending strategies, such as striving for perfection, rage, contempt for others, striving for power, or internal withdrawal, can so totally mask shame from view.

The therapeutic process, as Kell and Burow have described it, consists of the living out of a corrective emotional experience. Clearly, the therapist becomes significant in that endeavor. How that living out needs to occur in relation to shame is what I would like to make especially clear. The therapeutic processes necessary for the resolution of internalized shame can be most clearly understood by differentiating them from one another.

Interpersonal Bridging

We begin with building a bridge, an interpersonal one of course. The building of trust within the therapeutic relationship is slow and painstaking since the original failures were early and deep ones. Building the interpersonal bridge gradually lessens the need for defending strategies and makes possible experiences of vulnerability and openness between therapist and client, as Kell and Burow also have observed. Mutual understanding, growth, and change are thereby facilitated.

Once built, such a bridge needs to be maintained in a particular fashion in relation to shame. Bridging thus becomes an on-going process. Let me clarify. Shame feelings need to be actively approached and openly validated by the therapist. When this occurs, exposure fears become reduced, thereby enabling the client's awareness of his internal shame processes to deepen even further. In effect, the client learns an important interpersonal lesson, namely, that expression of shame will not be shamed again. Therapist approach and validation need to follow each time the client dips deeper into shame. Otherwise, the client will feel abandoned, shamed again, or experience his shame as too threatening for the therapist.

A related example comes to mind. A client I worked with, Ted, once asked if we could go canoeing together. Instead of responding directly to his request, I asked Ted if going canoeing was a "need" or a "want," implying that I would say yes to a "need" but not to a "want." He thought about it, decided his request was really a "want," and ambivalently dropped out of therapy. Let us enter Ted's experience for a moment. Asking Ted to examine his request induced sudden self-consciousness and exposure. The resulting sense of shame deepened as he felt there was something wrong with his need or wrong with him as a person. Why else would his request not be responded to? The secondary response Ted felt was fear of further exposure, and he consequently backed out of our relationship. When I failed to approach him, Ted felt confirmed in his shame, which became a growing barrier between us since he could not risk exposure of his badness. Then, when I did make several direct approaches to him, Ted's overt response was rage. While we eventually restored the relationship, I had learned an important lesson.

For several other clients of mine, their dip into shame has gone so far as to involve intense fears of literally "going crazy." I have had to sit on my own anxiety and go with them into their inner experience in order for them to begin to feel restored. Thus, interpersonal bridging is a basic underpinning of the therapeutic endeavor which also facilitates other important therapeutic processes.

Discovering the Original Sources of Internalized Shame

As the client's own awareness of shame gradually deepens through the bridging process, therapist and client increasingly are able to discover the original inducing events within the family. Our sense of worth and adequacy as human beings rests upon having certain fundamental needs responded to positively as we grow, thereby enabling us to feel secure in our personhood. Frequently, though certainly not always, shame internalization follows from parental rejection of the child's most fundamental needs, however unconscious that rejection may be. Such rejection may occur, for example, when one or both parents did not want the child at all or really wanted a child of the other gender. Shame can also be rooted in a parent looking to the child to literally be parent to the parent, or in wanting the child never to need anything emotionally from the parent—in a sense, to have been born an adult. Or the child may simply have been born the wrong temperament for the gender; quiet, more introverted boys and outgoing, aggressive girls have traditionally fared less well in our culture because they fail to match the expectations of significant others. Rejection may be clear and open, ambivalent and hidden, or defended against by overpossessiveness and overprotectiveness. Finally, parental behavior can have unintended rejecting impact upon the child through communicating failure to meet parental expectations, even when parental attitudes are not inherently rejecting.

Expanding awareness of and discovering the original sources of internalized shame, in conjunction with experiencing the emotional pain associated with defectiveness, together make possible the internalization of new affect-beliefs about the self. The developing new relationship with the therapist gradually enables the client to relinquish some of the old, shameful identity. And a new sense of identity tentatively begins to emerge.

I believe that historical exploration, along with discovering the original shame-inducing events within the family, have particular value in furthering therapeutic growth. While it is true that the conflicts so disabling to my client are being actively maintained in the present, searching the past can provide important information which helps us differentiate, more accurately identify and label, the conflicts which are especially troublesome in his present life.

In addition, such backward looking enables a client to understand, as best we are able, how his conflicts originated. So often people believe they have always been the way they are. I attempt to interest such a person in finding out how he got to be the way he or she is. Usually, we aren't just born that way and we didn't learn it from strangers, either. Through this seeing of how it all came about, a client is freer to begin making new choices for the future.

There is a third value to historical exploration. Through gaining knowledge of whatever developmental failures have occurred, a client has a clearer sense of his own needs *and* of the reality of those individuals to whom he had looked for his needs yet from whom he had never seemed able to get what was needed. Once a person accepts as unalterable fact that he can never go back and make up for past needs, he is freed to live his life from the present onward. And a new, more equal and adult relationship with his parents is able to come about. By making peace with the past and accepting that some of our core conflicts remain with us, that some holes are permanent, we can go about the task of becoming the best possible person we can be.

Dissolution of Specific Affect-Shame and Need-Shame Binds

In these cases, rejection has been partial and specific to particular affects, behaviors, or needs, whether that rejection was intentional or inadvertent. Affect-shame and need-shame binds can be dissolved by making both the bind and its source conscious for the client. The need or affect itself also needs to be validated. This can happen by encouraging the client through new, perhaps frightening experiences outside of therapy that are themselves corrective. This also happens through living out corrective experiences directly within the therapeutic relationship. For instance, a client deeply ashamed of needing to be held may eventually ask to be held by the therapist. Most frequently, such emotionally corrective occurrences are an ongoing, often unnoticed, part of the therapeutic process.

Making Conscious the Link Between Shame and Strategies of Defense

Defenses against shame are adaptive. They have been the client's only ways of surviving intolerable shame. Strategies of defense aim at protecting the self against further exposure and further experiences of shame. Several of the most prominent strategies are rage, contempt for others, the striving for perfection, the striving for power, and internal withdrawal. Both perfectionism and excessive power-seeking are strivings against shame and attempt to compensate for the sense of defectiveness which underlies internalized shame. None of these are unitary strategies; rather, they become expressed in unique and varied ways, with several often functioning together.

The therapeutic aim is not to eliminate those strategies but to enable the client to learn new, more adaptive ways of coping with the *sources* of shame. Gradually, the need for rigid defending strategies lessens as their meaning in relation to shame becomes clearer to the client. As the client's tolerance for shame thereby increases, the powerful need to interpersonally transfer experienced shame also lessens. We will return to the therapeutic handling of defenses toward the close of this chapter.

Enabling the Client to Learn to Cope Effectively With the Sources of Shame Without Internalizing that Affect

Whenever a client expresses bad feelings about self, the therapist needs to attend not only to those feelings but to the *source* of those feelings as well (a differentiation also emphasized by Tomkins). If the source of bad feelings is the self's autonomous activation of shame following some past or current precipitating event, the therapist needs to enable the client to learn how to cope effectively with the sources of shame without internalizing that affect. There are many ways in which this occurs during the course of therapy. One way concerns the appropriate handling of the client's shame spirals. The therapist needs to enable the client to learn to recognize, intervene consciously, and terminate that internal shame spiral.

Attempts at understanding the experience while it is spiraling or snowballing only embroil one deeper into shame. Deliberately focusing all of one's attention outside oneself by becoming visually involved in the world breaks the shame spiral and allows those feelings and thoughts to subside. Later, the precipitating cause can be explored and understood with one aim: to enable the client to intervene even sooner in the future. The therapist can both intervene directly when shame is spiraling within the session and enable the client to do likewise on his own. The client thereby gains active control over his internalized shame processes. In effect, the therapist helps the client know not only which bad feelings he needs to feel and which to let go of, but especially, how not to internalize them.

Equally basic to therapy is the therapist's need to provide the client with new ways of understanding his own experience in order to free himself from the paralyzing effects of shame. Defeats, failures, and rejections are inevitable in life. We need to learn how not to internalize the feelings of shame which naturally arise, while still being able to profit and learn from the very "mistakes" which may have contributed to those failures in the first place. One way Bill Kell did this was through the concept of "learning time." We need to give ourselves time to both make mistakes and live them out, without internalizing those mistakes as personal failures, precisely in order to gain eventual mastery. The therapist provides a very important new identification model in this regard.

A client, Ron, was deeply troubled about intimacy. He believed that he was defective in not being able to ever sustain an intimate relationship. One session, Ron came in expressing much hurt and pain because the group-living situation he had been heavily invested in was falling apart due to one of the other member's conflicts. He began sobbing about this being a repeat of his other failures. I listened to his feelings of shame, but I also pointed out to him that this time was different. Ron looked at me quizzically. I clarified for him that *this* time he had stayed in the relationship long enough to learn that it was not *his* personal failure which was causing the problem. His tears dried up, he sat up in his chair and said, "I'm done for today."

The sources of shame are not always externally based. They can be internal in the form of the self's own awareness of perceived limitations. Most frequently, we have learned to feel ashamed of those aspects of self which make us feel different from others. The therapist needs to enable the client to accept, even to find value in, those very aspects of himself which he finds most intolerable. Only then can change begin to occur.

Shame Inducement and Resolution Within the Therapeutic Relationship

If the source of shame lies within the therapeutic relationship, the therapist needs to recognize, hear, and validate those feelings, even acknowledging his own part in producing them. When the therapist becomes significant to the client and the therapist's caring, respect, and valuing begin to matter, the therapist himself becomes a potential inducer of shame. When he has induced shame within the client, however inadvertently, the therapist can restore the interpersonal bridge he severed by openly acknowledging his own part in that process. If the therapist, someone deeply valued, can acknowledge his imperfect humanness, even his part in making us feel shame, those shame feelings pass on. The growth impact is far greater than if the severing experience had never happened in the first place. When inducing shame is followed by restoring the bridge, internalization does not occur.

With one client, Martha, I had no idea anything was wrong until I received a letter from her expressing her intention to stop therapy, though feeling much hurt, pain, and rage. I called her and she decided to come in. Somehow she began to feel better about working with me, though still wondering if I really cared about her. The very next session was critical. We began fine but I gradually became aware that something was wrong again. Then Martha began talking of terminating. What emerged, as we tried to understand the sequence, was that whenever I looked out of the window, Martha felt abandoned and rapidly withdrew inside herself. Shame and rage followed. I acknowledged my part, that is, I do like to look out the window, but I did not intend to abandon her. I persisted in suggesting that somehow what I had done must also have happened before. Martha came in the following session having remembered similar occurrences with her step-father during childhood.

Developing the Client's Capacity to Affirm the Self from Within

The foregoing therapeutic processes interact with one another, gradually enabling the client to disinternalize shame, to learn to cope effectively with those potential sources of shame to which he is uniquely vulnerable, and to begin to affirm himself from within. The capacity to affirm oneself and the evolving of a separate identity are mutually enhancing. Self-affirmation is facilitated by therapist valuing of the client's uniqueness as a person, by enabling the client to increasingly tolerate shame feelings, and by enabling the client to learn to cope with the sources of shame without internalizing that affect.

Realization of the self-affirming capacity integrates the self around a new core. The self gradually becomes a primary source of its own caring, respect, and valuing, as it begins to recognize and value both our human communalities and those very things which make us uniquely different. Because the self can now continue feeling affirmed from within in the face of defeat, failure, or rejection, shame can remain a feeling which is activated or induced and then passes on. While we may always remain susceptible to shame, we have also begun to learn how not to internalize that affect.

THE TASKS OF INNER DEVELOPMENT: TOWARD A MORE SATISFYING INNER RELATIONSHIP

The inner life comprises what is conscious as well as what is unconscious, that which lies beyond the bounds of remembering or awareness. There are parts of the self, such as affects, needs, and drives, which are consciously available to awareness while others are barred from awareness. That barring occurs either actively through defenses or through never having learned to differentiate accurately and verbally *name* those parts of the self. That, in and of itself, is a failure in development of sorts, for what cannot be accurately labeled even to oneself cannot be understood and thereby mastered. Those conscious as well as unconscious parts of the self represent one important aspect of the inner life. There is a second integral part of inner reality, the self's relationship with the self. This is the way we currently relate to ourselves, those internal activities we engage in which, if engaged in with another human being, would be understood in relationship terms. Just as with the self, this internal relationship is partly conscious, partly unconscious. The third component to the inner life is the internal relationship with one or more identification images, again partly conscious, partly unconscious. With all three— the self, the self's relationship with the self, and the self's relationship with internal guiding images—conscious awareness can be deepened and expanded to enable the inner life to become increasingly accessible to the person concerned.

We have dealt at some length with failures in development, with the impact shame has upon the self. If internalized shame lies at one extreme of the process of identity development, what lies at the other? If an unsatisfying or even pain-inflicting relationship with the self might be an outcome, what might a more satisfying, inner relationship with ourselves look like? If disowning and splitting of the self represent one turn of development, what are more positive alternatives?

Integrity of the Self

Let us proceed by beginning to think about developmental tasks which need to be attained if the *process of the self* is to continue forward without undue impairment. As I think in these terms, a number of ideas begin to surface within me. The first is a sense of wholeness. If disowning robs us of the essential wholeness of the self, certainly this must suggest a vital developmental task to be accomplished. Maintaining the integrity of the self in the face of life's vicissitudes is paramount. Maintaining further suggests striving for reintegration of the self following some prior disowning or splitting. Let us place *integrity of the self* among our necessary developmental tasks.

Internal Security

The self begins to utilize defenses, but then may come to direct those defenses internally against specific parts of the self. The use of those defenses internally becomes the foundation for internalized insecurity. Inner peace has not merely been shaken violently, but replaced by internal strife waged against disowned parts of the self. It is that active disowning of an inherent part of the self which creates and then maintains internal insecurity. Because it has become perpetuated, we may speak of insecurity itself as having become internalized. Thus we must add internal security, inner peace, and safety within the inner life to our listing of tasks to be accomplished in the course of development. Both the order of these tasks and the age at which they are attained are not at issue here. They can happen as they do and at whatever point in the life cycle at which they come about.

Nurturance of Self

Let us proceed further. Integrity, security: what else? Two images emerge, one being the relationship which we come to have with ourselves, and the other, the need to nurture others. One of the most vital things a person must learn is how to care for himself or herself. And I do not mean some abstract love of self which only amounts to so much verbiage. What I am referring to are the very ways in which we can actively care for ourselves. Whether it is through buying a present for oneself, taking oneself someplace special, or simply giving oneself some time to be alone with oneself when necessary, these are activities which can nurture the self inside of us. These are specific actions we can engage in wholly with ourselves which directly and actively provide us with caring. And times come upon us when caring is precisely what we need, certainly from others, but no less so from ourselves.

When the self has experienced some disappointment or wound, actively giving oneself caring is a way of relating to oneself which heals. Talking to oneself comfortingly as one would to a wounded child provides the self inside, even the child within, with that much-needed nurturing. And daily tending to the inner self is a way of sustaining one's emotional stores. When real accomplishments have occurred, giving to oneself tangible rewards and feelings of pride, as well as permission to rest for awhile, make the act of accomplishing itself a satisfying activity. And when we have disappointed ourselves, broken some cherished internal value of our own, or done some regrettable deed, we have also to learn how to wipe the slate clean, to forgive ourselves. True nurturance of self embraces these two, caring and forgiveness. And as a more satisfying way of relating to oneself, nurturance of self further supports internal security. Let us add cultivating ways of nurturing oneself as another of our emerging developmental tasks.

Self-Affirming Capacity

When the interpersonally based need for affirmation has been responded to appropriately and an individual also is taught how to give that affirmation to himself, the capacity to affirm oneself from within emerges. Affirmation is the restoring need and the valuing need. By internalizing affirmation and developing a self-affirming capacity, an individual is able to restore good feelings about self when these have been disrupted. When belief in oneself or in one's adequacy has been shaken, or doubt has crept inside, that belief and adequacy can be restored internally. That is what I mean by the restoring function.

Affirmation also confers valuing. Through being valued by a significant other, we learn how to find value, inherent value, in ourselves even when others may not. There comes to be an inner source of valuing of the self which becomes the securest foundation for self-esteem. This internalization of valuing of self enables us to cease being wholly dependent on the evaluations or acceptance of others for our own sense of self-worth. One's inherent worth as a person is kept separate from life's uncertainties.

Being able to affirm oneself, especially in the face of significant defeat, failure, or rejection enables one to continue feeling whole, worthwhile, and valued from within. It is the development of this self-affirming capacity which can prevent internalization of shame and ensure a separate identity. Let us add the self-affirming capacity as another task to be accomplished in the course of development.

Differentiated Owning Capacity

These four—integrity of the self, internal security, nurturance of self, and self-affirming capacity—comprise necessary developmental tasks. But in order to accomplish these, the self must first have accurate knowledge of the self. Feelings must be differentiated from needs as well as one from another among feelings and also among needs. This means that a particular feeling or need is capable of being experienced and recognized, then consciously identified, and finally owned by the self as an inherent part of the self. Differentiating and then owning feelings, needs, and drives as distinguishable parts of an integrated self together comprise a necessary developmental task, certainly recognized by others such as Kell, Burow, and Mueller to name a few.

A differentiated understanding of one's basic temperament, of one's introvertedness or extrovertedness, is equally essential to productive living. There is no more disastrous path than to seek to violate one's basic nature. If an introverted individual feels deficient because of that introvertedness and seeks to become extroverted, *as though this were the better way to be*, the seeds of neurosis are already growing. Whatever the temperament or other native factors might be, these must be consciously understood and differentiated, that is, made accessible to the self. Then follows owning, saying, as it were, "This is a vital part of me. This is how I function." From owning of the differentiated part naturally flows reintegration within the self.

Differentiated owning embraces first, differentiation; second, owning; and third, reintegration. It is this differentiated owning of self which supports the essential integrity of the self and makes integration in conscious awareness possible. The realization of the differentiated owning capacity also makes possible the reowning of previously disowned parts of the self. Thus it furthers and maintains inner security as well. Conscious differentiation of inherent parts of the self enables the self to function ever more smoothly and with increasing mastery over the inner life.

We have seen that consciously differentiating specific parts of the self can be useful to the self. Just as useful is differentiating those internal identification images lodged in the inner life. But with these images, since they were acquired through internalization, the self must eventually *choose* whether to keep or attempt to relinquish its internal guiding images once these have been made conscious. That choosing is never an easy one, for no claim upon the self is stronger than a parent's. Just as separation from one's external parents is a struggle, so is separation from the parental images within.

When the external relationship with the parent has been an enhancing one, the internal relationship with the identification image also is a freeing, supporting, and sustaining one for the self in the absence of the parent. In such a case, conscious awareness of the role of the image within the inner life is already present. For the self has little need to bar from awareness what is satisfying and supporting to the self. And the self may even resort to recalling in visual imagery memories or other images of that positive identification figure at times when the self is wounded, lacking direction, or in need of preparedness. Through imagery, that much-needed experience of identification, which in turn restores the self, can still be found even when that significant other who provided it previously is either not available or no longer present. And here we have another instance not only of how the self can nurture the self but also of how the self can reaffirm the self.

When the external parental relationship has been limiting, unsatisfying, or outright destructive, the internal relationship with the identification image is equally disastrous for the inner life of the self. Such identifications are limiting for the self, not freeing; punishing or even persecutory, neither nurturing nor affirming; and weakening, never supporting. Yet the self will cling to its relationship with an internal identification image, however unsatisfying it may be, just as the self clings to the needs which never have been met by the parent, still hoping beyond hope that *this* time will be different. Letting go of that hope is one of the most difficult tasks confronting us. And when things go wrong, that internal guiding image will mete out swift judgment to the self much as the parent had done before. In such a situation as described here, conscious differentiation of internal identification images is necessary if inner security ever is to come about. And differentiation is followed, not by owning and reintegration, but instead by consciously disinternalizing that guiding image. The self must be weaned from it, must relinquish and let go of the parent's internal representative, just as separation must occur in outer living.

Attaining a Separate Identity

When the foregoing tasks of development are sufficiently accomplished, a secure, self-affirming identity which integrates interpersonal with internal living is enabled to come about. As a final developmental task, identity emerges as a *conscious integration of the self*. The mediating and integrating functions of identity, internally with ourselves and interpersonally with others, represent the developmental/psychodynamic base. Identity is that bridge linking inner and outer. There is a second, more spiritual base underlying identity as a motivator. Here is subsumed the need for meaning in life, for a sense of purpose to what we do, that quest for belonging to something greater than ourselves, the search for significance which springs from the identification need. And to the degree that shame has been encountered as well as internalized, we have a third motivational base underlying identity, the search for wholeness and worth, for our essential dignity as a human being.

CURRENT FUNCTIONING OF THE SELF: ACCOMPLISHING THE TASKS OF INNER DEVELOPMENT

As I began to appreciate the power of internalization as a dynamic process in human development, I already had glimpses of situations left unexplained by it. It was this searching which led me to think about the disowning of self as a fourth process dimension. My approach to therapy continued to change as these emerging theoretical ideas, based upon my own observations as well as those of others, filtered through.

I had learned from Bill Kell how to enable clients to complete undone developmental tasks that were interpersonally focused and thereby to get back in step, as it were. And I had already understood the importance of reversing the developmental sequence by returning internalized shame to its interpersonal origins. Now I saw that the internal functioning of the self needed direct therapeutic attention in order to accomplish that other series of developmental tasks which is equally tied to the very progress of the self in living.

Differentiated Owning

The nature of the therapeutic work that needs to be accomplished with the inner life of the self comprises several dimensions. Conscious awareness and differentiation of disowned parts of the self must occur. A client must be able to label to himself, have words for and so identify, parts of the self that had been shamed or disowned. When these can be consciously differentiated, those parts of the self can further be affectively experienced in consciousness. This initially brings on an acute inner pain. Putting words together with feelings, needs, and drives promotes the conscious reintegration of the self. Through identifying and then owning of the disowned parts, all done consciously, the self is enabled to begin the work of becoming whole.

In addition to such differentiated owning as comes about, and through it the fostering of the essential *integrity* of the self, work must be done to restore peace and safety directly within the inner life. *Internal security* must be worked for actively by the client, and the therapist needs to offer the way the client is to proceed in gaining that security within. In order to heal the splits within the self, one must also heal the internal strife waged against disowned parts of the self. That means getting the client to exert conscious will aimed at breaking the hold of those early, internalized patterns, that is, after they have first been made conscious. That is what defenses turned against the self are. It is this peculiar use of defenses which is the source of that inner insecurity. A client must be aided in making essential peace within himself and with himself.

We have already discussed several examples of disowning drawn from therapeutic experience. Recall how one woman, Martha, briefly disintegrated into two partial selves, the one contemptuous and persecutory and the other childlike—needy, frightened, and helpless. My efforts were directed at healing the split by aiding the self to own that child part, no longer seeking to destroy it. I knew she needed to symbolically reenact it just as her manner changed to fit either partial self.

After a time of it, I said to her, "Now, pick up that little girl who desperately needs your love and love her. Hold her in your arms, even holding yourself wrapped in your own arms, and give her what she needs." (My client convulsed into sobbing pain.) "Yes, love her, even cry for her. But you don't have to go on trying to hurt yourself anymore, as if this would finally kill that little girl." (She would physically seek to damage herself.) "She is a real part of you to nurture, and help her feel secure."

While my client had finally gotten some good mothering from a former therapist, and so had completed some of that interpersonal developmental step, she had been still continuing the internalized pattern learned a long time ago.

Another example. I first saw Molly in the midst of acute depression. It hurt so badly she wanted to take her life. What I saw was a worthless-feeling self because she had so turned rage and contempt against her very self. I sought to give her an ally, someone who thought there was another way out of feeling so bad, someone who happened to think that she was worth something. She began to withstand these assaults from within and even to redirect these defenses back outside where they belonged. Sure, there have been some recurrences of the depression, but from each one she recovers more easily and it does not get as severe as the last.

She has also learned an inner source of valuing. Molly came in one day and told me about her recently going to a women's conference. She sat in on a women's rap group, spoke her mind, and found most of them got angry with her. "Boy was I nervous," she said to me, "but nothing bad happened! I even got one of the women leaders who's a professional pissed off at me!" Was she ever pleased with herself and did I howl over it all. From standing up for herself came self-respect. What made that all come about was practicing and learning how to find value in herself.

A third client, Adam, had been withdrawn and isolated for much of his growing years. He would spend hours alone in his room working on projects. All this until one day he went into therapy while in college, prompted by some vague inner disquiet. When I saw him much later, I saw a little boy locked away inside, frozen with fear. How to release the self inside? With Adam I knew we had to start at the beginning. We first had to develop a real, honest human relationship in which he could feel cared about for the person he was. And to build trust, it had to be *real*.

From there we got to security. For Adam it meant learning to have elementary peace and safety within the inner life, *at least some portion of the time*. He had none of it. So we worked and I sought to quiet that inner battling which raged so insistently within him. He would start out every session with a written list of his problems, or defects as I came to call them. For every item amounted to something offensive to be gotten rid of. When he came down to problem number three, his *introversion* as he called it, I said rather sadly, "Well, that one I'm afraid you're just going to have to learn to live with,'cause it is a part of you. Can't get rid of that one. Besides, I think it's neat you're introverted. You can do things all alone. And besides, there are enough 'mouths' in the world."

I sought to change the way he related to those perceived "bad" parts of himself. I encouraged him to own rather than continue persecuting these most vital parts of self. Whether it be specific feelings, particular needs, or some insistent drive, whatever it is must first be owned consciously. Whether introvertedness, the needing child part, or homosexuality, *owning* is essential. One need not like the part of the self revealed, but it must be owned, saying, "Like it or not, this is a natural, inherent part of me."

I knew that further growth would be impeded until integrity or wholeness could be breached and internal security established for even a small portion of the time. And I leaned my whole weight, my support, behind it, suggesting that "He could literally take me inside of him as an ally" when his security felt threatened or was shaken. This would foster his internalizing me as, I hoped, a more freeing identification, almost a new parental image to contend with the ones plaguing him inside. And these images derive from parents mostly, even grandparents, or a sister or brother, from experiences with whomever consistently provided that mothering or fathering initially.

The Self's Relationship with the Self

Several other therapeutic dimensions have surfaced. We began with differentiated owning and considered integrity and security as outgrowths of owning. Implicit in such reowning of disowned parts of the self as I have been discussing is the developing of a new, more satisfying relationship with oneself, an inner relationship based upon nurturance of self along with self-affirmation. Learning to accept, respect, and love the young, needy child inside of her was one client's way of learning to nurture herself. Learning specific, actual ways to care for the child within us provides an inner source of nourishing when that is needed. Learning to accept, no longer fight against, being mortal, human, and imperfect is a way of talking to oneself which heals. And learning ultimately to forgive ourselves, no matter how grave the wrong we've done, is another side of true nurturance of self. We can never move beyond a failing until we can honestly forgive ourselves for it and in this way make peace both with ourselves and with the past. Otherwise, it returns forever to haunt us. And learning to internalize self-affirmation, literally to find value in ourselves at times when our very self feels wounded, provides the most secure source of valuing—from within. Talking to oneself in such ways enables a much more satisfying relationship with oneself to grow and evolve. It is as though one begins behaving toward oneself as worthy beyond question.

In fact, one's worth or adequacy ought never to be up for questioning. These are to be kept inviolate as best we ever can.

Active Imagery

In discovering and differentiating a client's needs, I often utilize active imagery while in the session in order to promote awareness of a vague though troublesome need or to free the *wanting*, impulsive part hidden inside. Engaging actively in fantasy is one way of aiding the unconscious to become conscious. And I frequently will suggest, to appropriate clients, that they try this on their own at times when some need or impulse is unclearly felt. In fact, learning to set aside time for getting in touch with oneself, and for becoming an observer of internal processes, is another way to become conscious of unconscious inner events. We let our feelings and needs become a conscious part of our motivational system by learning to consult them. In a sense, through this process of conscious differentiation, of which imagery is a tool, we discover the real self inside, validate its uniqueness, its right to be. In so doing, we give it its chance to grow.

How I work with imagery certainly varies from client to client or session to session. At times I will go with a client on a shared journey into inner space. First, we relax our bodies, close our eyes, and then wait for something to come up inside, a spontaneous visual image. We then speak out loud whatever we see in our mind's eye. An example would help. One young lady I worked with, Anna, came into therapy to discover what went wrong in her relationship with her father. She never knew her real father, nor could she ever get close to her stepfather. In the course of our working together, Anna acutely reexperienced her deprivation and the longing yet inside her for a father. One day, spontaneously, she asked me, "Will you be my Daddy?" I answered her honestly, gently, "Sure I will," for this I too felt inside. Some short time later, Anna came in voicing a wish that we could go somewhere together, doing something with her "Daddy." So I suggested we go to the circus—in fantasy. We closed our eyes, sat quietly a moment, and then we were off to the big circus. We each had visual images which we immediately described to one another to make the experience a shared one. The imagery felt vivid and real for both of us. When we completed the fantasy, we opened our eyes and talked about the meaning of the experience or how we felt. Anna left that day feeling nourished in a way she had never known before.

Now, not all individuals have free access to their own imagery. Some are more able than others to visualize images and then *enter* their imagery. Visual imagery can be a potent experience. With many clients, we emerge from a shared fantasy trip feeling as though we had actually just experienced the event in reality. Hence my concept that we live in two worlds, the one being inner reality and the other, outer reality.

Clients who already image easily are most able to participate in shared imagery during therapy. However, like anything else in life, imagery is not magic. It is not always profound, full of impact, or restoring. Hence, I have learned to rely upon my intuition to guide me in deciding when to try active imagery with a client.

In the course of an imagery experience, some clients may unexpectedly recontact powerful feelings that had been blocked from conscious awareness. One fellow discovered his inner loneliness and pain which until then had only been vaguely felt inside.

Another client's mother had died some months back following heart surgery, and he had not completed grieving for his loss. His relationship with mother had been a highly ambivalent one. This fellow, whom we'll call John, grew up experiencing his mother as controlling and manipulative rather than genuinely loving. John's temperament was very clearly an extroverted one. He was extremely verbal, socialized fairly freely with others and experienced large needs for human interaction, all characteristics of an extroverted temperament. One of John's primary defenses was precisely this ability of his to verbalize. He would run off at the mouth but without much affective connection. His words tended to remain disconnected from his own inner affective life. In one session we began to explore his relationship with his mother and what he had missed growing up. Rather subtly he moved away from this inner searching through verbalizing about some tangential matter. I simply observed his avoidance and then suggested we try something if he were willing. And he was. I had him sit comfortably, relax his body, close his eyes, and allow himself to visualize whatever images spontaneously arose inside. I told him I would close my eyes and go with him. Within a few moments, he was standing beside his mother as she was being wheeled into the operating room. It was the last time he would see her alive. John allowed himself to relive through imagery the emotional impact of his mother's death. As he described to me the images he visualized, tears rolled from his eyes, and he convulsed in sobbing pain. He began to realize that he was grieving not only for her death but also for what he had never had. John began to experience in full conscious awareness his deep inner pain, his own emotional deprivation. In this instance, visual imagery became an inner bridge, reconnecting John's conscious, verbal self with needs and affects that had been disowned and blocked from awareness.

Other ways I utilize imagery relate to troublesome or frightening dreams which clients bring into therapy. One woman, Rita, had been sexually assaulted by a man at knife-point about a year previously. She continued to have nightly terrors, dreams in which she relived this humiliating and terrifying experience. One day she came in quite anxious and upset. This recurring nightmare had happened again during the night, and she was so terrified she could not go back to sleep. I suggested that she "redream" the dream in waking fantasy. I had her relax, close her eyes and then visualize the dream in conscious imagery as it had just happened the night before. I told her I would go with her through it, but this time she was to regain *power* over this frightening dream image by any means possible. Before embarking on the imagery journey, she asked me how she could take back the power. I said she could disarm the rapist, call for assistance from dream friends, or, ultimately, kill the rapist in fantasy. So we embarked, and she took me through the dream by verbalizing the images as she visualized them. She came to the rape scene and froze. She could not do anything and felt paralyzed. I first waited a bit, but then I encouraged her to take action. In the midst of acute inner anguish as she relived the rape, Rita's fury suddenly spewed forth. She visualized herself knocking the man down and then kicking him over and over until her rage was spent.

I later suggested to Rita that whenever frightening dreams woke her, she could use much this same approach in order to regain power over her terrifying dream images. Subsequently, Rita reported that these nightly terrors had begun to diminish in frequency.

Active imagery can be utilized toward a variety of ends: to assist the unconscious in becoming conscious, in differentiating and reowning needs, in recontacting blocked affects, to assist the healing of early deprivation, and to regain power in the dream life. Imagery can also be a way of *practicing* how to cope with any unfamiliar or threatening situation. Through vivid imagery we can imagine ourselves going through a potential encounter. In so doing, we can discover how we might truly feel about that situation or person. We can also discover what our worst fears are and how we might cope with them when the situation actually presents itself.

Reversing Need Conversion

I ought to record here that I have begun to observe some connection between failures in identification due to a need-shame bind having arisen and homosexual manifestations at least in a portion of males seeking therapy. In no way am I suggesting a necessarily cause-and-effect relationship. Rather I would hope to point to a possible way of understanding *one* of the many complex contributors to homosexual expression. Sexual orientation certainly has both innate and environmental determinants. Homosexuality and bisexuality represent normal, not pathological, developmental variants which we will reexamine in Chapter 7.

For whatever set of complex reasons, a boy begins to consciously experience his need for male identification in explicitly sexual guise. There has been a conversion of the need into something quite different from it. At times when that need to merge with a man surfaces, that yearning for closest bonding with another, the internal imagery expressing the need takes on genitals as though *this* were the thing desired.

My initial reading of it suggests to me that somewhere in the client's life there had been a critical tear in the fabric of his male relationships starting with father or whoever filled that role. So we look for the tear and try to understand how it came about. And we seek to aid the client in having the power to differentiate internally and thereby come to know his own needs. As he becomes an observer of his own inner processes, he is able to say how what registers in sexual terms inside of him may in actuality be some quite other need instead. On the other hand, had a shaming, available father been passed over for a more satisfying other, older male figure (grandfather, neighbor, or teacher at school), the necessary identification could be made to him instead, in this way avoiding the shame by avoiding all significant dealings with the father. Turning to the other, more satisfying-to-be-with and consistently available figure can serve the need for relationship as well as identification.

Not always is it some need for identification which has been converted. For many, and this is as true for male-female relationships as any other, needs for touching and holding frequently become shamed and converted into something vastly different. Many of us believe that we must engage in sexual relations to fill a quite younger need, of which we may or may not be aware, though one which will recur throughout our adult lives. And the need motivating that touching may not be a young need so much as an adult one. Still, there is need for some disguise of it. Sexual play is one, athletic play another. The one more suits male-to-female touching while the other, male-to-male. And when competitive male-to-male play such as in sports or work fails for whatever reasons to provide for the underlying need (human touching), sexual male-to-male play can be one attempt at solution.

Society plays its role in fostering the conversion process. When so many voices tell us that the only reasons for wanting to touch, hold, or feel especially close to another human being are sexual, eventually we will listen. I cannot believe that this species of ours is motivated only to make love, compete, or destroy.

At any rate, needs for physical touching and identification with another man underlie *some* of the imagery in a portion of clients describing homosexual concerns. Of course this is not the whole picture. Every individual's development is a unique and complex affair. There are few simple meanings to anything which matters to us. And few things are as important as one's identity and sexual orientation.

Enabling the client to gain conscious awareness of his *currently active needs* as well as past deprivation has a most freeing effect upon the shame which I believe is the originating source and active sustainer of the conversion which has occurred. The more the client is able to accurately identify needs and seek appropriately to satisfy them, the more he reports increased inner well-being and more satisfying human relationships, whether male-male or male-female.

Avoidance of females due to prior disappointments, along with whatever shame has accrued, is a dynamic all its own to be contended with. New learning experiences with women will be necessary in order to overcome this developmental obstacle.

Disinternalizing Parental Identifications

We come to our last dimension now, at least for the present discussion. It is paramount to free the self from the hold which the past has upon it. Letting go of those troublesome, forever-to-be-unmet needs tied to those significant others who have failed us is one of the hardest of all things. For it means closing a door on the past and accepting what may be a painful reality: I cannot go back and get it the way I needed it then. Some holes will inevitably remain inside.

That painful separation from an unfulfilled childhood must come about in order to set the self moving again. Otherwise, one would be forever chasing after past needs and so miss the present moment, the needs of our current lives.

Even then the past retains a hold within. Internal parental images need to be differentiated consciously and then disinternalized. It is here that internalizing the therapist as a new inner ally exerts power. When the client has a new guiding identification within, even a new parent to internalize, he is enabled to gradually let go of prior self-limiting identifications made with parents.

And attitudes or values internalized in the past but which are no longer appropriate for the self can also be discarded, with consistent conscious effort, of course.

This brings us to the therapeutic handling of projection. While projection distorts the present relationship by confusing past with present, nevertheless the process of projection is the individual's initial and spontaneous attempt at self-cure. Projecting back into outer reality (the interpersonal realm) what was originally present there but had become internalized and hence installed in inner reality (the realm of "I with myself") can even be construed as an attempt by the unconscious to disinternalize that disruptive identification image by transferring the internalized unfinished relationship into the new current relationship. Almost always, the attempt fails. For unless conscious differentiation occurs, and, along with it, a resolution of the original failure which unleashed the process to begin with, what remains is an endless sequence of attempts to remedy defectiveness, in a word, a compulsion to repeat.

Effective therapeutic handling rests upon the following: (1) permitting the process of projection onto the therapist to proceed, i.e., to become ever more conscious for the client; (2) the living-out of the projection: therapist and client make conscious and differentiate their actual relationship from the projected one, though still *pretending* along with the projection *as if* it were also the present reality; (3) returning internalized shame, along with the internalized identification images, to their interpersonal origins, thereby reversing the developmental sequence. The client needs to let go of and relinquish those self-limiting, internal guiding images, which is perhaps the most difficult thing of all, and replace them by internalizing more freeing identifications derived from the therapeutic relationship.

CURRENT INTERPERSONAL FUNCTIONING

This too must be a prime dimension of focus. It is through new interpersonal learning that change comes about, provided that the old internalized learning also is sufficiently dealt with. But not all learning needs to happen in the actual therapy setting. Change does not solely come about there. Frequently, a therapist must guide a client through outside experiences which are themselves therapeutic. One thirty-five-year-old man was partially crippled from a childhood bone disease. He was still living at home with his parents. My active encouraging and support of his finding a place of his own enabled him to take the risk of separating. That was a significant step in his life.

With another client, we had uncovered his need for holding, something he missed growing up. Yet the corrective emotional experience occurred not in therapy but with his girlfriend. One night the need came upon him, and he was able to ask *her* for that holding. And she freely gave it.

Other clients need support in overcoming particular developmental hurdles. Clients who feel an acute sense of deficiency in relating either to people generally or to one or the other gender in particular, feel so because of sufficient prior encounters with shame, and need guidance from a therapist in learning to have relationships generally or with the avoided gender. Several clients had not avoided all relationships, but rather had experienced predominantly disastrous relationships. Here I seek to guide them, provided this is something they also wish to master.

In the case of Sam, we worked to enable him to become conscious of his internal shame processes, the very internal dialogue he engaged in which reproduced bad feelings about himself. One of these concerned his usual pattern of storing bad feelings while letting good ones evaporate. Whenever life events occurred as they inevitably must, Sam would retain and keep the bad ones while quickly letting good ones slip through his fingers. Thus, whenever he felt bad for any reason he was apt to snowball those feelings into a depressive episode, culminating in his feeling worthless, inherently defective as a person. He had never learned how to store good feelings inside of himself as well as to let go of bad feelings. Even though we had begun to make progress toward enabling him to gain active control over his internal shame processes, important interpersonal learning was yet to be done.

Failures in Sam's relationships, particularly with women, had been a continuing source of anxiety as well as shame for some time now. This had been one of the reasons for his seeking therapy in the first place. In spite of our having been able to break into this old internalized pattern which by now had become a part of his identity, a learned way of relating to himself, something would invariably go wrong in his human relationships only to rekindle his sense of failure as a person. It gradually became clear to me that Sam must be contributing in ways that brought on these failures.

Realizing this enabled me to recognize another failure in development. Sam never had learned how to be aware of and sensitive to the impact he was having on other people. He was so blinded by his own "neediness," the little boy inside of him so desperately needing to feel wanted and loved, that never could he see beyond his own deprivation to how others might *actually* be reacting to him, those subtle cues which tell us how others are feeling about us. He developed the ability to begin to keep a conscious hold on the deprived little boy inside of him so that his desperateness would no longer spill over and scare others away. And as I began to let Sam know about the impact he was having on *me* as we worked together, Sam began to accomplish another important developmental step.

He had always felt he was doing something to others, but no one had been willing to tell him honestly. Of course, I could appreciate why. Sam often would convey an air of fragility, of "Please don't hurt me, I can't take it." And others would mistakenly fall for it, in this way depriving Sam of most essential interpersonal learning. And I offered the guidance he had missed in learning the basic skills of having human relationships.

With one client, Martha, her relationships with men had never worked out and she wanted to improve them. So we explored her relationships of the past, and I told her she would need to practice some, that learning how to relate effectively requires giving oneself learning time (time to make mistakes) and ample opportunity to practice. It's really not all that different from learning any other skill, except this one is interpersonal. And as each relationship blossomed and either went nowhere or ended, she learned to stop internalizing each as a personal failure, as another confirmation of inherent defectiveness. Furthermore, we began to see some of the reasons why her relationships went poorly. For she never felt free to say no or to set limits in keeping with her own needs and wants. So I insisted that she now practice setting limits on others as well. As she began to, Martha came to a new sense of power in relation to others, a sense of having for the first time equal power. In this way, the learning of interpersonal competence was fostered along with the disinternalization of shame.

Another client, Sandra, was in much the same boat. She felt trapped into feeling powerless in her relationship with her parents, especially mother. Yet all of her relationships, with men particularly, followed a similar pattern: she felt powerless and trapped while raging underneath. After one of these encounters would happen, Sandra would inevitably embark on some self-destructive course such as eating everything in sight followed by making herself vomit it all up. So we worked to develop some elementary sense of dignity and self-respect, an inner valuing of herself. And I leaned on her heavily to decide what it was she wanted in each and every relationship she was in. One of these involved an older, married man. Sandra did not like having a sexual relationship with him, yet every time she said as much he talked her back into it. I finally supported her in stopping this part of the relationship. And I guided her through every step of it. She would report the last exchange, and we would figure out what to do next so she could disentangle herself. There was a while when this coaching went on by telephone as though I were right there in it.

This kind of guidance through interpersonal living is indeed a parenting function. A client often will need to learn how to navigate with competence the interpersonal realm we all find ourselves in. And the kind of guidance a client can need from a therapist may include assistance with freeing oneself from the relationship he or she has always been in with a parent. This is not historical exploration as much as it is changing the relationship a client *currently* has with the parent. Guidance here aims at having a new, more mutual, more satisfying relationship with the parent as though the parent were simply another adult. Through learning that one *now* can call the shots just as well as the parent, in this way attaining fully equal power with one's parents, one is enabled truly to let go of the past and to live life in the present. It is this letting go which makes a different future possible.

DIFFERENTIATION OF THE SELF

Therapy needs to accomplish the tasks of inner development just as it needs to complete those interpersonal developmental steps missed in the course of living. That the building and maintaining of inner security is essential must be clear. Reowning disowned parts of the self fosters wholeness, the very integrity of the self, and changing the way in which the self relates to the self through relinquishing the use of defenses directed inward brings peace and safety to the inner life. Learning how to actively care for one's inner self as well as to forgive oneself brings about a much more satisfying inner relationship. Such active, day-to-day nurturance of self provides a new and inner source of basic love as well as strength.

When an individual feels some especial threat to self, whether it comes as self-doubt, a fit of worthlessness, or some sense of deficient adequacy, turning to a significant other is likely. How that other responds to our need carries impact. In turning to a therapist a client, as any human being at such moments, needs reaffirmation. That need for affirmation of self must be understood to be responded to appropriately—understood not perfectly, but humanly. From therapist-provided affirmation of self, a client can learn to do this from within, thereby gaining mastery and increasing eventual separation. Here is an example of how *permitting* dependence and identification foster differentiation. Learning how to affirm ourselves from within enables us to retain an inner sense of valuing in the face of threat. We are learning to internalize a conviction in our fundamental worth as persons as well as our other most essential, our unquestioned adequacy. The power to determine how we feel about ourselves slowly comes to reside solely within the self. Implicitly, the self also is learning more flexible, much more adaptive defenses against external threat to self.

Differentiation of the self comes about interpersonally, and it comes about in the inner life as well. Such teaching of new ways of relating to oneself as are involved here also is a parenting function which a therapist can provide.

REGAINING CONSCIOUS CHOICE OVER DEFENSES: TOWARD INTERNALIZING CHOICE IN LIVING

I would like to draw out one of the more central implications of the particular conception of development arising here, that view of development based on the interplay among shame, identification, and the inner life of the self. I am referring to the idea that defenses are in some manner consciously chosen at the outset. Choice here may mean deliberate or merely modeled. The sample of defenses offered to choose from in all likelihood may be quite limited. The interpersonal realm called the family we all happen to get born into offers certain visible, available means of defense. Native endowment, whether with respect to innate temperament or innate strength of affect, likewise acts selectively in the sorting out of whatever useful means of adaptation may be at hand.

The ways in which a parent defends against threat to self can serve as model for the child. Or the manner in which the parent responds to the child's obvious displays of most imperfect humanness will likely be adopted through identification. Or yet again, a particular individual may literally renounce a part of the self much as one young woman had. After repeated disappointments when looking to her parents for vital emotional needs, she resolved to look no further. Every night before she fell asleep, she would recite what became her emotional litany: *"I'm never going to need anything from anyone ever again!"* Over and over she would repeat it, each night again and again. Now, as an adult, whenever she comes unavoidably face-to-face with her innermost self, most especially the needing part of her, the litany is repeated. She recites inside herself that same dialogue once aimed at her parents.

If defenses are in some manner selected, there is a conscious part of the self aware of its occurrence. Later, once internalization is underway, the defense comes to function increasingly removed from conscious awareness, much as any acquired habit becomes second-nature to the self. As the defense comes to function beyond our awareness, we begin relinquishing conscious choice.

It is that *choice* over defenses which clients must regain. That is what developing conscious awareness is all about. The loss of conscious awareness of *when* one defends, in response to *what* activators, and *how* one defends surrenders a measure of vital choice over inner living. To decide that a particular situation or person is not safe and that one is therefore wise to stay defended provides needed conscious choice over defenses. To choose to engage a particular defense also implies being able to let go of that defense when trust does finally get established.

If defenses are in some fashion chosen, the therapeutic aim is to regain that lost conscious choice, to free the client either to defend *or* not to defend. A client usually will have little or no awareness at the outset of how he or she goes about manifesting defenses. Conscious awareness of a defense is essential if one is ever to regain the choice over using it.

There are a number of ways of working which increase conscious awareness of the defenses used. First we seek to name the defense in a way that lends us more conscious control over it. As we name it, we grow to see it operating in the client's life. We track its origin in the past, for a client is better able to understand a defense of his own if he can see how or why it came about, to comprehend the meaning of the defense in relation to the client's earlier life. As we understand the meaning of the defense in relation to shame, how the defense currently functions within the self becomes clearer to us as well.

It is the internalizing of *choice* which works to free the self from the stranglehold of the past. And choice over the use of defenses is but the beginning. From choice grows increasing freedom in living one's present life, the active discovery of one's own unique way of going about the task life hands us all. Since choice confers a measure of power to say yes *or* no to prior internalized learning, choice becomes but a stepping-stone to a sense of inner strength or potency, that emergent perception of mastery. And from conscious considered choice, choice grounded securely in a differentiated owning of one's internal needs and values, emerges a compass for the philosophic vacuum of life.

THE POWER OF CARING

Two concepts which make sense to me in describing the kind of therapy which I have slowly been evolving are *reparenting* and *identity regrowth*. Perhaps these do not accurately reflect what happens. Perhaps these two notions which recur so often in my thoughts about therapy are but myths and not processes actually occurring. Still, myths are a vital source of meaning in what we do. Maybe reparenting and identity regrowth are my personal myths which give essential meaning to my efforts. And maybe still, these are something more, somehow pointing to possibilities inherent in the psychotherapeutic adventure.

In closing I would like to recount the experience of working with one particular young woman, a situation which captures some essentials of the healing process. I first met Jonie when she was just eighteen and a college freshman, and we worked together in therapy over several months. At first she struck me as certainly a bit odd. She seemed much younger than her years, with loud giggles coming most unexpectedly. She would jerk about and gesture quite a bit as we talked. Yet it all seemed like some big joke to her. She said she came to find out if she was as crazy as everyone said she was. I laughed and, yes, I could see some likely reasons why many upstanding individuals might be taken aback, shocked, or even insulted by this young upstart who had no respect for her elders. But I just laughed with her when she did and said that no I didn't think she was crazy. I added that some people weren't likely to like her very well if they were the kind that got easily threatened by her antics. She laughed, then howled and slapped her side and laughed some more. "That's right," she said and told me how once when she was four years old, a Catholic priest had asked her to cut some pretty flowers for the Virgin Mary. Jonie just looked at him and replied, "No, I'm not gonna cut no live flowers to put on no dead statue's head!" Well, you can imagine the reaction she got. I do believe she either was drummed out of the school or they were greatly relieved when she failed to return.

Jonie and I laughed together for an hour intermixed with serious talk, but I could see no particular current conflicts troubling the girl and I told her so. Then it came. We spent forty-five minutes reaching this point, and we spent another forty-five minutes in Jonie's agonizing struggle to face an emotional truth blocked from conscious awareness. I had no inkling of what was coming.

The carefree, laughing, giggling Jonie dissolved into a much younger, more frightened, helpless-feeling Jonie. She would grab hold of her sides, holding herself, and rock back and forth. She would mumble something about being four years old when it happened. Apparently, something painful had happened, not once but many times. "Then he lied, he lied," she cried out and she wrung her hands, her eyes staring off into another time, another place inside.

I sat listening, confused, at times mildly anxious, attempting to aid her but knowing not what to do. So I did nothing except be with her through it, whatever it was to be. Then she turned upside down in the big orange chair, feet straight up in the air, and curled up as a ball.

I let her know I was still there. At times she responded to me. At times I couldn't reach her. So I joined her inside and tried to experience her phenomenal world through my own imagery.

I grew impatient, wanting to end the mystery and find out what had indeed happened or else quit trying to and wait until she was ready to see it. I said this to her, and I helped her name for herself her own ambivalence about facing this thing. She felt deeply ambivalent about reexperiencing the traumatic events. Only then could they be recontacted affectively, reowned and made peace with, and the wound, however bad, be allowed at last to heal. I said this to her, saying also the choice was hers. That power I did not have. I would go with her through it, but I could not make her do it, nor do it for her.

She could continue living as she has, keeping whatever this was hidden away inside and cut-off, though perhaps always haunting her on the fringe of knowing, or she could choose to face whatever this ghost or demon was and then get on with the business of living. I said all this and I said one thing more. She would not do it until she was ready to and prepared.

Then it grew apparent she was going to have another round inside of her. So we went into it once more. Gesturing, holding herself, rocking, not being able to look at me. Indeed, when she was in this state, whatever it was, she could not look at me. If our eyes met for but an instant, she literally covered her face with her hands or buried her face under her arms. How old is this behavior, I asked myself. Then I remembered her prior laughing and giggling. These came most often, though perhaps not always, when I looked at her looking into my face.

I naturally began to wonder about shame. Was I witnessing a gross shame reaction that had become repetitively induced, shame grown so powerful as to totally engulf the self? I knew that if I became either impatient, intellectual, too detached, helpless, or threatened, the entire drama now beginning to unravel could abruptly hide once again. I told her and myself that we would see it out and eventually understand it, though it might take us more than several hours. Besides, it took Rome seven years to build, and it just might take us a bit of time to do what we need to. She laughed and I think I reached out and touched her hand.

We went on. And I began to put names together with feelings or needs or whatever I saw. Yes, she said she felt shame. I asked her if she felt exposed when we looked into each other's eyes. She grimaced and buried her head beneath her arms. I talked to her about shame and how I have come to understand it. And I told her some about how it was for me.

We went into active imagery, perhaps spontaneously, perhaps at my suggestion. She was standing there at the door. She was four years, no, five years, no, it was four years old, she finally decided. Every night she would have to go up there and into their bedroom. "And *she* knew." *How did mother know?* "She knew and still she sent me up there, to *him*, she heard my screams!" *What happened when you went in there?* "No, no, no, I don't want to see it, I don't want to know!" *Fine, then let's stop here.* "No!"

And then she saw, and she convulsed into sobbing, racking pain, pain from long ago, pain from her *deepest inside*. I listened to her anguished soul pour out, for never had she spoken of this to any person. More than comfort and support, though these I had to give her, she needed to name her ineffable. So we named the missing pieces, those shadows in her unconscious but dancing on the fringe of knowing. She went up to the room, night after night, had to, I said to her. "For how long?" I asked. "A year," she answered. My God, I thought, is this real or her creation? Yet my deepest instincts, my intuition, said it felt real.

She had to go in there every night and submit to sexual things done to her. She struggled and struggled to break free but he easily held her physically, she feeling quite trapped. And then father apparently began telling the whole family that Jonie was a little liar. He destroyed her believability, Jonie said, so no one would believe her if she told. This is what Jonie revealed to me and, finally, to herself. There was much work to be done to heal her shame and work the deprivation into inner peace. She still never once looked at me, not once in the entire hour after our first forty-five minutes together. She had done so at the outset but not since. I knew her shame yet bound her to the crime. This was still a vital part of her identity even now.

And then it came as if some telepathy had occurred in which she heard me think to myself about her shame. She said, "At my deepest darkest inside, I feel to blame." She has also carried the sense of responsibility for a crime done against her, culpability in a funda-mental human offense done by a parent to a child. It then occurred to me that, perhaps, a punitive *something* inside of her yet rides herd upon her inner life, dispensing shame and guilt. Is this conception of identification images an accurate or useful symbol of the self?

Well, the hour grew late, almost two having passed. We set up our next time together; she said she wanted that. I gave her a hug as we walked to the door, feeling real closeness with her in her struggle and liking her as well just as she was. When I hugged her, she spontane-ously convulsed again, crying between words that were pleading and desperate. "Please don't leave," she pleaded, each hand grabbing hold of me, then releasing, grabbing, releasing. "Please don't leave me, promise me you won't leave me." I said to her, "I won't abandon you. I will go with you through this. We'll see it out together."

She visibly relaxed, smiled warmly at me, turned and slowly walked away. I stayed after many minutes, simply experiencing my own self or reexperiencing, in imagery, moments in our time to-gether.

I, of course, had no idea whether she would ever return. As a result of preferring to always leave the choice freely to the client, I often get surprised. And this was no exception. Everything about our first session was a surprise. Everything about Jonie continued to surprise me. Our relationship twisted and turned in ways I could never have predicted if I had wanted to, which I didn't. I simply told myself I was in for a ride, and I wasn't to be the only driver. And when Jonie steered, taking me along for the ride, did we ever move. One session, maybe our third, she came in with nothing to talk about. When she started getting self-conscious and feeling exposed with me again, I suggested we go out-of-doors. We walked—I had to hustle to keep up with her. We went to see a couple of favorite places along the river which flows through the university campus. I took her to see my sitting place, a place I go to just be by the water. And then we literally sprinted quarter-way across campus to her sitting place, but other people were already sitting there, so we hiked around to avoid them. I said, "We could still go over there, nearby." "No," she said, "I'd feel too exposed." So we just looked and hiked back. Then we sat in the gardens next to the building my office is in and talked and did some therapy as needed. But mostly we just talked together.

In the middle of one session, Jonie pulled out a toy hammer and with absolutely no warning hit me squarely on the head. It squeaked. And she howled and so did I. At the end of that session, as we hugged and said good-bye, she said, "I like you." Then off self-consciously she fled.

One day she came in and told me in her most serious tone that she'd been up to the "room" again. "Oh," I replied, "I see." She went on describing what had happened, looking straight down at the floor all the while. But this time she could put words together with feelings or events or needs and name what had always been unspeakable. Then she said, after recounting just a bit more detail to what her father had actually physically done to her, "And I came to the worst thing of all. It's not what he did to me, it's what he *didn't* do." I looked puzzled. "It's that never, not once, did he ever hold me, just hold me. He didn't have to do nothin', just hold me and hold me and hold me and not let me go." Then she asked me, asked with much embarrassment, asked by casting down her eyes and stammering over words, asked me to hold her, but only if I wanted to, 'cause I didn't have to, and I was to remember I didn't need to do nothing, just hold her.

We sat together the rest of that session, with our arms around each other. We talked if she spoke first or if some thought or fantasy occurred to me, but mostly I silently held her.

Another session, perhaps the next or the one after, she came in and asked to be held pretty much from the outset. I had a fantasy, and so I asked her if she had ever had bedtime stories read to her, something every child ought to have had. She said, "No, no one ever read to me. I could read so early they said, 'Here, go read it yourself.' They were always trying to get rid of me." So I suggested reading her a story. Her eyes went big and round like a girl at her first circus. I got up and looked through some books and settled back to read a favorite little piece of mine from *The Velveteen Rabbit*. It's the part about, well, how toys become real and perhaps people too. I held her and read to her until the piece ended. We hugged a last hug and she was off into the big world.

At the end of one of our holding sessions, a session in which she asked me for holding, I made a parting comment about there being someone else due in I also "gotta care about." She grimaced fiercely, her face now furious and screamed, "Gotta care about! No gotta!" Well, evidently she felt wounded and shamed by my choice of language. I replied, "No, Jonie, my caring is real. What I give, I give freely. I certainly don't hold just anybody and not strangers and not people I don't choose to and want to hold. I don't have to care about you. Some people grow to matter to me and I to them and when that happens, our caring is indeed real."

"Sure you don't have to?" she replied.

"I don't have to, I want to. But there are others who are also special to me. And one of them is waiting for her turn. Jonie, you are special to me, but you're not *only*."

At the end of another session of holding, Jonie said, "What if I don't let go?" She said it teasingly. I said to her, "You'll let go," looking her squarely in the eyes. "How do you know?" she teased. "Cause I'm stronger," I answered. She let go.

During one moving session, Jonie said to me, "I love you, please let it be alright, you don't need to even love me back, I desperately need someone to love." I answered her gently, "It is good to love. Love me, love whomever you love. Besides, we do that for each other."

During other more tortured meetings, Jonie would wail, "But why, why didn't they love me?" That there was some disease within her, something so vitally wrong with her, was the only way she had had of understanding the deficiency of her shame. I told her we might never know the whole picture but that she wasn't really wanted, wanted as a separate human being, was clear enough by my reckoning. There was no doubt in my mind that she had missed some fundamental human needs, not the least of which was being treated with the same dignity and respect we ask of others. But somehow she had to make honest, lasting peace with the past, I told her, to make a different future possible. As long as the past haunts us within, part of the self remains identified with it.

And I also said one other thing. "You'd have been a neat daughter for me to have had." And she hugged me close and beamed and off she went.

As the months wore on and the academic year approached its summer hiatus, Jonie grew in a relaxed spontaneity. Less of her extreme self-conscious and paralyzing exposure, more easy being together and talking about most anything. Fewer requests for holding, though every session we hugged good-bye.

Active therapeutic work became intermixed with our simply having a real human relationship with each other, one hopefully restoring some of the developmental failures in her relationship with her father.

At our last session together, we looked back and admired the work we'd done together. And we felt both pleased and proud. She told me she would let me know after summer break about continuing therapy. I said that was fine and to have fun this summer and play and most of all, be good to you. And then she sprung her last surprise and gave me a drawing she had made of her favorite comic strip hero. I admired the gift and promptly hung it up on the side of a file cabinet. "There it will hang," I said to her.

"I didn't expect you to hang it," she countered, all blushing and ashamed.

"I want to," I answered. "It'll remind me of you and keep a part of you right here in this office beside me."

I knew beneath her shame secretly she felt proud.

We said our good-byes and fond wishes. I gave her a great big hug as she went out the door, and she was gone.

Once again, I learned to appreciate the power of shame and its healing.

PART III
Extending Shame
Theory in New Directions

6
Toward a Theory of Shame-Based Syndromes

The foregoing theory of shame and identity is necessarily an evolving one. The discussion of culture's impact (Chapter One) adds to our conception of the sources of shame. The discussion of the interplay between language and imagery (Chapter Two) further illuminates the internalization process. The next critical step is to extend shame theory further into the realm of pathological development. We have already considered the development of schizoid, paranoid, and depressive postures as distinct syndromes of shame. I am now conceptualizing a variety of shame-based syndromes. These are particular developmental patterns which are rooted in, and organized around, the affect of shame.

PHYSICAL ABUSE

One class of shame-based syndromes comprises *physical abuse.* These are disorders which are rooted in the conjoint states of powerlessness and intense humiliation (shame), two inevitable consequences of parental abuse. Repetitive beatings are a recurring source of shame for children whose parents cannot control and otherwise safely discharge their own mounting rage. Parental rage, which triggers the enactment of a scenario involving physical abuse, itself is part of the unfolding drama. Parents who physically abuse their own children were typically themselves abused when young. They felt equally humiliated, and continue to live with unresolved shame in their own lives. Children of shame-based parents will inevitably activate their parents' shame, and the cycle repeats itself with shame passed from generation to generation.

There is a critical intervening step in the development of such a shame-based syndrome. Parental shame is imbedded in a series of *governing scenes*. These original childhood scenes of the parents later become reactivated by their own children. Like a magnet, these scenes compel reenactment. Phenomenologically, a scene is like an entrance, a kind of psychological "black hole" drawing us inward, a portal in time. We are transported back into our scenes; we reenter and reexperience these original or nuclear scenes. Once a governing scene has been reactivated, we relive the original experience with all the affect present. Parents who are about to abuse their own children are simultaneously reliving scenes in which they were also beaten, but they relive the scene from the perspective of their own parents as well. They now play their parent's role, thereby *recasting* the scene. The internal image of the abusive parent mediates the process. Physical abuse can lead to a compulsive reenactment of abuse either toward self, spouse, or one's own children. And shame maintains the process, compelling reenactment. There is also secondary shame about being an abusive parent.

SEXUAL ABUSE

Compulsive disorders are rooted in internalized shame. That is why they are shame-based. Such disorders inevitably reproduce shame while, at the same time, attempting to reduce it. *Sexual abuse* comprises a second general class of shame-based syndromes. Incest and rape are two distinct types of sexual abuse which activate intense inner states of powerlessness, personal violation, and humiliation. In the midst of shame, one feels to blame. Childhood incest generates intense and crippling shame, which can and all too often does culminate in a profound splitting of the self. The experience of violation and helplessness itself is disowned, and the self withdraws deeper inside itself to escape the agony of exposure. Or else the self torments the self brutally with disgust or contempt turned against the self.

It is not only the victim of incest or rape who responds with a shame reaction or becomes shame-based as a person. The perpetrator of the assault or violation also is shame-based. Such acts are acts of power and revenge, born of impotence and fueled by shame. The scene of violation becomes emblazoned in the victim's imagination. That scene may hover at the periphery of awareness or instead actively replay itself over and over in consciousness, in fantasy, or in night terrors. Or the scene itself may be banished from awareness, disowned, and the self becomes frozen, statue-like. That scene of forcible violation, as experienced by the victim, is itself somehow a reenactment, a transformation of a scene of equal powerlessness and humiliation experienced by the perpetrator at the hands of a different tormentor. The rapist is equally haunted by scenes of torment, driven to reenact them, but this time as tormentor. The roles at last have become reversed. The victim, the target of revenge, is confused with the *source* of the perpetrator's shame. By defeating and humiliating the victim, the perpetrator momentarily becomes freed of shame. Indeed, theirs is a shame-based relationship.

ADDICTIVE DISORDERS

Addictive disorders comprise a third general class of shame-based syndromes. Here, addiction is understood broadly. Certainly, there are the specific substance addictions such as to alcohol and various chemicals. However, addiction itself can spread. Any object, real or imagined, potentially has the power to become compulsively desired. Sexual addiction is only one extension of the *addictive process*. The object of any addiction must be distinguished from the process by which an addiction develops and continues to maintain itself. Relationships can represent another form of addiction. Addiction to gambling or to work, as in the familiar "workaholic" syndrome, add to a growing class of disorders which reflect a distinctive addictive process. By its very nature, the addictive process is compulsive. It is repetitive, highly resistant to change.

There is one particular feature of every addiction, whatever the object, which is central to an understanding of the addictive process: a profound, often discouraging sense of powerlessness over the addiction. The tail increasingly comes to wag the dog, engendering secondary shame about the addiction itself. We feel humiliated whenever we feel controlled by an addiction to *anything* and whenever we fail to break it, to regain power over it. We feel defeated by our addiction. We grow to hate ourselves, disgusted at our helplessness, our lack of resolve, our lack of inner strength. The addictive process is repetitively reenacting a scene, but the scene is not necessarily a literal one. The affect, however, is literal. The repetitive reenactment of a scene which creates intense shame, disappointment in self, is not coincidental.

Addictions are rooted in internalized scenes of shame. The objects are repetitively longed for, repetitively a disappointment.

The addiction functions also as a *substitute* for shame-bound interpersonal needs. The alcoholic who has a relationship with his bottle has substituted something else for a human relationship. The addiction to a *sedative for negative affect* is the substitute for interpersonal needs. There has been a critical failure in the human environment, and a sense of shame surrounds those vital interpersonal needs we all experience.

This is only one perspective on the development of addictions. Certainly a host of factors will have to converge to shift the balance toward any particular line of development. One of those factors is Tomkins' concept of *scene*. Children with addictive parents will internalize images of those individuals. These scenes continue to shape the self, but the self is not merely a passive recipient of events. We participate actively, directly in how we organize those events, how we interpret them, how we make meaning out of experience as it is lived. Alfred Adler reminds us: "Do not forget the most important fact that not heredity and not environment are determining factors. Both are giving only the frame and the influences which are answered by the individual in regard to his styled creative power."

If those governing scenes continue to shape our lives, we *can* gradually learn to actively reshape them. The first step is learning to consciously recognize governing scenes when they are operating. We must discover our governing scenes and fully reexperience and thereby release the affect imbedded in those scenes. These are the first steps toward change.

The addiction functions also as an escape from intense shame. Feelings of shame encountered anew are reduced through becoming addicted to something. Addictions can sedate intense negative affect. However, the addiction also reproduces shame, which only reactivates the entire cycle. The presence of shame ensures that governing scenes will become reactivated over and over.

One specific class of addictions must be further distinguished. Alcohol addiction adds a complicating factor. When the expression of affect becomes chronically inhibited, a condition of *affect hunger* is created, according to Tomkins. Affect hunger is "the wish to express openly the incompletely suppressed affects." For centuries, Tomkins further argues, alcohol has provided therapy for affect hunger, "releasing the smile of intimacy and tenderness, the look of excitement, sexual and otherwise, the unashamed crying of distress, the explosion of hostility, the intrusion of long-suppressed terror, the open confession of shame, and the avowal of self-contempt."[1]

Alcohol may be resorted to initially to release suppressed affects, particularly shame. At "the time of intoxication the promise of relief from the communication of shame overwhelms the impulse to hide it."[2] The morning after, the alcoholic becomes seized with shame at his or her alcoholic shamelessness.

Alcoholic intoxication is a *de-inhibitor* of suppressed affect. It minimizes the inhibition of shame and self-contempt as well as other affects, permitting the emergence of suppressed affect.

EATING DISORDERS

One further class of shame-based syndromes comprises the group of compulsive eating disorders. Again there is a sense of powerlessness over the process and also intense secondary shame about it. Eating disorders such as bulimia, anorexia, and bulimarexia are largely disorders of shame. Such a person feels inherently deficient, worthless, disgusting, a failure.

---

[1] Tomkins, S.S., *Affect, Imagery, Consciousness,* Vol. 2., New York: Springer, 1963, p. 268.
[2] *Ibid,* p. 269.

Let us follow the process by which bulimia develops and maintains itself through the perspective offered by the concepts of *shame* and *scene*. Bulimia comprises two distinct phases which recycle. The first is *bingeing* and the second is the *purge cycle*. Shame is present in each phase, though differently experienced and coassembled as Tomkins describes it. The scenes motivating behavior in bingeing and purging are different. Bingeing on food is a substitute for interpersonal needs which are shame-bound. When one feels empty inside, hungry to feel a part of someone, desperate to be held close, craving to be wanted and admired, respected and loved—but these have become taboo through shame—one turns instead to food. But food can never truly satisfy the inner need. Longing turns to shame. And so one eats more to anesthetize the longing.

The shame about eating—eating that remains hidden, secret—represents a *displacement of affect* (shame) away from the original source (self). The shame about bingeing on food is a displacement of the deeper, internalized shame about self.

During the bingeing cycle, shame intensifies. The purge cycle adds something crucial to this: the affect of *disgust*. Vomiting is frequently resorted to by bulimics to purge themselves of the shameful food they so shamelessly devoured. Vomiting is the *disgust reaction* experienced on the drive level. We have all had occasion to react with an urge to vomit in response to an emotional situation. The purge cycle, vomiting, represents the affect of disgust expressed directly on the level of the hunger drive, and overtly in action.

Why vomiting? Why such an intense form of purging? There is a kind of emotional cleansing that occurs if one literally bathes in shame. Magnifying the intensity of shame will rapidly bring it to its peak intensity, imploding the self and thereby automatically reducing shame. This is Tomkins' concept of *affect magnification* applied to bulimia. While bingeing gradually accelerates shame, purging quickly magnifies it, bringing it to peak intensity through self-disgust. When the shame peaks, there is a "bursting effect," and one feels purged, cleansed, even purified. Self-purging through vomiting continues until defeat and humiliation are complete. The bulimic behaves so as to guarantee complete humiliation, acting to magnify and accelerate humiliation because these feelings have become intolerable. They can be reduced only by first magnifying them until they reach their peak intensity. By magnifying feelings of humiliation in intensity and duration, they are finally spent, their fire burned out. This is what creates the sense of cleansing.

This is a masochistic strategy, according to Tomkins, of reduction through magnification: "A species of masochistic behavior, the aim of which is to increase negative affect to such a point that it produces an explosive overt eruption of affect which ultimately thereby reduces itself."[3]

Tomkins' concept of affect magnification is central to my thesis of how bulimia develops and maintains itself. It is a disorder rooted in shame and in the masochistic strategy of reduction through magnification. By affect magnification, Tomkins refers to any systematic increase in intensity and/or duration of affect, with or without supression of the overt expression of affect. Affect magnification can feed equally well on expression as on suppression, and affects can also be minimized and reduced either through overt expression or through suppression. There is no necessary relationship between expression and intensity or duration of affects, or between suppression and intensity or duration of affects.

Magnification is one of the prime reasons for the vicarious expression of humiliation. After insult and incomplete suppression of humiliation, the inability to suppress selfcontempt or shame can be reinforced by a circular intensification of humiliation and the nature of the insult as this is re-experienced again and again upon review. The smouldering ashes of humiliation recruit images and reinterpretations of the antagonist so that he grows more and more offensive. As this happens, the embers of shame and self-contempt are fanned into hot flames which in turn recruit cognitive reappraisals that provide fresh fuel for the magnification of the negative affect. Just as individuals fall in love at a distance, so may they fall in hate with one who has humiliated

---

[3]Tomkins, S.S., *Affect, Imagery, Consciousness*, Vol. 2., New York: Springer, 1963, p. 283.

them. The mutual, circular magnification of humiliation and insult following humble withdrawal from insult is a prime condition for producing a level of humiliation such that the individual is forced into the vicarious avowal of his feelings. It, of course, also happens that the individual fortified by righteous indignation and incensed by the monster of his own imagination now returns to vanquish his original antagonist.[4]

Finally, with regard to bulimia, the internal imagery of the bulimic is hypothesized to reflect the internalized relationships with internal parental identification images (Fairbairn's internal object). These internal relationships mirror the original parental relationships in which shame and self-contempt were rooted. Relationships with identification images recreate the shame process. They reproduce shame. These inner relationships also mirror the sources of shame and the primary interpersonal needs which had become bound by shame.

CONCLUSION: TOWARD A SYNTHESIS

This view of compulsive disorders as reflecting distinct classes of shame-based syndromes is a synthesis. It represents an integration of three distinct theoretical perspectives: first, the *object-relations theory* developed by W. R. D. Fairbairn and Harry Guntrip; second, the *interpersonal theory* formulated by Harry S. Sullivan, Karen Horney, and Bill Kell; and finally, Silvan Tomkins' *affect theory*. Each syndrome is rooted in significant interpersonal failure and displays a characteristic pattern for reproducing shame. Each syndrome undergoes further transformation which is mediated by language and imagery .

Affect, imagery, and language are the central processes shaping the self and identity. Governing scenes of shame lie at the heart of addictive, compulsive, and narcissistic disorders. While other nega-

---

[4]Tomkins, S.S., *Affect, Imagery, Consciousness*, Vol. 2., New York: Springer, 1963, pp. 282-283

tive affects can certainly play a key role in particular cases, the role of shame is central in each of these syndromes. Disorders of self-esteem and disorders of mood, such as depression, have resisted therapeutic intervention as well as theoretical understanding because we have largely failed to grasp the primary role of affect, and its primacy over other subsystems within the self. Affect fuses with and thereby amplifies both the group of physiologically based drives (drive system) and the equally important group of interpersonally based needs (need system). Compulsive and addictive syndromes, which continue to elude effective intervention, are rooted in *affect dynamics* in general and *shame dynamics* in particular.

Psychotherapy must mirror development by actively engaging the identical processes which shape the self. Psychotherapy must attend to the full range of the primary affects. It must provide a reparative, security-giving relationship, one that heals shame through experiences of identification. And it must directly engage imagery, not only language, in order to make conscious and reshape governing scenes. I conceive of psychotherapy as an evolving integration of four central process dimensions: the *therapeutic relationship,* which involves restoring the interpersonal bridge; the *developmental process*, which involves returning internalized shame to its interpersonal origins; the *internal process* of the self, which comprises identity regrowth and healing shame; and the *interpersonal process*, which centers on developing equal power. Psychotherapy must be grounded in knowledge of how the self develops and actually functions.

Accepted models of the psyche, our fashionable metaphors of the self—from Freud's, Jung's, Adler's, and Sullivan's, to Fairbairn's, Roger's, and Berne's—have become outworn. What began as a metaphor to describe inner experience has since become reified and disconnected. Psychology needs a new vision, a coherent image of the self to guide it. Science inevitably begins by making new observations within its domain which are then translated into descriptive relational language. Anyone can, potentially, repeat the observation by working backwards from the concept (linguistic symbol) to its referent (phenomenological event). Science advances by such continual conversation between the brain and the senses, and it advances by discovering a new potential of meaning in an old concept, whether it be gravity, time, scene, or shame.

Like science, psychotherapy is an experiment, this time between two (or more) human beings. Each will inevitably become changed through their relationship. In order for shame-based clients to fully enter and experience their shame, psychotherapists have to be willing to do likewise. Shame will activate shame. We will not enable our clients to experience feelings or needs we cannot allow in ourselves. Every psychotherapeutic relationship is an experiment of the self in living just as every book is an experiment in knowledge.

We have examined the critical roles of shame and identification, of affect, imagery, and language. The continuing task is translating that expanding awareness into effective strategies for healing shame and developing a competent self. Only through evolving an accurate language of the self will psychology have a sound base from which to construct both a science of the self and an effective psychotherapy for shame-based syndromes.

7

The Significance of Shame for Gender, Culture, and Society

Shame is a multidimensional, multilayered experience. While first of all an *individual* phenomenon experienced in some form and to some degree by every person, shame is equally a *family* phenomenon and a *cultural* phenomenon. It is reproduced within families, and each culture has its own distinct sources as well as targets of shame. Shame also occurs from birth to death: it is a *life cycle* phenomenon. There are distinctive sources of shame during childhood, adolescence, adulthood, and old age, and because it is invariably passed from generation to generation, shame is an *intergenerational* phenomenon. That transmission of shame is mediated by scenes of shame which become internalized through imagery, and then reactivated and reenacted. All individuals live within families which, in turn, exist within cultures, and these cultures comprise nations—making shame a central *international* phenomenon as well. To view shame from only one of these perspectives is therefore necessarily limited.

It is this multilayered nature of shame that we will now focus on with a wider lens. In Chapters One through Four we examined shame as it relates specifically to personality development. In Chapter Five we explored the implications of shame theory for the treatment of shame in psychotherapy. In Chapter Six we considered how shame becomes embedded in the patterning of various forms of psychopathology. The centrality of shame in dysfunctional family systems is now an established fact. The pivotal role of shame in both addiction and recovery can no longer be ignored since shame has moved from obscurity to center stage within the therapeutic community. Still, we have merely skimmed the surface of the phenomenon and just begun to probe the significance of shame. In further extending our inquiry into the role of shame, we will examine shame in this chapter specifically in relation to aging and disability, the school and work settings, culture and gender, and sexual orientation and gay identity. Then in the following chapter we will widen our focus still further and explore both affect in general and shame in particular as they manifest in the context of international relations and of war. This study of shame will conclude with an examination of three central interrelated phenomena: identity, culture, and ideology. First, however, we must define the central constructs that will inform and focus our inquiry.

AFFECT, SCENE, AND SCRIPT: THE CENTRAL CONSTRUCTS

A general theory must account equally for differences as well as communalities. In constructing such a theory, I will employ three fundamental concepts: *affect*, *scene*, and *script*, as formulated by Silvan Tomkins. What follows is partly a review and partly an elaboration of what has been considered earlier.

Affects are inherited subcortical programs involving correlated sets of responses, including facial, glandular and muscular. Affect is the primary innate biological motivating mechanism, according to Silvan Tomkins; it is more urgent than the drives or even pain. Affect is experienced primarily on the face; only secondarily is affect experienced in the body, including the outer skeletal and inner visceral apparatus. When we become aware of our facial responses, we become aware of our affects. It is the feedback from the face that produces the distinctive feel of affect. Affect in turn amplifies all other subsystems within the human being; for example, when I feel excitement affect, my thoughts race, or if I am walking, my pace quickens. When I feel enjoyment affect, however, my pace slows in relaxed contentment, and when I feel ashamed, my eyes and head lower. The affect mechanism is thus capable of simultaneously capturing the face, the heart, the endocrine system, as well as both cognitive and motor responses. Nine innate affects have been identified by Tomkins, described in terms of their corresponding facial responses, and also have been cross-culturally validated. Like the primary colors, these innate affects blend to form all of our more complex inner states, such as compassion, love, and ecstasy, or jealousy, envy, and hatred.

Affective experience becomes stored in memory in the form of scenes. Tomkins' script theory defines the scene "as the basic element in life as it is lived."[1] A scene must include at least one affect and one object of that affect. An event must be "amplified in its urgency by affect" in order for any scene to be experienced. "The perception of a scene, at its simplest, involves a partitioning of the scene into figure and ground."[2] Affect first imprints and amplifies scenes; those scenes subsequently become interconnected with and thereby magnified by other affect-laden scenes. This is the process which Tomkins refers to as psychological magnification.

These scenes next give rise to scripts which embody specific rules for interpreting, responding to, controlling, and predicting any magnified set of scenes. Whereas the scene is a happening, perceived with a beginning and an end, the script encompasses the individual's developing rules for dealing with scenes. For example, the various defending strategies described in Chapter Three can be viewed as *defending scripts*, actual rules governing responses to shame scenes. While initially scenes determine scripts, those scripts increasingly determine future scenes. Scripts comprise rules for action, for cognition, and for decision.

Three distinct processes interact in the initial construction and subsequent reactivation of scenes: *affect*, *imagery*, and *language*. All experience becomes amplified by affect which, in turn, then partitions the event as a scene by causing it to stand as figure to the ground. Any affects present during the actual event as it is lived become imprinted in the scene. Similarly, any people present, facial

---

[1]Tomkins, S.S. "Script Theory: Differential Magnification of Affects." *Nebraska Symposium on Motivation*, 1979, 26, p. 211.
[2]*Ibid*, p. 221.

looks, actions performed, or words spoken become equally embedded in the scene. In this way, all experience becomes stored in memory in the form of discrete scenes which also comprise visual, auditory, and kinesthetic features. In most cases, the scene itself recedes from full conscious awareness, increasingly operating at the periphery of consciousness. Scenes constitute a more dynamic view of what typically have been called memories. The following diagram illustrates the above formulation of scene.

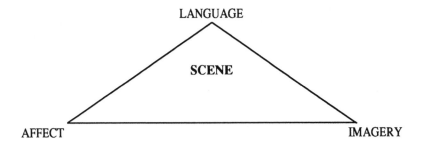

For a large group of individuals, only the language component of the scene remains available to consciousness. These individuals typically experience an *inner voice* which is the conscious residue of the scene; this voice is the language component of the scene. The inner voice experienced in this way is either the actual voice of a particular individual embedded in the scene or an auditory linguistic signifier permanently attached to the scene.Therefore, for this first group of individuals the language channel remains accessible, both open and connected. Through this language channel, the entire scene itself can be reactivated, even out of awareness, though the affect embedded in the scene all too often becomes reexperienced fully.

Individuals comprising a second group hear no inner voices but have full visual recall of the scene. While for these individuals the imagery channel remains open and connected, they experience no affect when visualizing the scene. Both the affect and language channels remain blocked or disconnected. They are able to recall and describe in vivid detail the most traumatic or shaming events without any affective experience connected to those events.

Individuals comprising the third group hear no inner voices and experience no visual images. Yet they become overwhelmed by intense affect often for no apparent reason. For them the process of scene reactivation is essentially silent. The language and imagery channels have both been disconnected in this latter case. It is as if these particular individuals become unexpectedly taken over or swept away by affect storms.

Psychotherapeutic treatment, then, must aim at the full conscious recovery of scenes. It must further accomplish the complete reconnection of all three channels—affect, imagery, and language— by which scenes become reactivated. For any given individual, it will be necessary first to utilize whatever channel remains connected or open, thereby working gradually toward accessing the blocked channels. The foregoing model of scene construction and reactivation has wide application in psychotherapy.

THE AFFECT OF SHAME

According to Tomkins, shame is innately activated by any perceived barrier to the continued expression of the positive affects, interest or enjoyment. The interpersonal activator of shame, explored in Chapter One, is breaking the interpersonal bridge between individuals who are significant to one another. Consider closely the many layers embedded in the experience of shame as we review the earlier discussion in preparation for extending shame theory. Phenomenologically, to feel shame is to feel *seen* in a painfully diminished sense. Our eyes turn inward in the moment of shame and suddenly we are watching ourselves, and it is this acute inner scrutiny that generates the torment of self-consciousness. Inherent to the experience of shame is this sudden, unexpected sense of exposure: we stand revealed as lesser. Exposure is an important characteristic of shame and is, therefore, central to understanding its dynamic impact. And exposure can be either to others or to the self alone. Developmentally, shame begins as a wordless affective experience; only later does it take on qualities of cognitive self-evaluation.

The principal effects of shame on the self are *hiding, paralysis*, and perceived *transparency*. The urge to hide, to disappear from view, follows quickly in the wake of shame. Reducing that often agonizing scrutiny is critical, and all hiding behavior therefore originates in the necessity of covering the self. Furthermore, exposure itself creates an experiential paralysis: speech is silenced, movement is interrupted, the self becomes frozen. Even the contents of consciousness may become experientially erased by the sense of exposure inherent to intense shame, thereby causing eventual repression of whatever has become associated with shame. Finally, we feel transparent because we feel painfully revealed in the moment of shame; others seemingly can see inside of us and know our innermost being.

If the inner experience of shame is exposure, the outer view of shame is captured in its characteristic facial signs: eyes down, head down, eyes averted, and blushing. These various, though universal, facial displays signify the experience of shame. They also serve to communicate shame both to the person who is feeling it and to any others present or watching. The shame response of lowering the eyes or head is a direct consequence of heightened visibility. But this response also reduces that painful visibility, thereby producing the universal symbol of the head hung in shame. From this poignant image comes the historical equation of shame with "loss of face." Shame *is* loss of dignity, fallen pride, damaged self-esteem.

Shame is typically followed by various secondary reactions, most notably other affects. The three most frequent are *fear*, *distress*, and *rage*. Fear of further shame experiences is a natural secondary reaction that is widely observed to follow shame. Fear, which often manifests as anxiety, frequently functions in anticipation of further shame. Distress—the crying response—is another affective reaction to shame; many children and adults will respond to their own shame by crying. The third principal secondary reaction is rage, which is an inflation of anger affect. Rage serves a vital self-protective function: it insulates the self, creating a protective cover, actively keeping others away.

The affect of shame typically manifests in various forms. The principal variants of shame are discouragement, embarrassment, shyness, self-consciousness, inferiority, and guilt. While these various inner states are certainly experienced overall as distinctly different, they do not reflect different affects but rather the same affect differently coassembled. Embarrassment is shame before an audience, while shyness is shame in the presence of strangers. Discouragement is shame over a temporary defeat, while inferiority is shame that is permanent. Self-consciousness is shame over performance, while guilt is shame over an immorality. Other phenomena rooted in shame include alienation, failure, worthlessness, and defectiveness.

SHAME AND THE AGING PROCESS

Now let us turn directly to the aging process and consider it more closely. The earliest organized scene during infancy is one of powerlessness, which first activates negative affect, including shame, and then becomes further amplified by that affect. Powerlessness activates shame. In childhood, there are distinct sources of shame which are connected directly to the child's relative lack of skill or developmental maturation. Children are vulnerable to shame precisely because they cannot match older siblings or peers in skill or accomplishment. During adolescence, the body becomes a source of shame owing to the inevitable bodily changes that now call attention to the self, thereby exposing it to view. Finally, toward the close of life the body once again becomes a universal source of shame, this time because of its decline.

As vitality and functioning diminish in the later years, shame is continuously activated. Though greatly telescoped in time, we can see this identical process in a stroke victim—the sudden loss of bodily functioning immediately generates shame. The aging process inevitably returns us to that primary scene of infant powerlessness.

In contemporary American culture, the quest to perpetuate youth and deny, disguise, or delay the visible signs of aging constitute this culture's dominant script for responding to and controlling the shame unleashed by aging. The problem has been made paradoxically worse by the advances of medical science—by lengthening the life span, a longer period of decline is made possible. Even when one's mind remains alert and active, the body slowly deteriorates. And to lose command over one's body is to be defeated by the simple passage of time.

The failure to hear as well, see as well, or move about as easily as one did before eventually results in a loss of power over one's own life. What was once an agile body—a source of enjoyment and excitement, of pride in body and in self—slips ever so gradually into decline. Some elderly people can become like infants, requiring benevolent caretaking, and the roles of aging parents and their adult children reverse. Through aging we are inevitably returned to the helplessness of infancy and to the shame ensuing therefrom.

Shame itself is contagious, for it will transfer interpersonally via empathy or identification. Adult children who watch their parents grow old will feel empathic shame in response. And they will feel equally powerless to delay or prevent the advance of time and the inescapable decline which it brings. Adult children of aging parents may be ashamed of the resentment they feel over the unexpected or unplanned role reversal they are confronted with. They may also be ashamed of having to weigh their parents' needs against their own, especially if they also have children or for any reason feel burdened by their parents' disability. Complicating this still further is the cultural expectation placed upon adult children to care for their parents. Clearly, aging is a source of shame for the elderly and others—especially their children. Every facet of the aging process is a doorway into shame.

DISABILITY AS A SOURCE OF SHAME

Learning disabilities and physical disabilities also recruit shame, magnifying the feelings that both infants and the elderly must contend with because of their developmental stage in life. No wish of the child is greater than to be like the beloved parent, but disability collides with that wish, thereby fueling shame. Children who fail in their efforts to identify experience shame and their disability makes failure permanent, a confirming deficiency. While infants eventually grow up and gain mastery over bodily functions, the disabled person may be forced to live with permanent deficiency. To be *differently*-abled, as Riger describes it,[3] and not experience oneself as *deficiently*-abled—therefore shameful—is a monumental challenge. For if one must live each day confronted anew with shame, the failing can only reside within the self.

The sense of shame inevitably experienced by anyone who is disabled is only confirmed by the response of others, a response which mixes shame and contempt, as Riger also notes.[4] The nondisabled onlooker inevitably experiences shame via an immediate, empathic identification with the disabled individual. The onlooker then quickly distances the disabled other through expressions of contempt and disgust in order to purge his or her empathic shame.

Even children who are learning-disabled learn all too quickly that they are not merely different from their peers but deficient. They are marked as lesser by their peers and by our schools, one of the principal institutions through which cultural values and taboos are transmitted.

Illiteracy is an example of a learning deficit about which there is considerable shame. Adults who have not learned how to read and write will feel acute shame over their deficiency. When faced with situations likely to expose their illiteracy, they will hide it because hiding is a natural response to shame. Exposure is the essence of shame. And the shame experienced over illiteracy often matches, in intensity, the shame experienced over incest.

---

[3] Riger, A. L. , *"When Differently-abled Girls Grow Up: The Legacy of Sexism and Shame and Their Healing."* (Paper presented at the National Conference of the Association for Women in Psychology, 1990).

[4] Riger, A.L., *"The Evocation and Healing of Shame in Differently-abled College Women."* (Paper presented at the symposium, The Role of Shame in Psychopathology and Psychotherapy, at the Meeting of the American Psychological Association, Boston, 1990).

SHAME IN THE SCHOOL SETTING

Teachers and the peer group at school have enormous power to influence the development of children. Much shaming actually takes place not in the family but in the school setting. Even the simple partitioning of a class into different ability groups, however that is disguised, will inevitably generate shame for the slower or less advanced among them. One man was forced to sit in the "dumb row" during math in fourth grade. From that time forward, he would experience a reactivation of that early shame scene whenever he was forced to manipulate numbers, such as when making change or balancing his checkbook. He not only avoided math but felt completely incapable of mathematical reasoning. Another child, a girl, was told by a teacher, "You can't carry a tune," during rehearsal for a class sing in sixth grade. For this individual, singing became bound by shame. She literally froze whenever she had to participate in group singing, and she could not freely sing even when entirely alone. Another young girl was told by her art teacher in fifth grade, "You can't draw," and she stopped trying. Finally, an adolescent boy was ridiculed by his teacher whenever he spoke in her class; increasingly this young fellow retreated from talking whenever he found himself in any kind of group situation. Teachers certainly have enormous power to shame children and that shaming can be crippling.

The peer group at school is also a source of considerable shame. Children who are excluded from various cliques that form will experience the shame of being outcast. Anyone singled out for ridicule, mockery, or teasing becomes subjected to shame. Anyone who is ganged up on or physically beaten will suffer the humiliation of defeat. The shaming by peers that occurs can be prolonged over time and relentless, lasting months or in some cases even years. One young boy was continuously ridiculed for wetting his pants once in third grade, and the ridicule he was subjected to continued for the next three years. Another child who was picked on and beaten up suffered such insults over the course of an entire school year. Because each child, each adolescent, yearns to feel identified with the group, to belong, the peer group has great power to inflict shame.

And the shaming power of peers matches that of teachers in school, just as it matches that of parents in the family setting.

SHAME IN THE WORK SETTING

When we turn to consider the work setting, another key instrument of culture, the dynamic which comes immediately into view is power vs. powerlessness. There is an inverse relation between shame and power: to the degree that one is powerless in any work environment, one is most vulnerable to shame. Powerlessness breeds shame, as we saw in connection to aging. This principle holds for many different interpersonal settings as well as developmental epochs. People need to feel consulted at work, to feel they have an impact. When this occurs, the individuals involved will experience a measure of power. Power vs. powerlessness is one critical feature of the work setting, and a second feature concerns each individual's need for identification, a sense of belonging. When employers and supervisors arrange the work climate to encourage positive identification, then the organization and its aims become prized along with those of the individual. But in the absence of identification, shame in the form of alienation will magnify. We will feel disconnected from the very establishment in which we work and from the people with whom we work. A third critical feature of any work setting concerns each person's need for affirmation. Each of us needs to feel recognized and admired; we need to feel valued and respected. To the degree that this need is not provided for at work, shame will inevitably ensue, and we will feel like outcasts, devalued, where we most need to belong and to be admired.

The needs for power, identification, and affirmation are the ones most critically involved in the work environment from an interpersonal standpoint. Certainly, competence, achievement, and performance play an enormously important role. But as a society we have generally paid more attention to accomplishment than to power, belonging, and recognition. Most work settings operate on the principle that if employees do not hear anything about their performance, then they should conclude that they are doing fine. The work setting constitutes a new family, if you will, a work family. This is a group of individuals who live together during a major portion of each day, and return daily to combine their efforts toward a common set of objectives. Coworkers form a distinctive social group, just as the family of origin and family of procreation also are unique social groups.

In every social group, scenes of shame are reenacted. Two shame-based individuals who marry, procreate, and thereby create a new family will inevitably reenact their individual shame scenes in that newly constituted, recombined social group. In a similar way, individuals who join an organization also enter and cocreate a parallel social group in which each employee's own scenes of shame become reactivated and reenacted. These occurrences may involve analogs of old shame scenes, newly synthesized and imported into this new setting. Or they may involve entirely new, previously unencountered shame scenes that are generated at the hands of people with power.

Various scripts observed on the individual and family levels can also be observed in the work environment. In particular, blame-transfer scripts operate in order to point the finger somewhere, to accuse someone, so that the accuser might be deemed free of the contamination of shame. Blaming someone else when things go wrong is a dominant script in the work setting. Just as potent is comparison making. Remember when you first began looking at a classmate's grades in school and compared yourself, either favorably or not? We are all inevitably socialized in this culture, perhaps in all cultures, to translate differences into comparisons and to experience ourselves as lesser precisely for the comparison. It is essentially no different for adults, however mature or successful, in the work setting. Raises and promotions, to consider two examples, become occasions for often agonizing comparison making. The self-shaming that can result generates self-torture. Finally, contempt scripts operate to partition the inferior within any social group from the superior. Certain individuals or a particular class of individuals are now looked down upon, found inferior, considered beneath contempt. These dominant scripts play out on two levels: directed primarily toward others or directed inward against the self.

Morale becomes deeply affected through the general failure of work settings to provide for certain of our fundamental needs, through the inevitable reenactment of shame scenes directly in those settings, and through the operation of shaming scripts. Discouragement can be pervasive at work. Powerlessness fuels the intensification of shame, whether in the form of alienation or discouragement. When devaluing is added to these, if only in impact, then the work setting or organization becomes shame-based, paralleling the family.

DIFFERENTIAL GENDER SHAMING PATTERNS AND THE EMERGENCE OF GENDER IDEOLOGIES

Central to the process of gender socialization within any culture is the affect of shame. Gender identity is profoundly shaped by this elusive emotion. As already noted, experiences of shame become internalized in the form of scenes which, in turn, generate rules for interpretation, response, and control. These developing scripts effectively govern action and imagination. There is a distinct progression from cultural and gender shaming to the development of gender scripts and ideologies. Identity, culture, and ideology are rooted in affect in general and shame in particular.

From this perspective, the role of shame is crucial in the partitioning of affects/drives/needs/purposes deemed acceptable versus those deemed unacceptable. Let us briefly review this process. The positive affects are: Interest—Excitement, Enjoyment—Joy, and Surprise—Startle. The negative affects are: Distress—Anguish, Fear—Terror, Anger—Rage, Shame—Humiliation, Dissmell, and Disgust. The drives most important to examine in terms of gender socialization are the sexual and hunger drives. I have furthermore distinguished the following interpersonal needs: need for relationship, need for touching/holding, need for identification, need for differentiation, need to nurture, need for affirmation, and need for power—which fundamentally is a need to predict and control and thereby experience inner control. Finally, our purposes are those enduring scenes we first imagine in the future with ever-deepening enjoyment and excitement; then we command into being those scenes in which we cast ourselves as hero. Affects, drives, interpersonal needs, and future purposes are shamed differentially for women as compared to men, thereby producing the *appearance* of quite different psychologies, of different developmental paths.

Consider more closely the socialization of affect. Expressions of *anger* affect and *excitement* affect have been traditionally shamed for women in American culture whereas expressions of *fear* and *distress* (crying) affects, as well as *shame* itself, have received parallel shaming for men in this culture. The specific affects targeted for shaming differ for women and men, but this pattern generally remains stable within a culture throughout a particular historical period. As we look across different cultures, however, the pattern of targeted affects will be observed to vary. In American culture, men are heavily shamed for expressing distress (crying), fear, and shame. Women typically have been especially shamed for expressing the affect of anger. They have been shamed as well for expressing excitement affect, and it is this shaming which is the source of the cultural disparagement of the so-called "tomboy," the girl who openly expresses excitement affect and who typically seeks out excitement-producing activities.

Analogously, the interpersonal needs have been differentially shamed: *power* and *differentiation* needs for women, *touching/ holding*, *identification*, and *affirmation* needs for men. Consider more closely the shaming pattern for women concerning expression of their interpersonal needs. Expression of their need for power has been severely shamed. Women have been shamed into relinquishing their natural and rightful half of the power in relation to others, particularly men. Their natural need to differentiate, to separate from others while placing their own needs first, has also been suppressed through widespread shaming. Related to the striving to separate is the parallel striving to gain mastery, competence. Together, these are twin expressions of the fundamental human need to differentiate, to define oneself as different and unique. Yet for women, to be powerful is shameful. To be different and separate from others is equally shameful.

The shaming pattern for men is different, but no less pronounced. Expression of the natural interpersonal need for touching and holding has largely been denied to men because of its widespread association with shame. For men, the need to touch, even more so the need to be held, has become poignantly bound by shame. Touching is taboo. Similarly, men have been shamed for expressing needs to identify, to merge or fuse with others, especially with other men. This is a universal human need observed from birth among both females and males. One of the earliest identification scenes involves infant and mother, or infant and father, gazing into one another's eyes during feeding—locked in a facial embrace. That is fusion, and it is experienced directly through the eyes. It is the later experience of shame about this important need that ultimately constricts its expression. Finally, men are also shamed for expressing the need for *affirmation*, to be openly valued, recognized, directly admired.

Because of shaming, the only culturally acceptable avenue remaining open to men for expressing these three interpersonal needs is through triumph during adversarial contests. Wars, fights, and sporting contests provide a culturally approved arena in which the open expression of these needs can occur without shame. In the context of adversarial contests, men can touch each other and embrace openly, men can identify with each other and feel *one*, and men can directly admire one another.

The result of such differential shaming on identity is striking: women are left to seek their identity through relatedness and identification whereas men must continually seek their identity through power and differentiation. These are the principal avenues remaining free from shame for each gender. This pattern of differential shaming must be viewed as culture specific because the particular targets of shaming, as we have already seen, will vary across different cultures.

The new conception of women's development offered by Gilligan[5] and others can be viewed from the perspective of affect theory. It is the differential shaming that women receive in comparison to men, along with the resulting partitioning of affects and interpersonal

---

[5] Gilligan, C. *In a Different Voice*. Cambridge, Massachusetts: Harvard University Press, 1982.

needs along gender lines, that produces the apparent differences in their development.

One further consequence of these shaming patterns that we have already considered in depth in Chapter Two is the development of internalized *shame binds*. To summarize briefly, the various affects and needs that are shamed actually become bound by shame; that is, shame is now permanently linked with anger or distress, with identification or differentiation, and so on. The result is that the subsequent activation of shame-bound affects or needs will, in turn, spontaneously activate shame, inhibiting their expression. Just to *experience* these affects or needs itself is shameful. Through the creation of these specific or multiple shame binds, shame exercises a powerful, indirect control over behavior, eventually constricting personality.

To recapitulate, these various shame binds become stored in memory in the form of *scenes* which progressively capture the individual woman or man. Next, particular *scripts* develop in order to avoid or escape from shame scenes. Scripts embody specific rules for predicting, controlling, responding to, and interpreting scenes of shame.

Feminine and Masculine Gender Scripts

What are the consequences of differential gender shaming? In response to the differential patterning of gender socialization, two distinct scripts emerge: a *feminine gender script* and a *masculine gender script*. These scripts partition personality by gender and simultaneously govern the development of gender roles, identity, and interpersonal relations from that point forward. These gender scripts become dominant over other types of scripts and increasingly determine the various scenes that will be sought after, celebrated, or avoided. Gender scripts govern the continuing evolution of gender components of identity by defining the principal pathways along which identity must now develop. Gender scripts also stratify and shape interpersonal relations.

In the feminine gender script, women *should* express the affects of distress, fear, enjoyment, and shame. Women *should* also express the need for relationship, the need for touching/holding, the need to identify, and the need to nurture others. Women *should* therefore search for identity primarily through relationships to other persons, particularly men. Women *should* also be popular and conform.

In its counterpart, the masculine gender script, men *should* express the affects of excitement, anger, dissmell, disgust, and contempt, which is a learned affect blend of dissmell conjoined with anger. Men *should* express the power need and the differentiation need in particular. Men *should* therefore search for identity principally through differentiation and through power. Men *should* also compete, succeed, be independent, be self-sufficient, and men *should* in addition engage in adversarial contests.

These are the predominant scripted roles for women and for men in American culture. They have evolved over the last century within contemporary culture, and only in the last two decades have these dominant and entrenched scripts been shaken loose. The impact of these gender scripts and gender ideologies on interpersonal relations has been enormous.

From Gender Scripts to Gender Ideologies

Ideological scripts define one's general orientation in the universe, in one's society, and in one's relationships to others. They embody values and injunctions by evaluating what is good and what is bad. They also embody sanctions, positive ones for the fulfillment of central values and negative ones for their violation. Ideological scripts are the most important class of scripts "because they endow fact with value and affect."[6] Orientation, evaluation, and sanctions are the defining characteristics of ideological scripts according to Tomkins.

---

[6]Tomkins, S.S. "Script Theory." In J. Aronoff, A.I. Rabin, and R.A. Zucker (Eds.), *The Emergence of Personality*. New York: Springer, 1987, p. 170.

Gender scripts evolve into gender ideologies. Relationships between and among men have typically been oriented toward competition and the pursuit of adversarial contests. The expression of particular affects—anger, excitement, disgust, and contempt—are evaluated positively; therefore their expression is elevated. The negative interpersonal sanctions are shame, dissmell, disgust, and contempt for expressions of identification or touching/holding needs toward other men—except when in the context of adversarial contests. Any other expression of identification or touching between males is equated with being feminine and hence unmanly. Because of this entrenched ideological gender script, the homosexual male is inevitably viewed as an inferior male, or even as a female, and homophobia actually comprises not fear, but disgust and contempt for any such sign of perceived masculine inferiority. The consequences are revulsion, hatred, and lynching-like contempt, either directed outward at others or turned inward against the self.

The gender ideology in relationships between women and men embodies power as control: men exercise power, women do not. A second feature is dominance-submission: men *should* dominate, women *should* be submissive. And a third critical feature of this ideology is nurturance: women *should* nurture men.[7] Because women are scripted to pursue their identity through a relationship with a man, that becomes the defining characteristic of their place in the cosmos. The successful woman has a secure relationship with a man whom she supports and nurtures, while the successful man has attained power and prestige through adversarial contest, now equated with his advancement in a career. Men are equally scripted to find their identity, not through relationships, but through achievement and competence.

In relationships between women, the elevation of the identification need allows for a greater degree of fusion and merging experiences to occur. Women are scripted to identify with one another and are freer to openly express other interpersonal needs as well, particu-

---

[7] Westkoff, M. *The Feminist Legacy of Karen Horney*. New Haven, Connecticut: Yale University Press, 1986.

larly their needs for touching/holding, nurturing, and for being in a relationship itself. Women are also scripted to compete for men since that has been their primary path toward identity. Identification versus competition with other women therefore become conflicting subscripts within the feminine gender ideology that serves to govern the enduring vision of the good life and how to attain it.

Identity, interpersonal relations, even imagination, have been held prisoner by these deeply entrenched gender scripts and ideologies. But imagination has been set free.

Reversing the Stratification of the Affects

Gender scripts and ideologies are indeed undergoing transformation. We are standing on the steps of the next century. Examining the early evolution of civilization from an affect theory perspective will illuminate the transformation now underway. The stratification inherent in society and between the sexes has its origin, according to Tomkins, in the stratification of the affects inherent in adversarial contests. "When the relatively undifferentiated hunter gatherers split into predatory big game hunters and sedentary agriculturalists, differentiation ultimately became increasingly specialized and finally stratified into warrior nomads who subjugated peasant agriculturalists, in the formation of states, empires, and civilizations." [8] The full spectrum of the innate affects became partitioned into two distinct sets: the masculine/warrior affects and the feminine/defeated affects. Men and warriors *should* experience surprise, excitement, anger, dissmell, and disgust, whereas the remaining affects of enjoyment, fear, distress, and shame were assigned to the losers in adversarial contests, to women, to children, and ultimately to the lower classes.

It is this stratification of the affects that the Women's Movement began to reverse. A new ideology was born. Women began to reclaim the affects previously denied them: surprise, excitement, anger,

---

[8] Tomkins, S.S. "Script Theory." In J. Aronoff, A.I. Rabin, and R.A. Zucker (Eds.), *The Emergence of Personality*. New York: Springer, 1987, p. 174.

dissmell, and disgust. Women are now more validated in both their experiencing and expression of the full range of the innate affects. Like men, they *should* become angry, or disgusted, express distancing dissmell, or become contemptuous, or become openly excited either during adversarial contests or during sexual intercourse. Women *should* express their power needs and search for identity equally through differentiation and identification. Either alone produces only a partial identity, an incomplete self.

Unfortunately, there is also a negative side to this transformation in gender scripts. The acceleration of such eating disorders as anorexia and bulimia over the last twenty years signals this cultural shift for women to differentiate, to assert power, and to embrace the once denied affects of anger, dissmell, and disgust. That rapid acceleration of eating disorders began at a point paralleling the emergence of the Women's Movement, even though the existence of various eating disorders certainly predates it. Bulimia becomes organized around the affects of shame and disgust, just as anorexia becomes organized around the affects of shame and dissmell. Bulimics repeatedly devour and then spit out the shameful food via disgust, while anorexics distance themselves via dissmell from the food that now must be controlled and thereby kept at a safe distance. For anorexics, food has become almost like rotten eggs, toxic. Bulimics are driven to perpetually devour and spit out, as though reenacting through food the wider cultural conflict between identification and differentiation which the Women's Movement has magnified. Anorexics, in contrast, not only keep food safely controlled via distancing dissmell, but also suffer from excitement and enjoyment affects permanently yoked by shame.[9] Their zest for life, as for life-giving food, is so completely bound by shame that it is utterly silenced, leaving them the shameful prisoners of the food they must forever keep at a distance.

The affects of anger, disgust and dissmell, which were previously assigned to men, have become increasingly available to women since the dawn of the Women's Movement. These affects also fuel

---

[9] Palombi, B. Personal Communication, 1990.

differentiation. For women, the need to differentiate was once shamed into suppression, but the renewed cultural pressure for self-definition has thrown into turmoil and struggle what had previously remained in silence and shadow. Conflict is inherent between the old and the new ideologies, between the warrior/slave script that once defined clearly and forever the place of both women and men in the cosmos and in the culture in which they lived, and the new egalitarian script that has replaced it. This conflict itself is given expression in the acceleration of such psychological syndromes as bulimia and anorexia, just as conflicting cultural and gender scripts have always found expression in psychological form.

If women have been reclaiming the lost affects and interpersonal needs long denied them, men have been doing the same. The Women's Movement has generated a new script for men, a new ideology to place them differently in the universe. Now men *should* express distress, fear, enjoyment, and shame. Men are allowed, actually encouraged, to cry, to become vulnerable, to expose their shame. Men *should* also express openly their needs for affirmation, for touching/holding, and for identification with other men *without* the necessity of adversarial contests. Herein lies the impetus for the current flourishing of the Men's Movement. For men, as for women, power becomes equal power, power that is shared equally in a relationship that itself evolves between respected equals.

The Ideology of Wholeness and Integration

Reversing the stratification of the affects has been one of the principal outcomes of the Women's Movement, providing fuel for the development of a new vision of integrated identity. Imagination has been freed from older scripts and the psychological and social consequences will be profound. Each gender is reclaiming and redeeming what had been previously disallowed. Each gender is now moving toward a more complete expression of the full range of affects and interpersonal needs. The dissolution of affect-shame binds and need-shame binds, which have been patterned differentially for women and men, is crucial to the full realization of what it means to be human. Dissolving the binding effects of shame, along with actively embracing and openly validating all affects, and all needs, is essential to the attainment of wholeness, to the full integration of the self.

Integration and wholeness ultimately lie in reversing the centuries-old stratification of the affects and interpersonal needs. To become a complete self is to have conscious access to all affects and all needs. To be integrated as a self also means to be in relationship with others significant to us. Human beings aspire to be both social and solitary, as Jacob Bronowski once observed,[10] to identify as well as differentiate, to merge and fuse with others but also to separate from others and in so doing define themselves as distinctly different, unique. In this vision is a new ideology, a new synthesis, that must inspire a more hopeful future for humankind, and carry us into the next century with the excitement of self-discovery and self-realization, with the mutual enjoyment of communality.

SHAME AND GAY IDENTITY: TOWARD A GENERAL THEORY OF IDENTITY DEVELOPMENT FOR MINORITIES

The development of identity is rooted in both positive and negative *identifications*. The need to identify is the need for rootedness, connectedness, and belonging. It is a need to feel identified with, to belong to, particular individuals or groups. Individuals identify in order to emulate those they admire, to feel *at-oneness* or belonging, and to enhance their own sense of inner power. Experiences of identification enable the self, providing strength and healing. The need to belong to something larger than oneself is one principal source of identity, and shame is another because this affect is at the root of all negative self-images.

For any minority, internalized negative cultural images must first be consciously confronted and then assimilated in the search for a secure, positive identity. By examining the process of identity development for lesbians and gay men, we will then be able to

---

[10] Bronowski, J. *The Ascent of Man*. Boston: Little, Brown, 1973.

articulate a general theory that ought to hold true for any minority group. Among minorities in general, the striving for identification is a need to feel a sense of pride in self precisely *because* of belonging to one's group. For gays it is a need to create a positive, self-affirming identity specifically as a gay man or lesbian.

Identity Development in the Context of Conflicting Identifications

The development of identity—whether personal, religious, racial, ethnic, gender, or sexual—is rooted in both positive and negative *identifications*. Individuals develop within changing social milieus, a family, peer group, an ethnic or religious community, and a wider culture. The need to identify presses for expression within each of these interpersonal settings. It is through feeling identified first with parents and peers; next with a particular ethnic, racial, or religious group; then with one's own gender; and finally with the wider culture, that one ultimately experiences rootedness. Only through positive identification with others can a sense of belonging grow. For any specific minority group—ethnic, racial, or sexual—negative cultural images inevitably will be confronted. Because these negative images also become internalized, they must eventually be assimilated in the search for a coherent minority identity.

The process is analogous irrespective of whether the focus is ethnic, religious, racial, or sexual identity. Despite differences, the process of identity development is universal in fundamental respects. An African American man or woman struggling to reach a positive identification with other African Americans as a racial group will experience a process that is analogous to a gay man or lesbian grappling with identification with other gays or lesbians within a predominantly non-gay and homophobic culture. Each has in varying ways felt like a stranger, and each is journeying from being an outsider to belonging somewhere.

The striving to experience positive identification with other gays means creating a self-affirming identity as a gay man or as a lesbian. It means experiencing a sense of pride in self precisely *because* of belonging to that group. To illustrate the complexity involved, consider the dilemma for a young man who is both a Catholic and a homosexual yet refuses to sacrifice either identification; of necessity each identification conflicts with the other. His search for a coherent identity dissolves into a struggle to resolve contradictions that appear to be irresolvable. Internalized negative cultural images about being gay will have to be confronted directly, neutralized, and assimilated in the quest for a coherent self, a positive identification with that group, an equally positive self-image, and a secure identity.

Belonging to any minority group—whether African Americans, Jews, or gays—within a dominant culture creates an inherent conflict of identification. Lesbians and gays inevitably experience conflicting identifications—on the one hand, pressures to embrace their particular group, on the other, pressures to assimilate in the wider culture. For individuals living in contemporary American society, this conflict is further fueled by the three cultural scripts discussed in Chapter One which become additional sources of shame: compete for success, be independent and self-sufficient, be popular and conform. The awareness of being gay or lesbian inevitably translates into being different, and therefore potentially inferior, in a culture that prizes social conformity. Insofar as an individual's gay or lesbian identification is predominantly positive, one solution to the inner conflict is to react with contempt toward the dominant culture, rejecting assimilation. However, insofar as one's lesbian or gay identification is predominantly negative, assimilation into the dominant culture is aided by contempt for one's own minority group. Rejecting group identification is the consequence of that particular solution. One cannot simultaneously belong to the minority group and the wider culture without conflict.

Contempt: A Strategy of the Powerless

Historically, gay men and lesbians have been persecuted, but they also have been discriminated against or disenfranchised in subtler ways in contemporary society. Becoming publicly known as gay has always put one at risk if not in direct jeopardy. Powerlessness, as we have repeatedly observed in other contexts, is invariably a seedbed for shame. Whenever people are relegated to an inferior status within a wider culture, they begin to doubt themselves and question the worth of the group to which they belong. Whenever people are rejected because of belonging to a particular group, shame becomes radically magnified into inferiority. Whenever homosexuals are persecuted, humiliation is imposed with a reign of terror.

In such a context, contempt becomes a strategy of the powerless. A persecuted or disenfranchised minority can insulate itself against humiliation by responding with contempt toward the dominant cultural group. However, when the barriers to assimilation are gradually removed, the pressure to assimilate and identify with the dominant culture intensifies, and contempt turns against one's own group, even against one's own self.

Scenes of Shame

For lesbians and gays, negative identity is invariably rooted in scenes of shame. In a culture that neither recognizes nor values individual differences, the awareness of difference between self and other inevitably translates into an invidious comparison. The awareness of being gay in a predominantly nongay society calls attention to the self, exposing it to view. To be different in a culture which prizes social conformity and popularity is to be marked as lesser, stigmatized. For that reason, minorities in general, and gays in particular, frequently experience themselves as lesser in comparison to members of the majority culture. Inferiority is always rooted in shame.

Lesbians and gays are likely to compare themselves to others and feel deficient for the comparison. They are made poignantly aware of being different from others in various critical scenes around which shame accrues. In every case there will be a lasting impression of one's essential differentness from others, a difference that translates immediately into deficiency, into shame.

To illustrate the nature of the operation of such scenes, consider first the experience of Jews, African Americans, Native Americans, and also women in general living in contemporary American culture.

For Jewish children, three critical scenes involving the early awareness of being different, being an outsider, are: absence from school due to Jewish holidays, attending synagogue, and Christmas programs in school or the media. Knowledge of the Holocaust must produce for a Jewish child what knowledge of slavery does for an African American child, and what knowledge of the Indian Wars accomplishes for a Native American child: caution against identification with such a repudiated people. Other critical shame scenes for African Americans include ones less remote than slavery: having to sit at the rear of buses, attending separate schools, living in separate neighborhoods. Scenes involving segregation were commonplace in the United States only thirty years ago. They were *then*, and still remain, poignant scenes of humiliation, lasting reminders for any African American. Finally, for women generally, rape is a governing scene which magnifies their powerlessness and consequent humiliation, the violence that women have suffered at the hands of men. The scene of rape is both immediate and historical, for women have always been vulnerable to rape. It is that scene which fuels the rage some women now express—at least in American culture—toward men and also toward the dominant male culture at large. Scenes form around past events that become retold in the present, just as they crystallize around interpersonal events experienced more immediately.

Gay men and lesbians experience countless scenes of derision, ridicule, and often vicious contempt; these shame scenes occur prior to, during, and after adolescence. Peers generally have been merciless in persecuting anyone suspected of being gay or lesbian, and scenes of disparagement are universal for homosexuals. Youngsters learn early on, certainly by third grade, to avoid doing anything that will earn them the slur "faggot." Even when they do not understand the meaning of that particular aspersion, they know to avoid it. That word is wielded as a weapon to humiliate others. Being seen by one's peers as gay or lesbian, whether accurate or not, is equivalent to public disparagement. To be gay is to be unfit to belong—the equivalent of a leper to be shunned publicly. Gays are judged to be contaminated, and therefore must be permanently distanced. To be gay is to be an outcast. And the phenomenon of gay bashing that recently has become even further magnified in response to the AIDS crisis is not unlike lynching for African Americans and pogroms for Jews living in Eastern Europe. These are all magnified expressions of contempt for the outcast.

Identity Scripts: Comparison Making, Self-Blame, and Self-Contempt

When isolated shame experiences become further magnified and fused via imagery and language, discrete shame events become linked together, reinterpreted as signifying essential meanings about the self. Identity itself is a relational pattern within the self that originates in interpersonal scenes within the family, peer group, and school setting, along with the wider culture. Interpersonally based scenes of shame first become internalized and subsequently reproduced.

Attitudes of the wider culture become internalized through the various scenes of shame that are encountered initially in interpersonal settings. These scenes later generate scripts which then fundamentally shape gay or lesbian identity. First, avoidance and escape scripts develop in order to protect the individual from further encounters with shame at the hands of others. But those defending scripts, which initially are directed outward, now turn inward and invade the self, creating analogs. These negative identity scripts now reactivate those original scenes of shame, and they also reproduce them. By reproducing shame, these scripts become the source of the pervasive self-hatred attached to being gay or lesbian.

The predominant identity scripts which reproduce shame for lesbians and gay men are self-blame, self-contempt, and comparison making. Each script becomes activated by, and directly targeted to, being gay or lesbian, and each of these negative identity scripts originates in governing scenes of shame. These scripts furthermore produce a shame-based identity.

A *comparison-making* script evolves directly from the awareness of difference between self and other which inevitably translates into an invidious comparison. A gay man may look at heterosexual men, become immediately aware of the obvious or perceived *difference* between them, and then translate that difference into a comparison. When such comparisons are invidious ones, the individual will feel lesser, deficient, precisely because he is gay. In an analogous manner, a *self-blame* script reproduces shame by fixing blame directly on the self for perceived failings or defects. A self-blame script recruits the affect of anger but directs it in a self-accusatory manner: the self accuses the self. Invariably the target of self-blame is the inescapable awareness of being gay, and the self repetitively blames the self for being deficient in that regard. The self now angrily accuses the self, in effect blames the self, for being gay or lesbian. Such a script is intropunitive in the extreme. *Self-contempt* is a third prominent script for reproducing shame among gays and lesbians. Contempt is both a punitive and distancing affect blend; it aims to permanently distance and eradicate whatever is perceived as offensive. When contempt is turned directly against the self, the equivalent of psychic surgery results as Tomkins views it; the self becomes fractured and one part of the self brutally torments another part of the self. The judging self actively, mercilessly persecutes the offending self. Being gay is now something to be abhorred, repudiated, disavowed—in effect, permanently distanced from the "purer" self.

These negative identity scripts reactivate governing scenes of shame and thereby continuously reproduce shame. In so doing, these scripts become the source of internalized homophobia.

Homophobia

On closer inspection, then, homophobia is the direct result of conjoined shame, disgust, and lynching-like contempt (anger plus dissmell)—whether expressed by the dominant culture or its representatives toward homosexuals or by gays and lesbians toward one another or themselves. In the latter instance, homophobia itself has become internalized and is experienced directly from the self against the self. It is principally in the dynamics of contempt that the source of homophobia is found. Homophobia is the product of shame, disgust, and contempt. The aversion for things homosexual, however expressed, is fueled not by fear, but by shame and disgust which are further magnified by contempt.

Resolving Conflicting Identifications

To illustrate the process of resolving conflicting identifications, consider the phenomenon termed "coming out"; for homosexuals it is a declaration of positive identification with their minority group. The conflict has not been resolved permanently, but the weight of the struggle has definitely shifted. As a metaphor, coming out signifies moving out of hiding into openness; it is fundamentally a coming out of shame. The process of coming out necessarily involves the resolution of shame about homosexuality. Coming out is a process of self-definition, a process of identity co-creation; the self partly detects and partly creates its own identity. But coming out also signifies something else: taking back the power over information. By openly declaring one's own sexual orientation, one no longer lives in dread of exposure, of shame, but is instead now directly in control of disseminating that knowledge.

Toward a Theory of Minority Identity Development

Answers to the questions "Who am I?" and "Where do I belong?" are predominantly shaped by experiences of identification and shame. By examining the process of identity development as it occurs specifically for lesbians and gay men, we can furthermore begin to articulate a more general theory of identity development that will hold across minority groups. Certainly, differences will be found. Nevertheless, there are general dimensions of the process of identity development, and these transcend the differences observed across particular groups.

THE PATTERNING OF SHAME BY CULTURE

Culture influences personality development through the operation of cultural scripts, which are the equivalent of cultural rules for the governance of various types of affect-laden scenes. One particular set of cultural scripts develops in response to shame scenes. These scripts function to control the experience of shame at the wider cultural level. While different cultures will certainly organize shame differently—with different cultural sources and targets as well as vastly different rules governing the return to honor—shame is nevertheless a dynamic observed in all cultures. Previous attempts to classify cultures as either guilt or shame cultures are, from an affect theory perspective, obsolete and misguided.

Three prominent cultural scripts in contemporary American culture, previously discussed in Chapter One, are *to compete for success*, *to be independent and self-sufficient*, and *to be popular and conform*. These three scripts function to prescribe certain behaviors deemed culturally acceptable and to proscribe others that are negatively sanctioned. To recapitulate the earlier discussion, in response to the success script, failure is inherently shameful; failing at anything becomes a source of shame. In response to the independence and self-sufficiency script, needing is shameful. To need assistance, help or directions is a sign of the self's inherent deficiency, and emotional needing is all the more potent a source of shame. Finally, in response to the popularity and conformity script, being either different or alone is shameful. To be seen as different from others marks one as lesser, and to be less social than others is equally a mark of shame.

These three cultural scripts influence the development of personality in contemporary American culture by utilizing the affect of shame to negatively sanction undesirable behavior. These scripts are cultural rules for action, decision, and interpretation within particular life contexts. They shape the contours of identity within a culture by placing a distinctive cultural stamp upon personality, one that is also differential by gender, as we have seen.

But different scripts will dominate in different cultures and thereby place a different cultural stamp upon their people. Even within a particular culture, there are markedly different subcultural groups. Within American culture, for example, we have African Americans, Native Americans, Chicanos and Hispanics, and Asian-Pacific Islanders, and each group organizes shame somewhat differently. Native American children are typically socialized to keep their head down and not look too directly into the face of strangers, as a sign of respect. Contrast this for a moment with French culture, where looking into the eyes of strangers is culturally permitted to a greater extent even than is true of American culture in general. Looking into the eyes of another, particularly a stranger, is deemed disrespectful in Native American culture. But the head down posture *is* a shame posture. Even the head bowed before royalty or deity is a shame posture; we pay homage through shame. A Chicano man once told me that as a young boy, the dinner table became a daily shame scene; someone was invariably singled out by father for derision and humiliation. The entire family was encouraged to participate in this public shaming of the designated child. This, he believed, was a typical occurrence among Chicano families. Among Eskimos, to consider a third example, young children are taught to discriminate thin ice from solid ice by public shaming by the entire family whenever their foot slips through thin ice into water.[11] An obvious survival skill in this way becomes indelibly learned.

As a final example, let us consider shame within a particular geographic region, the South. Among the Southern States in the United States, what was once a shame-honor culture remains so. The humiliation handed the South by the North during and after the Civil War has been neither entirely redeemed nor forgiven. The return to dignity, honor, and pride is a long and lonely journey, for individuals and for nations. Yet for many, repairing shame is never fully completed. For them, shame lives on if only in memory.

---

[11] English, F. "Shame and Social Control." *Transactional Analysis Journal, 5,* 1975, 24-28.

When we look beyond our own culture, we can also readily observe the dynamics of shame. Both Mediterranean and Eastern cultures are shame-honor cultures, though what becomes shameful in one culture need not be deemed necessarily shameful in the other. In these particular cultures, shame is quite visible; it is neither hidden nor disguised. These cultures are organized more *openly* around shame in comparison to contemporary American culture. To bring shame upon oneself in traditional Chinese and Japanese cultures, for example, inevitably means bringing shame, and therefore dishonor, upon one's family and ancestors.

The strong identification with the group that is fostered in these cultures tightly links the individual's shame with the family's shame. And in these cultures, identification with the group predominates over differentiation—individuation and separateness.

In these, as in many other shame-honor cultures, there are prescribed rules for either purging shame, avenging dishonor, or restoring honor. In traditional Japanese culture, for example, *hara-kiri* or ritual suicide was the culturally prescribed route for returning to honor from shame. Such an extreme remedy can also be observed in other cultures. I was recently informed by a Korean physician that traditionally the greatest source of shame, and hence dishonor, for Korean women was becoming pregnant out of wedlock (even as a result of rape) and the only culturally acceptable remedy was suicide. Traditionally, the greatest source of shame for Korean men, in contrast, was failing to provide for one's family. Here is an example of how a culture differentially patterns the sources of shame by gender.

Cultures can be examined in order to identify their characteristic sources of shame, particular targets of shame, and the various culturally patterned remedies for shame. In addition, the degree to which any given culture fosters the identification of the individual with the group, in contrast to differentiation from the group, will significantly influence the patterning of shame, even the experience of shame. Such an analysis can proceed by identifying for each culture the predominant scripts that become organized around shame. Those cultural scripts dominating a given culture, in turn, produce its *national character*. Modal personality characteristics will vary widely in response to these cultural scripts. These scripts also determine any culture's patterning of interpersonal relations specific to its targets of shame. Just as misunderstandings arise between individuals and even families in response to shame, certain misunderstandings between nations will likely occur partly because of failures in sensitivity to each culture's unique sources of shame and to its equally unique, culturally patterned scripts governing shame.

The particular affects that are deemed appropriate for expression, such as anger, distress, and joy, also reflect culture-specific patterns. The rules governing the expression and public display of affect—scripts—vary widely across cultures. In Mediterranean cultures, for example, distress affect is publicly displayed in response to the death of a loved one; even the specific *cry* of distress affect largely remains uncensored. Contrast this for a moment with American culture where the "stiff upper lip," the anti-distress response, is the governing rule for mourning, certainly in public and often in private as well, because distress affect has been systematically and uniformly shamed. As one illustration of the operation of this particular cultural script, recall President Kennedy's assassination in 1963; news commentators repeatedly remarked with approval how "strong" Jacqueline Kennedy was because she did not cry.

Another example of differential shaming across cultures concerns the behavior of individuals when eating in public. As a culture, for example, the French have no shame about eating food, and no shame about eating in public. They can eat and be seen eating without shame; perhaps this accounts for the many street cafes. Strangers passing by typically look directly at people who are eating, and they also look directly at the plates of food before them. The passersby display no shame at looking, and the people who are eating display no shame at being seen. On one occasion I was dining in a restaurant in Paris; the family at the adjacent table sighed with enjoyment as each new course was brought to *my* table. Contrast this with the cultural rules governing public eating in American culture, where eating is considered private, not to be intruded upon by strangers. Many people experience acute shame in this culture when eating in public or when seen eating. To verify this observation, simply violate the cultural rule and look directly at the food on the plate of someone as you pass by their table. This will immediately activate shame.

The primary interpersonal needs will vary widely in expression from one culture to another. Touching will be considered quite acceptable in certain cultures, even between members of the same gender, while in others it will be negatively sanctioned, even abhorred. The needs for identification and differentiation also become differentially magnified across cultures. In the West, for example, it is the need to differentiate, both to separate from others and also acquire mastery, that has marked Western culture so distinctively. In the East, in contrast, it is the need to identify—to merge with others, with the group, and in so doing, belong—that instead has dominated that culture for centuries. Differentiation is fueled by the affects of excitement and disgust whereas identification is amplified by enjoyment affect. The differential magnification of affects and interpersonal needs, as these were defined earlier, is a principal determinant of cultural development.

The socialization of affect scenes, drive scenes, interpersonal need scenes, and purpose scenes will determine their differential magnification for individuals living within a given culture, just as their socialization within a particular family is a prime determinant for any individual family member. The socialization of individuals within any culture, then, will vary around the modal pattern observed for that culture. Socialization variants will be further influenced by minority group status within a particular culture. The socialization pattern and consequent shaming patterns, observed for Native Americans or African Americans living in contemporary American culture, would therefore be expected to vary from the modal pattern observed for the culture at large.

THE MULTILAYERED NATURE OF SHAME

The significance of shame extends well beyond its role in the process of individual development, or even in the family as a functioning system. Narrowing the field of observation only to those particular domains unnecessarily limits the potential application of affect theory and shame theory. These perspectives have wide utility. The multilayered nature of shame reflects an essential layering of various domains of experience, each of which must be viewed in relation to the others. The school and work settings, along with gender, sexual orientation, and culture are examples of particular domains. Each represents a rearrangement of the phenomenal field, a reordering of experience. Aging and disability likewise represent different ways of ordering experience over the life cycle, and they permit observations that other domains do not. This way of ordering domains and viewing them as embedded within one another allows for the examination of various dynamic processes that intersect those domains. Among the more important of those processes is shame.

8
Affect and Ideology Among Nations

The foregoing examination of shame in relation to gender, culture, and minorities brings us to include the global community in that study. The relationship which exists between nations is governed by affect, and by each nation's various scripted responses to affect. All of the affects will undoubtedly play a role to varying degrees in the complex dynamic termed international relations. But if we consider international relations more closely, we will discern the particular affects already found to be central in the domains involving individual development and interpersonal relations. Rather than attempt an exhaustive treatment of all affects involved, we will instead focus on shame. And we will also examine the interrelation between affect and ideology that was previously noted in the last chapter when we considered gender.

THE ROLE OF SHAME IN INTERNATIONAL RELATIONS

National shame is analogous to family shame and to individual shame. The defeat of Germany at the end of World War One is one example of national shame; Germany was not only defeated in war, it was humiliated as a nation. Certain features of the Versailles Treaty, such as the war guilt clause imposed on Germany, further magnified the shame of defeat. And that climate of national shame set the stage for identification with a hero, Adolf Hitler, as this particular nation's way out of shame. Humiliation intensifies the need for identification, the need for merging or fusion with another, for belonging to something larger than oneself. Identification can lift one out of despair. Hitler captured the imagination of the German people, magnifying their excitement and joy over their shame and distress. Much as spectator sports in contemporary society provide a team to identify with, a winning team to belong to, a victorious group to feel a part of, Hitler was the heroic vision of pride and honor regained, of triumphant feeling restored. But that pride was not true pride, enjoyment invested in self; it was arrogant *contempt* for all others. Contempt made Germans the master race, inherently superior. The blend of distancing dissmell and punitive anger that produces lynching-like contempt, furthermore, resulted in the repudiation of other peoples, the literal stamping out of the impure, the rejection of the contaminated, including Jews, Gypsies, Slavs, Communists, and homosexuals. Contempt reinforced excitement to vanquish national shame. Identification with a hero, amplified by enjoyment affect and excitement affect, became the new dream, the national purpose, the manifest destiny of the German people, the now revealed Master Race.

What Hitler was able to accomplish in Germany can be seen, in somewhat different measure, on the football field or basketball court of any major university. Here, triumph and defeat play out for all to witness and revel in. The spectator is not merely passive, but actually a participant enacting in imagination what the team enacts on the field or court; one has only to observe other spectators at any sporting contest to demonstrate the point. The German citizen listening to Hitler was seized by affect, as is the spectator at a sporting event. The spectator in either setting, Germany in 1936 or a contemporary sporting event, feels a part of something larger, merged with the group, identified with another—a hero, people, cause, or even an idea. The electrifying excitement of triumph or the demoralizing humiliation of defeat are as visible today as they were in Germany. And the events culminating in World War Two were in large part the legacy of the new cultural script, transformed from even older ones, that Hitler rewrote for the German people as a way out of shame.

To consider a second example, the defeat of Japan at the end of World War Two was accompanied by a considerable national humiliation. Given that defeat, we might expect an equally strident, though altogether different, strategy to overcome their national shame. Perhaps theirs has been to achieve an economic reversal. The aggressive assault by the Japanese on the United States' economy might be construed as their unique response to shame: defeat the victor economically; become like the victor, only better. And the difficulty of economic access to Japanese markets is almost a confrontation with contempt: Japanese markets exclude and distance goods deemed inferior.

In more recent years, the Falkland Islands War was a direct response to the humiliation handed Great Britain. In response to Argentina's invasion of the Falkland Islands, newspaper headlines around the world resounded with the challenge, "Argentina *Humiliates* Great Britain." The effect was immediate; Great Britain launched an armada and went to war with Argentina to avenge its national honor. While it is certainly not the only cause of war, shame does play a central role in fueling the recurring cycle of war.

Terrorism is a disturbing contemporary phenomenon that is essentially a strategy of the powerless. Groups who have felt decidedly powerless and humiliated for decades now have reversed roles and *recast* the original scene in Tomkins' sense. The tormented now become the tormentors. The phenomenon of terrorism is, psychologically, analogous to physical abuse syndromes in which adults who were themselves beaten as children now reenact their original childhood scenes of abuse, but with one important difference: they recast the scene and reverse roles, becoming the active abuser to others instead of remaining the passive, abused victim. Likewise, groups who have felt victimized in the past now victimize others. Terrorists are reenacting a governing scene in which all of their actions are entirely scripted. They also depend on the spectators watching via television as well as other principals to play their own scripted parts. Television magnifies the affects of terror, rage, and shame for everyone involved. But the medium accomplishes something else as well: it transports us directly into the scene, thereby making distant events immediate and personal.

Each new terrorist incident adds to the growing family of scenes, which become further magnified; the parts of the principal players become additionally scripted as well. In response to terrorist incidents, we are all rendered powerless and experience conjoined terror, humiliation, and rage in response. Might the invasion of Grenada by the United States have been fueled, partly, by the powerlessness and humiliation experienced when a U. S. Marine barracks was destroyed in Beirut just before that event? Certainly the attack on Libya by the United States was a distinct response to terrorism, and to the powerlessness, terror, and humiliation it generates.

Violence is always stimulated by powerlessness and by humiliation; that is true in the family and it is also true on the playground. Apparently it is equally true among nations. The only viable solution is to rewrite the script, to create a new scene.

Invariably the dynamics of diplomacy on the international stage are the dynamics of shame and honor. We have only to recall the events of the recent Iran-Contra Scandal as witness; those events embroiled various individuals in different nations in efforts to salvage dignity, to reclaim honor. Diplomacy between nations always hangs on shame; in every instance diplomacy depends on avoiding loss of face by any nation. Shame is ubiquitous. By illuminating its multilayered role, we can draw implications for a psychology of international relations, for a more general psychology of groups, peoples, even nations. Science, after all, is an ever-expanding enterprise. We must become a truly scientific civilization, not remain merely a technological one, if we are to survive on this planet.

IDEOLOGY, AFFECT, AND WAR

As I conclude this chapter, the Gulf War is moving into its fifth week, compelling some discussion of the impact of war on affect and ideology. The Vietnam War provides us with a clear example of the impact of shame, both for this nation and for the veterans who served in that war. The Vietnam era was marked by great national debate and controversy over the wisdom of deploying United States' troops in a distant country gripped by an internal civil war. The national purpose, so stated, was to stop the advance of "Godless Communism." Such was one ideological position on the issue. But debate gave rise to an ideological dispute that divided this nation and eventually turned its citizens against its returning soldiers. Ideologies further magnify the affects embedded in their organization; of particular note are the affects of shame, dissmell, disgust, and contempt. To further illustrate the operation of ideologies, remember how Galileo was burned at the stake *just a few centuries ago* for espousing an idea that both challenged and violated the cherished and dominant ideology of his day. That is an example of responding with *contempt* to someone whose ideas differ from our own—an affect blend that both punishes and permanently distances, actively repudiating the offending other.

The ideological dispute concerning continued United States presence in Vietnam divided this nation. Eventually, the issue was settled, but only in regard to its outward form. Withdrawal of troops from Vietnam did nothing to heal the nation's inner strife and shame. The fact that more than a decade passed in silence about the war only attests to our national shame. The natural response to shame is hiding, and hiding breeds silence which further deepens shame. Not only did this nation give up its fight and withdraw its troops—and, in doing so collide with the prized claim of never having lost a war— but the response to its returning veterans was a mixture of shame and contempt.

Indeed the veterans themselves experienced a profound sense of shame and humiliation upon their return. They were not welcomed home like heroes. Instead, they felt like outcasts in their own land, repudiated. We can only imagine what the impact must have been.

If we have not ourselves directly risked our lives in combat, then we can only approximate it. We can enter the experience by imagining ourselves bombarded in a fire fight: bullets, shells, bombs, and rockets making a deafening roar; confusion, chaos, and death all around. The density of stimulation reaches a crescendo that does not abate, unleashing unlimited affect—terror, rage, anguish. Then there is the struggle to contain affect, to remain in control, and the sudden eruption of affect that overwhelms control; the shame over losing control; shame at being afraid, at succumbing to fear, or over actual cowardice in the face of the enemy; and shame because of one's own real transgressions in battle, violations of one's internalized moral code, committed under the grip of intense affect that clouds judg-ment; the desperate running to escape, or suddenly being gripped by rage and madly fighting on; the sense of powerlessness and being trapped that only fuels the endless cycle of affect. Becoming unex-pectedly frozen in the paralysis of conjoined fear and shame is like being trapped in a nightmare that has no end.

These are the conditions of unlimited magnification of affect. To risk one's life and then return from battle, grateful though shaken and ambivalent about returning when so many died and did not return, and then *not* to be welcomed, but instead to be greeted with contempt and a nation's silence—this is humiliation beyond endurance.

The experience of unrelenting terror conjoined with humiliation is potentially psychotic-making for human beings, as Tomkins notes.[1] Scenes of terror and shame, terror and rage, or terror and endless crying in distress become seared in memory. It is these scenes of unending and unrelenting affect that now replay themselves in nightmares, in night terrors, and in waking fantasy, as if they were actually happening all over again. So-called *post-traumatic stress disorder* is organized precisely around these recurring scenes of overwhelming negative affect that have not been assimilated, but instead continue to seize the individual. These past scenes intrude themselves forcefully; they are continually reactivated and then become imported directly into present day consciousness, with the raw affect reexperienced fully, utterly unnerving us. We enter the scene and become lost in it.

I want to digress now and discuss a clinical case that bears on the present discussion of scene intrusion. I recently treated a woman in psychotherapy who as a child was sexually molested repeatedly by her father, beginning at about age three. Her father would enter her bedroom each night and slip into bed with her, forcing her to submit to sexual acts. She felt deeply humiliated and to blame. Physically violating the body invariably generates profound shame; and in response to shame one naturally feels to blame. Shame is thus inherently self-validating. If she tried to get away, he would pull her back harshly by her hair. If she tried to cry out, he quickly covered

[1]Tomkins, S.S. *Affect, Imagery, Consciousness, Vol. 2.* New York: Springer, 1963.

her mouth tightly with his hand or a pillow. She became immediately terrified because she could not breathe; she felt like she was choking. Each night the scene of conjoined shame and terror played itself out—for well over five years. After he was finished with her each night, he silently left her room. She lay there awhile alone, crying. Then she crept to the bathroom and hid under the sink. For this woman, terror and shame became magnified conjointly.

When she sat with me and I looked into her eyes, I saw her terror. It was still present. When I suggested that we would eventually need to reenter these scenes in order to heal her shame, she quickly blurted out, "But I'm already there—I'm in them right at this moment. I'm in that room while I speak to you and he's coming in, he's climbing into my bed. Now he's grabbing me, hurting me. *I can't get him out!"*

She was vividly reexperiencing those terror/shame scenes in full waking consciousness. And then she indicated that these scenes would recur daily, often several times each day. On every occasion, she would feel overwhelmed, both terrorized and deeply humiliated.

I knew intuitively that I needed to intervene. As I continued to gaze into her face and into her eyes, I said, "Imagine me right there beside you, right there in that room with you. See me standing there."

She nodded agreement, saying, "Yes, I can see you . . . with me."

"Now, I'm pushing him out of your bedroom," I continued. "He doesn't belong there, and I'm stronger than he is. I'm pushing him back through the doorway, back into the hallway, and now I'm closing the door and locking it. He will not come back in. He won't be able to hurt you while I'm here. And I'm going to stay right here in this room with you for as long as you need me. I will guard the door and I will protect you. It's safe now."

Visibly, she relaxed. I further suggested to her that she imagine me right there guarding the door whenever the abuse scene returned and intruded itself. She said she would try to do so.

In many cases I will have my client imagine his or her adult self actually present in the original shame scene, and then imagine becoming the protecting, nurturing parent to the child self in that scene. Often, however, my client will not be able do so. In these instances I have learned that I must first involve myself directly in the scene before my client is ever able to do so.

Several sessions later, I suggested we actually construct in her imagination a new house for her child self, that abused girl still inside of her, because the only home she had ever known was always filled with terror and shame. The necessity for doing this became evident during an imagery experience that we shared one day. She was imagining herself as a young girl sitting on a fence watching the sunset with me beside her. She was feeling a quiet calm inside, contentment, only to become instantly terrified and ashamed upon realizing that sundown had always lowered a blanket of gloom. Sundown struck terror into her because it meant returning to her house and then to her bedroom. Following my new suggestion, she became immediately excited and joyful at the prospect of creating a new house. I suggested that she could use crayons or paints to draw it, or she could use cardboard or wood to actually build it. And it was to be a safe place, one where only she could live. And in *this* house she had the power to let inside only safe individuals that she wanted to allow in.

After several months, she was able to feel increasing inner peace and freedom. Our work together was certainly far from finished, but she was now able to imagine me present within her as a guardian, an inner ally. Scenes of her father no longer intruded quite so unexpectedly. When they did, she quickly imagined me present in the scene, stopping the abuse. Or, she picked up her child self and took her to the new house to be safe. We had been able to successfully create a *container* for those acutely disturbing childhood scenes of abuse.

Now let us return to the principal discussion. This clinical case suggests a potential treatment approach which can be adapted for working with other forms of scene intrusion. The reactivation and intrusion of affect-laden scenes is the principal dynamic, I believe, that occurs in different kinds of post-traumatic stress disorders, from survivors of a disaster to survivors of battle. In every case of survival from trauma, there will also be *survivor shame*. When the fact of having survived itself becomes a new source of shame, living inevitably is made deeply ambivalent. This shame, produced because one has survived when others did not, will have to be assimilated and resolved in addition to containing the intrusion of scenes.

In the last several years, numerous films about the Vietnam War have been produced after more than a decade of relative silence. The need to make such films is both a response to that silence and to the prior shame which caused it. Breaking the silence means coming out of shame. By exposing our national shame through films, our nation at long last begins to openly confront its shame and express it, to reclaim its dead soldiers along with its living veterans, redeeming those who fell along with those who survived, and thereby returning to dignity, pride, and honor. The need to retell the Vietnam story through film is a need to expunge shame, to tell it and to show it until there is no longer any need to do so.

Literature, theater, and films have always enabled the identification process. Art is a mode of knowledge, according to Jacob Bronowski, specifically knowledge of self. By identifying with characters in fictional dramas, we enter their experience; we become *one* with others, and see deeper into ourselves in so doing. We actually move through the experience and transcend shame. Through watching recurring films about this conflict, Vietnam veterans themselves can identify with one another by entering the experience depicted and thereby have their own personal story told as well. These films also serve to bridge the generations, to unite those who lived through those tumultuous years, witnessing them directly, with those who were born in the aftermath of Vietnam. The process of healing shame and returning to honor is as vital to nations as it is to individuals.

Ideological scripts become a matter of faith. They are both self-validating and self-fulfilling, and "are lived out as if true and good against others as false and bad."[2] These are the scripts that human beings believe in with the most fervent passion and absolute conviction, and about which there is the greatest ambiguity and least certainty. Ideological scripts "endow fact with value and affect."

The Gulf War commenced in the third week of January, 1991, unleashing yet another ideological dispute. Groups of individuals in

---

[2]Tomkins, S. S. "Script Theory." In J. Aronoff, A.I. Rabin, and R.A. Zucker (Eds.), *The Emergence of Personality.* New York: Springer, 1987, p. 170.

the United States emerged and began protesting the war; they drew immediate parallels between this newest conflict and the earlier Vietnam era. Other groups sprang up just as quickly and began refuting that analogy, espousing support for the troops and/or the war effort itself. These deeply felt affective reactions to the war intensified rapidly and became increasingly polarized. Even President Bush declaimed, in effect, "We will never have another Vietnam—we will never again fight with one hand tied behind our back." The parallel he perceived was not with Vietnam, but with Adolf Hitler and World War Two.

The psychological impact of this war, like any other, is one of accelerating powerlessness and uncertainty. The sudden loss of the ability to predict and control events renders any individual or group of individuals initially powerless. Whenever the need to predict and control is thwarted—without which human beings appear unable to thrive—the resulting powerlessness activates any or all of the negative affects, including any combination of negative affects. Anyone with family or friends in military service will feel immediately powerless upon learning of their deployment, or even the possibility of their deployment. Anyone with young adult children or friends of potential draft age will likely worry about the military draft being reinstituted, causing further powerlessness coupled with uncertainty. Together, these conditions prompt the rapid magnification of negative affect. The children of military personnel serving in the Gulf feel especially threatened by the imminent possibility of their parents' death or capture. There is further concern about who will care for these children if both parents are in combat and are lost. Finally, anyone with family or friends living in any of the countries in the Gulf area will experience powerlessness and uncertainty as a direct result of the conflict.

Is this a *just* war? The ideological dispute turns on exactly this moral question. Even when polarized positions are defended visibly and vocally, is there not some secret inner doubt that whispers in the mind of protestors on either side of the dispute even if only occasionally? Many people are indeed ambivalent about the war, feeling themselves divided within, even when the weight of their inner struggle ultimately comes out on the side of favoring the war. That inner division within individuals is matched by division between opposing groups. The pro-war vs. anti-war advocates are engaged in a dispute of opposing and irreconcilable ideologies. But division can also be observed to emerge within a seemingly cohesive group espousing one particular, coherent ideology. Ideology itself breeds divisiveness. Even previously shared ideologies break down and intact groups become partitioned by conflict and by polarity. Ideology invariably polarizes individuals. It does so between groups, and it also does so within groups. This controversy is like the pro-abortion vs. anti-abortion ideological dispute that has been raging in this country in recent years. This is true with regard to the intensity of affect displayed, and it is equally true with regard to the fervor and passionate claims expressed on both sides of the dispute. The anti-war group is as ideologically fixed as the anti-abortion group.

President Bush addressed the nation in a recent visit to a military base; in his speech to the assembled soldiers, he called them heroes. Here we have honor and shame once more contending both in the present circumstance and in the lasting memories of earlier conflicts. Those who now remind us of parallels with Vietnam remind us of a war deemed inherently unjust in its aims and therefore dishonorable, shameful. It was a war also judged as shameful in its conduct. But it was a war that this nation, in effect, lost. That defeat only further magnifies the other, moral source of shame about the war in Vietnam. Therefore, those who now reject any connection whatsoever between the Gulf War and Vietnam are claiming that this war *is* a just war in its inception, in its very purpose. In so doing, they furthermore are striving to redeem a nation's honor from its past shame. And the openness of the current debate concerning the Gulf War, its wide public support, and the early military successes are helping to heal the shame of Vietnam.

Renewed affect springs from the competing and opposing claims of clashing ideologies. The resulting further magnification of affect serves, in turn, to further fuel the ideological dispute. The cycle of affect and ideology is a continuously recurring one, whether it is found in religion or politics, in science or war. Ideologies give people something vital to believe in, something to live for, and something equally vital to die for. Ideology is the cradle of civilization.

IDENTITY, CULTURE, AND IDEOLOGY

In examining the general significance of shame for gender, culture, and society, three broad, interrelated phenomena have emerged: identity, culture, and ideology. This perspective represents an extension of the prior work into new domains. We have extensively examined the psychology of shame, identity, and the self on the level of the individual. The next level of analysis involves the development of group identity, the dynamics of intergroup relations, intergroup violence, and ideological disputes both between and within groups. The final level of analysis concerns international relations. The theoretical framework at the heart of this study posits that all experience becomes amplified by affect or emotion. These affective experiences are then partitioned in the form of specific, discrete scenes. Next, actual rules develop for predicting, controlling, interpreting, and responding to any magnified set of affective scenes. These various sets of rules comprise distinctive scripts. Identity scripts determine the patterning of identity, whether individual or group, just as cultural scripts determine the patterning of culture. Our analysis has enlarged and extended the prevailing view of identity in terms of individual self development to include the emergence of various group identities, examples of which include ethnic, racial, religious, gender, and sexual identity. A further extension of this formulation of group identity is the development of national identity. Recent events in Eastern Europe and the Baltic States bear witness to the undiminished power of national identification and national identity.

But identity always evolves within a particular culture and at a specific temporal-spatial location within a historical time period. Cultural scripts give shape and definition to a culture, but also become the socialization tools of that culture. Culture, therefore, significantly impacts identity development, while culture becomes equally impacted by identity. This leads me to posit a theory of the reciprocal evolution of personality and culture.

Both the human being and culture are continuously evolving and reciprocally evolving entities. We must consider the broader sociocultural milieu along with the more limited family and peer group milieus as all significantly interactive in the evolution of both the self and civilization. Even the forms of psychopathology have changed over the last one hundred years. The acceleration of eating disorders during the preceding twenty years demonstrates the impact of cultural values regarding appearance and thinness on both personality and psychopathology. And the prominent disorders of today are unlikely to be the same ones observed twenty years from now. Humans live in a social group. Because individuals strive to identify with one another, to belong, culture is able to wield considerable power over any particular person. The emergence of a highly technological society has, in turn, created the necessity for that lengthy cultural apprenticeship known as higher education. Such a cultural development has itself prolonged and transformed the developmental epoch of adolescence. The presumably innate progression of developmental phases has been directly altered by sociocultural changes. The lengthening of adolescence, in turn, accords the peer group even greater influence over personality formation. Certainly Harry S. Sullivan was one of the first personality theorists in the early decades of this century to recognize the importance of peer relations; that Sullivan's own early development was marked by an absence of peer relations should come as no surprise. Yet the role and impact of the peer group in a highly technological society is different still from that in an agrarian or even an industrial society. The peer group that has evolved in contemporary American culture now rivals the family in its power to socialize adolescents. This helps explain the recent phenomenon of organized urban *gangs*, which are able to meet the interpersonal needs of their youthful members in ways that the family does not. These observations point to the reciprocal impact of family, peer group, and culture on personality, on both its expression and development. Personality influences culture, just as culture determines personality.

Ideological scripts transcend both the individual and society, linking them tightly together within a cosmology that both communicates and defines one's orientation in the universe, delineates the evaluation of what is good and what is bad, and determines various sanctions, both positive and negative. Ideological scripts unite identity with culture. The current dispute raging about abortion in the United States is one example of an ideological dispute. The individual's right to die promises to become another ideological dispute paralleling that presently surrounding abortion. And still other ideological disputes are looming on the horizon, most notably centering on introducing self-esteem curricula in the elementary school classroom and gay rights.

Examining the dynamic interaction of identity and culture is critical to the understanding and eventual resolution of intergroup rivalry and hostility. The hatred and violence that historically has played out between various groups—for example, between African Americans and Caucasians, men and women, or heterosexuals and homosexuals—is inextricably rooted in the dynamics of identity and culture. Central to this phenomenon is a third dynamic, ideology. An ideology, in effect, is a systematic and self-validating "ideo-affective posture" toward the world, as Tomkins views it. It is fueled by affect or emotion, and further shaped by language or cognition. The ideology of intergroup hatred and violence is fueled by particular affects: shame, dissmell, disgust, and the affect blend, contempt. Racism, sexism, anti-Semitism, heterosexism, and homophobia are particular examples of the ideology of group hatred, prejudice, and violence. It is lynching-like contempt in particular which causes the punitive distancing of the repudiated other, now deemed unfit for the human community. The contaminant must be permanently distanced via dissmell and equally punished via anger—in a word, lynched. The psychology of personality must evolve into a psychology of peoples in order to effect resolution of continuing intergroup violence, whether in the United States, Northern Ireland, or what was once the Soviet Union.

Furthermore, examining the dynamics of affect and script illuminates the phenomena of group prejudice, discrimination, and violence. The origins and dynamics of group tension and violence viewed broadly are vital issues of contemporary significance. Group tension and violence in any culture or nation are invariably fueled by the affects of shame, contempt, and rage. Violence directed at particular groups is furthermore shaped by distinct ideologies of superiority and hate. The actions and reactions that repeatedly play out between various groups are indeed scripted actions. Each participant, each group, enacts its own scripted part. Furthermore, belonging to a particular group is equivalent to being seen as different and therefore lesser in any culture that devalues differences. The sense of inferiority, alienation and feeling outcast that is experienced invariably by members of distinct minority groups is the direct product of the affect of shame, further compounded by contempt for perceived differences. And it is the affect of contempt which partitions the inferior from the superior in any culture or nation. As such, contempt is the principal dynamic fueling prejudice and discrimination.

The examination of various intergroup dynamics from the perspective of affect, scene, and script will furthermore yield a new theory of ethnic, racial, religious, gender, and sexual identity development. A first approximation of this theory has already been elaborated above in the context of the development of gay identity. Such a theory of group-based identity development will complement the theory of individual identity development. Examining the interaction of identity, culture, and ideology is equally important to the expanding focus on multicultural awareness and valuing diversity that is emerging on many levels in this society as we approach the close of the twentieth century. Either we will solve the problems of hatred and violence both within and among nations, or else we as a species will not long survive on this planet.

New answers will be found in the examination of affect and the various scripted responses to affect. And that knowledge must be made widely available, so that dignity, pride, and honor may finally triumph over shame and humiliation—not only for individuals, but for families and for nations. Just as the self must reown and embrace all those rejected orphans within it, and in so doing become whole, so must the human community reclaim its outcasts if we are to continue to thrive. That is the evolutionary challenge of the twenty-first century.

Bibliography

Alexander, F. "Remarks About the Relation of Inferiority Feelings to Guilt Feelings." *International Journal of Psychoanalysis, 19*(1938): 41-49.

Ausubel, D. "Relationships Between Guilt and Shame in the Socializing Process." *Psychological Review, 62*(1955): 378-390.

Barry, M. J. "Depression, Shame, Loneliness and the Psychiatrist's Position." *American Journal of Psychotherapy, 16*(1962): 580-590.

Bassos, C. A., and Kaufman, G. "The Dynamics of Shame: A Therapeutic Key to Problems of Intimacy and Sexuality." (Paper presented at the Meeting of the American Psychological Association, Montreal, Canada, 1973).

Bronowski, J. *The Ascent of Man.* Boston: Little, Brown, 1973.

Broucek, F. J. *Shame and the Self.* New York: The Guilford Press, 1991.

Buss, A. H., and Plomin, R. *A Temperament Theory of Personality Development.* New York: John Wiley and Sons, 1975.

Campbell, J. (Ed.) *The Portable Jung.* New York: Viking Press, 1971.

Colby, K. M. "Appraisal of Four Psychological Theories of Paranoid Phenomena." *Journal of Abnormal Psychology, 86*(1977): 54-59.

Ekman, P., Levenson, R.W., and Friesen, W.V. "Autonomic Nervous System Activity Distinguishes Among Emotions." *Science, 221*(1983): 1208-1210.

English, F. "Shame and Social Control." *Transactional Analysis Journal, 5*(1975): 24 -28.

Erikson, E. H. *Childhood and Society.* New York: Norton, 1963.

Fairbairn, W. R. D. *Psychoanalytic Studies of the Personality.* London: Routledge and Kegan Paul, 1966.

Fossum, M., and Mason, M. *Facing Shame.* New York: Norton, 1986.

Frankl, V. E. *Man's Search for Meaning: An Introduction to Logotherapy.* Boston: Beacon Press, 1962.

Frankl, V. E. *The Will to Meaning: Foundations and Applications of Logotherapy.* New York: World, 1969.

Frankl, V. E. "Paradoxical Intention and Dereflection." *Psychotherapy: Theory, Research and Practice, 12*(1975): 226-237.

Gilligan, C. *In A Different Voice.* Cambridge, Massachusetts: Harvard University Press, 1982.

Guntrip, H. *Personality Structure and Human Interaction.* New York: International Universities Press, 1961.

Guntrip, H. *Schizoid Phenomena, Object-Relations and the Self.* New York: International Universities Press, 1969.

Guntrip, H. *Psychoanalytic Theory, Therapy and the Self.* New York: Basic Books, 1971.

Hawthorne, N. *The Scarlet Letter.* New York: New American Library, 1959

Horney, K. *Neurosis and Human Growth: The Struggle Toward Self-Realization*. New York: Norton, 1950.

Johnson, G., Kaufman, G., and Raphael, L. *A Teacher's Guide to Stick Up For Yourself*. Minneapolis, Minnesota: Free Spirit Publishing, 1991.

Jung, C. G. *Psychological Types*, translated by H. G. Baynes. London: Routledge and Kegan Paul, 1923.

Jung, C. G. *Memories, Dreams, Reflections*, translated by Richard Winston and Clara Winston. New York: Vintage Books, 1965.

Jung, C.G. *Analytical Psychology: Its Theory and Practice*. New York: Pantheon, 1968.

Kaufman, G. "The Meaning of Shame: Towards a Self-Affirming Identity." *Journal of Counseling Psychology, 21*(1974): 568-574.

Kaufman, G. "On Shame, Identity and the Dynamics of Change." (Paper presented at symposium, Papers in Memory of Bill Kell: Issues on Therapy and the Training of Therapists. The Meeting of the American Psychological Association, New Orleans, 1974).

Kaufman, G. "Dynamics and Treatment of Shame-Based Syndromes." In *Proceedings of the Eighth and Ninth Annual Adult Psychiatric Day Treatment Forum*. Minneapolis: University of Minnesota, 1986.

Kaufman, G. "Disorders of Self-Esteem: Psychotherapy for Shame-Based Syndromes." In P. A. Keller and S. R. Heyman (Eds.), *Innovations in Clinical Practice: A Source Book, Vol. 6,* 53-62. Sarasota, Florida: Professional Resource Exchange, Inc., 1987.

Kaufman, G. *The Psychology of Shame: Theory and Treatment of Shame-Based Syndromes*. New York: Springer, 1989.

Kaufman, G. "The Role of Shame in the Differential Patterning of Gender Socialization: A New Psychological Perspective." (Paper presented at the National Conference on Re-Visioning Knowledge and the Curriculum: Feminist Perspectives, Michigan State University, East Lansing, Michigan, 1990).

Kaufman, G. (speaker). "From Shame to Self-Empowerment: Origins, Healing, and Treatment Issues." Newton, Massachusetts: Lifecycle Learning Cassettes, 1990.

Kaufman, G., and Raphael, L. (speakers). "Listening to Your Inner Voices" (Cassette Recording No. 20275). Washington, DC: Psychology Today Tapes,1983.

Kaufman, G., and Raphael, L. "Relating to the Self: Changing Inner Dialogue." *Psychological Reports, 54*(1984): 239-250.

Kaufman, G., and Raphael, L. "Shame as Taboo in American Culture." In R. Browne (Ed.), *Forbidden Fruits: Taboos and Tabooism in Culture.* Bowling Green, Ohio: Popular Press, 1984.

Kaufman, G., and Raphael, L. "Shame: A Perspective on Jewish Identity." *Journal of Psychology and Judaism, 11*(1987): 30-40.

Kaufman, G., and Raphael, L. *Stick Up For Yourself! Every Kid's Guide to Personal Power and Positive Self-Esteem.* Minneapolis, Minnesota: Free Spirit Publishing, 1990.

Kaufman, G., and Raphael, L. *Dynamics of Power: Fighting Shame and Building Self-Esteem, Second Edition.* Rochester, Vermont: Schenkman Books, 1991.

Kell, B. L., and Burow, J. M. *Developmental Counseling and Therapy.* Boston: Houghton Mifflin, 1970.

Laing, R. D. *The Divided Self.* New York: Pantheon Books, 1960.

LeShan, L., and Margenau, H. *Einstein's Space and van Gogh's Sky: Physical Reality and Beyond*. New York: Macmillan, 1982.

Levin, S. "Some Metapsychological Considerations on the Differentiation Between Shame and Guilt." *International Journal of Psychoanalysis, 48*(1967): 267-276.

Levin, S. "The Psychoanalysis of Shame." *International Journal of Psychoanalysis, 52*(1971): 355-362.

Lewinsky, H. "The Nature of Shyness." *British Journal of Psychology, 32(1941)*: 105-112.

Lewis, H. B. *Shame and Guilt in Neurosis*. New York: International Universities Press, 1971.

Lewis, H. B. (Ed.) *The Role of Shame in Symptom Formation*. Hillsdale, New Jersey: Erlbaum, 1987.

Lynd, H. M. *On Shame and the Search for Identity*. New York: Harcourt, Brace, 1958.

MacCurdy, J. T. "The Biological Significance of Blushing and Shame." *British Journal of Psychology, 71*(1965): 19-59.

Mahler, M. S., Pine, F., and Bergman, A. *The Psychological Birth of the Human Infant*. New York: Basic Books, 1975.

Marsella, A. J., Murray, M. D., and Golden, C. "Ethnic Variations in the Phenomenology of Emotions: Shame." *Journal of Cross Cultural Psychology, 5*(1974): 312-328.

Modigliani, A. "Embarrassability and Embarrassment." *Sociometry, 31*(1968): 313-326.

Modigliani, A. "Embarrassment, Facework, and Eye Contact: Testing a Theory of Embarrassment." *Journal of Personality and*

Social Psychology, 17(1971): 15-24.

Money, J., and Ehrhardt, A. *Man and Woman, Boy and Girl: The Differentiation and Dimorphism of Gender Identity From Conception to Maturity.* Baltimore: Johns Hopkins University Press, 1972.

Montagu, A. *Touching: The Human Significance of the Skin.* New York: Harper and Row, 1972.

Morrison, A. P. *Shame: The Underside of Narcissism.* Hillsdale, NJ: Analytic Press, 1989.

Mueller, W. J., and Kell, B. L. *Coping With Conflict: Supervising Counselors and Psychotherapists.* New York: Appleton-Century-Crofts, 1972.

Nathanson, D. L. (Ed.) *The Many Faces of Shame.* New York: Guilford Press, 1987.

Nuttin, J. "Intimacy and Shame in the Dynamic Structure of Personality." In M. L. Reymert (Ed.), *Feelings and Emotions.* New York: McGraw-Hill, 1950.

Peristiany, J. G. *Honour and Shame.* Chicago: University of Chicago Press, 1974.

Perlman, M. "An Investigation of Anxiety as Related to Guilt and Shame." *Archives of Neurological Psychiatry, 80*(1958): 752-759.

Piers, G., and Singer, M. B. *Shame and Guilt: A Psychoanalytic and a Cultural Study.* Springfield, Illinois: Charles C. Thomas, 1953; reprint edition, New York: Norton, 1971.

Raphael, L. *Edith Wharton's Prisoners of Shame: A New Perspective on Her Neglected Fiction.* New York: St. Martin's Press, 1991.

Riezler, K. "Comment on the Social Psychology of Shame." *American Journal of Sociology, 48*(1943): 457-465.

Riezler, K. "Shame and Awe." In *Man: Mutable and Immutable.* New York: Henry Regnery, 1951.

Riger, A. L. "When Differently-Abled Girls Grow Up: The Legacy of Sexism and Shame and Their Healing." (Paper presented at the National Conference of the Association for Women in Psychology, 1990.)

Riger, A. L. "The Evocation and Healing of Shame in Differently-Abled College Women." (Paper presented at symposium, The Role of Shame in Psychopathology and Psychotherapy. The Meeting of the American Psychological Association, Boston, 1990).

Sattler, J. "A Theoretical, Developmental, and Clinical Investigation of Embarrassment." *Genetic Psychology Monographs, 71*(1965): 19-59.

Schneider, C. D. *Shame, Exposure and Privacy.* Boston: Beacon Press, 1977.

Shapiro, K. J., and Alexander, I. E. *The Experience of Introversion: An Integration of Phenomenological, Empirical, and Jungian Approaches.* Durham, North Carolina: Duke University Press, 1975.

Stierlin, H. "Shame and Guilt in Family Relations."*Archives of General Psychiatry, 30*(1974): 381-389.

Straus, E. "Shame as a Historiological Problem." In *Phenomenological Psychology: Selected Papers,* translated by Erling English. New York: Basic Books, 1966.

Sullivan, H. S. *The Interpersonal Theory of Psychiatry.* New York: Norton, 1953.

Tomkins, S. S. *Affect, Imagery, Consciousness: The Positive Affects, Vol. 1.* New York: Springer, 1962.

Tomkins, S. S. *Affect, Imagery, Consciousness: The Negative Affects, Vol. 2.* New York: Springer, 1963.

Tomkins, S. S. "Affect and the Psychology of Knowledge." In S. S. Tomkins and C. Izard (Eds.), *Affect, Cognition and Personality.* New York: Springer, 1965.

Tomkins, S. S. "The Phantasy Behind the Face. "*Journal of Personality Assessment, 39*(1975):551-562.

Tomkins, S. S. "Script Theory: Differential Magnification of Affects." In H. E. Howe and R. A. Dienstbier (Eds.), *Nebraska Symposium on Motivation, Vol. 26,* 201-236. Lincoln: University of Nebraska Press, 1979.

Tomkins, S. S. "The Quest for Primary Motives: Biography and Autobiography of an Idea." *Journal of Personality and Social Psychology, 41*(1981): 306-329.

Tomkins, S. S. "Affect Theory." In P. Ekman (Ed.), *Emotion in the Human Face.* Cambridge, Massachusetts: Cambridge University Press, 1982.

Tomkins, S. S. "Affect Theory." In K. R. Scherer and P. Ekman (Eds.), *Approaches to Emotion.* Hillsdale, New Jersey: Erlbaum, 1984.

Tomkins, S. S. "Shame." In D. L. Nathanson (Ed.), *The Many Faces of Shame.* New York: Guilford Press, 1987.

Tomkins. S. S. "Script Theory." In J. Aronoff, A. I. Rabin. and R. A. Zucker (Eds.), *The Emergence of Personality.* New York: Springer, 1987.

Tomkins, S. S. *Affect, Imagery, Consciousness: The Negative Affects, Anger and Fear, Vol. 3.* New York: Springer, 1991.

Wallace, L. "The Mechanism of Shame." *Archives of General Psychiatry, 8(*1963): 80-85.

Ward, H. P. "Aspects of Shame in Analysis." *American Journal of Psychoanalysis, 32(*1972): 62-73.

Westkott, M. *The Feminist Legacy of Karen Horney.* New Haven, Connecticut: Yale University Press, 1986.

White, R. W. "Motivation Reconsidered: The Concept of Competence." *Psychological Review, 66(*1959): 297-333.

Winnicott, D. W. *Through Pediatrics to Psychoanalysis.* New York: Basic Books, 1975.

Wurmser, L. *The Mask of Shame.* Baltimore: Johns Hopkins University Press, 1981.

Index

BIOGRAPHICAL SKETCH

GERSHEN KAUFMAN was educated at Columbia University and received his Ph.D. in clinical psychology from the University of Rochester. Currently he is a professor in the Counseling Center at Michigan State University.

He is the author of *The Psychology of Shame: Theory and Treatment of Shame-Based Syndromes* (Springer Publishing Co., 1989) and Journey to the Magic Castle (forthcoming 1992, Double M Press). He is the coauthor with Lev Raphael of *Dynamics of Power: Fighting Shame and Building Self-Esteem* (Schenkman Books, Inc., 1991) as well as *Stick Up For Yourself! Every Kid's Guide to Personal Power and Positive Self-Esteem* (Free Spirit Publishing, 1990) and A Teacher's Guide to Stick Up for Yourself (Free Spirit Publishing, 1991).